DEAF
EDUCATION

DEAF EDUCATION

By

M.Alice Raj Kumari
M.A., M.Ed., (Ph.D.)
Principal
Tarlupadu College of Education
Tarlupadu, Prakasam Distt., A.P.

D.Rita Suguna Sundari
M.Sc., M.Ed.
Principal
St. Paul's College of Education
Giddalur, Prakasam Distt., A.P.

General Editor
Dr. Digumarti Bhaskara Rao
M.Sc., M.A., M.A., M.Ed., Ph.D.
Reader
R.V.R. College of Education
Srinivasa Nagar Colony
Guntur-522 006
Andhra Pradesh
India

SONALI PUBLICATIONS
NEW DELHI-110002

Edition : 2026

ISBN 81-88836-45-1

Published by

SONALI PUBLICATIONS
4228/1, Ansari Road,
New Delhi-110 002 (India)
Phone: 23279245 • Fax: 91-11-23253475

Printed by :
Navya Digital, Delhi - 110092

PREFACE

The excellent research relevant to children who are deaf, very little of the resulting information trickles down to the people who need it most: parents, teachers, and other professionals involved with deaf children on a day-to-day basis. My goal, therefore, has been to take what we know from a wide variety of investigations and explain it in everyday language. Because of my own perspective on the field and the needs and sensitivities of many people who hopefully will read this book, the endeavor turned out to be rather more time-consuming and difficult than I originally expected. I wanted to be sure that readers got "the whole truth and nothing but the truth," but that sometimes required decisions about whether it was worth even starting on some important points that I knew would seem trivial unless they were put in what would be a rather complex context.

This book is in no way intended to be a how-to manual. Instead, I have focused on broad issues like alternatives for effective communication, the importance of diverse social experiences, and the need for consistency in parenting. In a variety of situations I have been quite specific, but only going so far as I could with confidence. For example, it should not seem odd to parents and teachers when I suggest that they need to read to their children and students. Nor should it surprise anyone when I suggest that this activity is all the more important for deaf children, who may lack other opportunities for exposure to English. I hope I have explained fully the bases for these recommendations.

Editor

Contents

1

Defining Learning Disabilities

For a field that was officially recognized only about 25 years ago, learning disabilities has experienced unprecedented growth and has had significant impact on special education. Besides being the largest category in special education, LD is also among the most problematic because of continuing controversy, conflict, and crisis. Many of the difficulties experienced by the LD field appear to emanate from a failure to answer the seemingly straightforward question, "What is a learning disability?" The vagaries and antagonisms associated with any response has placed the LD field at a critical juncture. The purpose of this chapter is to explore the enduring problem of definition and to suggest positive and rational approaches for resolving many fundamental problems.

Problem Area

On the surface, LD should not be any more problematic than other areas of special education. Although both mild mental retardation (MR) and behaviour disorders (BD) — its partners in the large designation "mildly handicapped" — also experience definitional problems, the difficulties experienced by LD appears to take center stage. The problem of defining LD, after so many attempts, appears to defy resolution, and discussion seems only to result in an ever-increasing tangled web from which escape seems impossible.

Such language is not mere hyperbole: No other area of special education has ever been called on to defend its very existence. There is ever increasing depiction of LD as myth, questionable construct, or imaginary disease, and, even though usually without merit, require a response defending LD that deflects attention away from more substantive issues. The MR and BD literature does not reveal any similar discussion about their existence, and it is only LD that is referred to as a "phantom category."

For a condition whose reality is continuously challenged, LD is seemingly doing quite well. Since the passage of PL 94-142, the LD population has increased about 150% to a level where it now represents almost 5% of all students in school and 50% of all students with disabilities. The prevalence ranges from 1.51% to 6.11% with LD as percent of students with disabilities ranging from 31.9 to 64.5. To provide perspective, the prevalence rate for MR is slightly less than 1% across states with the range being from. 16% to 2.52%. For BD, the prevalence rate is .69% with a range from .04 to 1.69. On average, LD reveals anywhere from 2-3 times more students even in states with the highest prevalence rates for MR and BD. As a percent of students with disabilities, MR ranges from 3.1% to 28% with an average of 12.3% while BD ranges from .5% to 20.1% with an average of 8.9%. At about 50%, the LD category includes anywhere from 4-5 times more students than other categories in special education.

The sheer number of students with LD may eventually strain resources, and LD may be trapped by its own "success." Is there any justification for LD being the largest category in special education? Could anyone have anticipated in 1970 that LD would expand to its present proportions? Answers are difficult and may result from a failure to achieve consensus about the nature of LD as manifested in the "problem of definition," the inability to achieve agreement about how best to define LD. Definitions of LD have remained vague and have not presented precise statements. The result is varying interpretation, and this seems the fate of the LD field: It is known when seen, but accompanied by an inability to bring those views into an exact and unencumbered statement.

History and Definition

In many respects, the LD field appears to have advanced far ahead of itself. The lack of comprehensive and unified definition suggests that LD cannot attain two critical elements: understanding-a clear and unobscured sense of LD, and explanation-a rational exposition of the reasons why a particular student is LD. Without understanding and explanation, statements about LD remain conditional, and this conditionality becomes the source of much debate.

Historical Considerations

The history of LD is well documented. For example, Weiderholt conceptualized the historical development of LD along two dimensions: a developmental sequence delineating historical time periods, and a type of disorder analysis. The development phases included foundation , transition, and integration with Lerner adding a contemporary phase bringing the field to the present. The types of disorders included spoken language, written language and process disorders. Each phase and disorder was placed in a matrix where the work of significant individuals was described to show how their contributions advanced toward the LD concept.

Kavale and Forness analyzed the development of LD within the context of special education. From clinic-based treatment for aphasia and dyslexia, to classes for neurologically impaired students, to misclassification in special classes for MR and BD, and, finally, to a need for an educational focus-rather than counseling and guidance services — for underachievement, LD filled a void in the spectrum of special education. Previously, there were a variety of LD-like students requiring special education but no provisions except in either non-school arrangements or inappropriate special education arrangements. The needs of such students were best met through what eventually became LD programmes.

Historical analyses point to the fact that there was a need for a category like LD. A variety of pressures led to a convergence on the concept of LD as a foundation for a new category in special education. By bringing disparate elements under a single rubric, there was the potential for more focused diagnosis and treatment.

Definitional Considerations

With a need for an LD category established, attention was directed at formulating a definition that could describe the parameters of the condition. It is at this point that the definition problem began. The basic problem with LD definitions is the failure to provide insight into the nature of the condition. The most widely used definition is the one found in IDEA that was formalized by the United States Office of Education in the *Federal Register*:

> *The term "specific learning disability" means a disorder in one or more of the basic psychological processes involved in understanding or in using language, spoken or written, which may manifest itself in an imperfect ability to listen, speak, read, write, spell, or to do mathematical calculations. The term includes such conditions as perceptual handicaps, brain injury, minimal brain dysfunction, dyslexia, and developmental aphasia. The term does not include children who have learning disabilities which are primarily the result of visual, hearing, or motor handicaps, or mental retardation or emotional disturbance, or of environmental, cultural, or economic disadvantage.*

After reading this definition, it is not at all clear that one could answer the question, "What is LD?" There is some indication about process disorders specifically in the language area that interfere with basic academic achievement but the descriptions and relationships remain vague. There is a statement that LD is like other conditions as listed, but definition by analogy introduces much imprecision because indications about how similar and how different the other conditions are from LD is lacking. There is a relatively clear statement about what LD is not, but this is not equivalent to stating what LD is-a missing aspect of this definition. The fundamental difficulty is that no sense of LD emerges beyond that of a general and indistinct learning problem even though it is presumably defining "specific learning disability." The definition is marked by a rather nonspecific description of the elements contributing to LD.

Analysis and Critique of LD Definitions

The IDEA definition is widely used, but it is not the only LD definition. To see how the problem of definition emerged, it would be useful to trace their development and determine what they say and don't say.

Precursors to LD

The seminal work of A. Strauss and H. Werner in the development of the LD field is well documented. Their study of brain-injured MR students laid an important foundation for LD. A brain-injured student was defined as one:

> *Who before, during or after birth has received an injury to or suffered an infection of the brain. As a result of such organic impairment, deficits of the neuromotor system may be present or absent; however, such a child may show disturbances in perception, thinking, and emotional behaviour, either separately or in combinations. This disturbance can be demonstrated by specific tests. These disturbances prevent or impede a normal learning process.*

The importance of this definition lies in the fact that it introduced behavioral criteria to diagnose a biophysical phenomenon. Within the context of this definition, brain injury became a rather broad and elastic category spanning gross damage easily documented to slight damage not easily documented but presumed because of the presence of behavioral symptoms. The dilemma created surrounds the tautological reasoning established as suggested by Sarason , "The logically minded may of course object to a reasoning which appears to go like this: Some individuals with known brain damage have certain behavioral characteristics, therefore individuals with these same behavioral characteristics must be presumed to be brain damaged".

The next precursor is found in the concept of minimal brain dysfunction (MBD). Strauss and Lehtinen recognized a "minor brain damage" where "behaviour and learning may be affected by minimal brain injuries without apparent lowering of the intelligence level". The term was formalized by Clements, where MBD was defined as a disorder affecting:

> *Children of near average, average, or above average general intelligence with certain learning or behavioral disabilities ranging from mild to severe, which are associated with deviations of functions of the central nervous system. These deviations may manifest themselves by various combinations of impairment in perception, conceptualization, language, memory, and control of*

attention, impulse, or motor function. The aberrations may arise from genetic variation, biochemical irregularities, perinatal brain insults, or other illnesses or injuries sustained during the years which are critical for the development and maturation of the central nervous system or from unknown causes. During the school years, a variety of learning disabilities is the most prominent manifestation of the condition which can be designated by this term.

Although lacking precision with respect to symptomatology and etiology as well as permitting wide latitude with respect to intellectual and severity levels, the definition again affirmed the possibility of diagnosing a biophysical phenomenon on the basis of behavioral characteristics. More specifically, disorders in learning were among the most prominent behavioral characteristics defining MBD.

These two definitions are important because they served to conjoin central nervous system (CNS) dysfunction and LD. There was little question that LD was associated with neurological impairments and that they represented the most prominent etiology of LD.

Early Definitions of LD

Kirk offered the first formal definition in the text Educating Exceptional Children, which was disseminated further by Kirk and Bateman. The definition reads:

A learning disability refers to a retardation, disorder, or delayed development in one or more of the processes of speech, language, reading, writing, arithmetic, or other school subjects resulting from a psychological handicap caused by a possible cerebral dysfunction and/or emotional or behavioral disturbances. It is not the result of mental retardation, sensory deprivation, or cultural and instructional factors.

The definition introduced the notion of psychological process disorders as the foundation of LD. The focus was on process problems and how they interfered with academic performance. The actual problem might be either a retardation, disorder, or delay, but the differences among these possibilities was not specified. With respect to etiology, CNS dysfunction was affirmed but some confusion was introduced by suggesting that LD might be caused by emotional or behavioral disturbances (E/BD). The possible confounding with the "emotionally handicapped" category seems apparent. The definition also introduced the exclusion clause, the suggestion that LD cannot be due primarily to some other condition.

The definition offered by Bateman emphasized underachievement as an important component of LD. The definition reads:

> *Children who have learning disorders are those who manifest an educationally significant discrepancy between their estimated intellectual potential and actual level of performance related to basic disorders in the learning process, which may or may not be accompanied by demonstrable central nervous system dysfunction, and which are not secondary to generalized mental retardation, educational or cultural deprivation, severe emotional disturbance, or sensory loss.*

The notions about process deficit and exclusion were affirmed and the concept of discrepancy was introduced as a critical factor. A stipulated level for the discrepancy was not provided, however, and no indication of how best to measure estimated intellectual potential or actual level of performance was provided. No etiological statement was included and the CNS dysfunction idea became equivocal with the statement "may or may not."

Legislative Definitions of LD

The definition offered by the National Advisory Committee on Handicapped Children provided the basis for federal legislative definitions:

> *Children with special learning disabilities exhibit a disorder in one or more of the basic psychological processes involved in understanding or in using spoken and written language. These may be manifested in disorders of listening, thinking, talking, reading, writing, spelling, or arithmetic. They include conditions which have been referred to as perceptual handicaps, brain injury, minimal brain dysfunction, dyslexia, developmental aphasia, etc. They do not include learning problems that are due primarily to visual, hearing, or motor handicaps, to mental retardation, emotional disturbance, or to environmental disadvantage.*

The NACHC introduced the notion of specific LD; the learning failure was not a generalized problem, but rather one predicated on a discrete number of deficits. The specific notion appears to be undermined, however, by the phrase "one or more," because there is no stipulation about the point where, in terms of the number of problems, a disorder is no longer specific. The definition also appears to introduce a hierarchy of processes with language, spoken and written, being most prominent. The range of potential manifestations from process problems was also expanded to include "thinking disorders," which then related LD to a variety of cognitive deficits in addition to basic academic skill problems. Although not as explicit with respect to CNS dysfunction, the assumption that LD is similar to conditions emanating from neurological impairments is clearly indicated. This definition by analogy strategy introduces an inherent vagueness, however, because of the lack of specification about how LD may be similar or different from the conditions noted. No statement about requisite severity levels was included. An exclusion clause was included and appears to have become an integral component in defining LD.

In an effort to halt the proliferation of definitions, the U.S. Office of Education funded an institute whose charge was to resolve the perceived difficulties in existing definitions. Kass and Myklebust reported the following definition:

Learning disability refers to one or more significant deficits in essential learning processes requiring special education techniques for remediation.

- Children with learning disability generally demonstrate a discrepancy between expected and actual achievement in one or more areas such as spoken, read, or written language, mathematics, and spatial orientation.
- The learning disability referred to is not primarily the result of sensory, motor, intellectual, or emotional handicap, or lack of opportunity to learn.
- Significant deficits are defined in terms of accepted diagnostic procedures in education and psychology.
- Essential learning processes are those currently referred to in behavioral science as involving perception, integration, and expression, either verbal or nonverbal.

- Special education techniques for remediation refers to educational planning based on the diagnostic procedures and results.

The definition affirmed LD as a condition emanating from process deficits that were deemed "essential." Although statements defining "essential learning processes" and "significant deficits" were included, they were predicated on the assumptions that they are known from "accepted diagnostic procedures" and the way they are "currently referred to in behavioral science." The unarticulated and contentious nature of these statements, both then and now, makes it difficult to perceive how any consensus might be forged with this definition.

An exclusion clause was included and, while incorporating accepted conditions, also suggested an exclusion based on the "lack of opportunity to learn." This is a far less tangible condition that introduces an inherent vagueness because of difficulties in circumscribing boundaries for defining opportunity to learn. With sensory, motor, intellectual, or emotional handicap, classification criteria exist, and the decision becomes a dichotomous one; however, decisions about whether or not a student has had sufficient opportunity to learn are far more subjective.

The definition is noteworthy in two respects. First, the notion of discrepancy was explicitly articulated, thus affirming the relation between LD and underachievement. There was, however, the strange designation of "spatial orientation" as a disorder where a discrepancy might exist. It is unclear why this particular process was included and given equal status with language, reading, and mathematics. Second, the definition emphasized the educational foundation of LD by suggesting that special education techniques are a basic requirement for remediation. By providing an educational focus, no etiology was specified and thus there is no statement about CNS dysfunction. The emphasis was thus on essential learning processes with no presumptions about their origin being some form of neurological impairment.

Committee Definitions of LD

The failure to achieve consensus with respect to defining LD has resulted in repeated efforts to formulate an acceptable definition.

An analysis of these efforts reveals many of the difficulties involved in achieving consensus about LD.

As part of the National Project on the Classification of Exceptional Children, Wepman, Cruickshank, Deutsch, Morency and Strother proposed the following definition:

> *Specific learning disability refers to those children of any age who demonstrate a substantial deficiency in a particular aspect of academic achievement because of perceptual or perceptual-motor handicaps, regardless of etiology or other contributing factors. The term* perceptual *as used here relates to those mental processes through which the child acquires his basic alphabets of sounds and forms.*

In this definition, the notion of specificity was affirmed by limiting LD to perceptual process-based academic failure. The focus on perceptual or perceptual-motor deficits was introduced because of a concern that too many diverse types of learning failure were being subsumed under the LD rubric. To alleviate this concern, this more restrictive definition was offered but, in all likelihood, would be too limiting. Severity level was not specified but ensconced in the context of "substantial." The definition also eliminated an etiological statement and an exclusion clause.

The National Joint Committee on Learning Disabilities was formed by representatives from eight major organisations that had an interest in LD. Although endorsing the federal definition, it was believed that it could be improved with the following modifications: (a) reinforcing the idea that LD can exist at all ages, (b) deleting the contentious notion of *basic psychological processes,* (c) eliminating spelling as a specific disorder and subsuming it under *writing,* (d) eliminating the list of analogous conditions, and (e) clarifying the "exclusion clause" to indicate that LD may coexist with other handicapping conditions. The resulting NJCLD definition reads:

> *Learning disabilities is a generic term that refers to a heterogeneous group of disorders manifested by significant difficulties in the acquisition and use of listening, speaking, reading, writing, reasoning, or mathematical abilities.*

These disorders are intrinsic to the individual and presumed to be due to central nervous system dysfunction. Even though a learning disability may occur concomitantly with other handicapping conditions (e.g., sensory impairment, mental retardation, social and emotional disturbance) or environmental influences (e.g., cultural differences, insufficient or inappropriate instruction, psychogenic factors), it is not the direct result of those conditions or influences.

The NJCLD definition appears to be the antithesis of earlier definitions promoting "specific" LD. Instead, LD is now a general term that is quite likely to manifest a variety of symptoms. The notion of discrepancy is not stated explicitly and level of severity is only indicated by "significant." The notion of CNS dysfunction was affirmed as well as the assumption that the disorder emanates from disorders within the individual. Unlike earlier definitions where process deficits were the most direct manifestation of CNS dysfunction, no such relationship is specified, and it is not clear what neurological impairments "cause." The "intrinsic" notion also excludes the possibility of LD being associated with social or educational influences. The focus is on what deficits the individual brings to the situation, and complex environmental interactions and transactions seem not to be recognized. The "exclusion clause" is now modified to move away from an "either-or" dichotomy to one where LD may coexist with other conditions. Although LD is assumed primary, the lack of specification makes it difficult to determine precisely the nature of the relationships with other conditions.

The NJCLD definition was based on the efforts of eight major organisations, and its adoption was predicated on approval by all member organisations. The definition was accepted by all organisations except the Learning Disabilities Association of America, who chose to write their own definition:

> *Specific Learning Disabilities is a chronic condition of presumed neurological origin which selectively interfered with the development, integration, and/or demonstration of verbal and/or nonverbal abilities. Specific Learning Disabilities exist as a distinct handicapping condition and varies in its manifestations and in degree of severity. Throughout life, the condition can affect self-esteem, education, vocation, socialization, and/or daily living activities.*

The notion of specificity is included through the word "selectively," but the possible manifestations span an undefined range of verbal and nonverbal abilities. This introduced considerable imprecision, and it is unclear what type of problems are being defined. For example, are nonverbal abilities primarily social skill deficits? Although verbal abilities would include reading and writing difficulties, what is the status of difficulties in mathematics? The notion of CNS dysfunction as the primary etiology is affirmed, and the most direct problems might be either in the "development, integration, and/or demonstration" of abilities but the differences among these possibilities is not stipulated. The longstanding consequences of LD are recognized through the word "chronic," and a number of possible areas that might be affected adversely, in addition to education, throughout the life span are specified. An exclusion clause is not incorporated and presumably indicates no relationship between LD and other handicapping conditions. This seems to be affirmed through the inclusion of the word "distinct," which suggests LD be perceived as a syndrome, a discrete cluster of symptoms. The "distinct" idea appears to be undermined, however, by phrasing that indicates manifestations may vary as well as severity level.

In an effort to formulate an improved definition, the Interagency Committee on Learning Disabilities (ICLD) was formed from 12 agencies within the federal government. A number of papers were commissioned to determine the state of knowledge and, after deliberation, the following definition was proposed:

> *Learning disabilities is a generic term that refers to a heterogeneous group of disorders manifested by significant difficulties in the acquisition and use of listening, speaking, reading, writing, reasoning, or mathematical abilities,* or of social skills. *These disorders are intrinsic to the individual and presumed to be due to central nervous system dysfunction. Even though a learning disability may occur concomitantly with other handicapping conditions, with socio-environmental influences,* and especially attention deficit disorder, all of which may cause learning problems, *a learning disability is not the direct result of those conditions or influences.*

If the definition looks familiar, it is; the ICLD, rather than formulating a new definition, believed that the NJCLD definition was the best available and required only some modification . Questions about the NJCLD definitions are equally applicable to the ICLD definition but with new points of contention. Most contentious was the addition of social skills to the list of potential primary manifestations. Although recognizing that an individual with LD might also possess social problems, the desirability of including social skill deficits as a primary form of LD was questioned. First and foremost, there is the problem of diagnosing LD without academic deficits; a student without difficulties in reading, writing, or mathematics could be diagnosed as LD and placed in an LD programme solely for treatment of social disorders. The confounding with the federal definition for serious emotional disturbance (SED) is substantial given that one of the five diagnostic criteria for SED is an inability to learn that cannot be explained by intellectual, sensory, or health factors. Additionally, the research is unequivocal with respect to the nature, extent, and assessment of social skill deficits in LD. The perceived difficulties led to the Department of Education not endorsing the ICLD definition because including social skills would (a) require a change in IDEA, (b) increase confusion concerning eligibility, and (c) increase the number of students classified as LD. Finally, by stipulating attention deficit disorder (ADD) in the definition, the problematic relationship between ADD and LD comes to the fore.

Definitions in Perspective

What can be learned from this examination of LD definitions? First, the LD concept has generated a number of definitions. Unlike MR with a single definition, the LD field has generated a number of competing definitions. Second, LD has not been defined with much exactitude; what emerges is a generalized picture of a portion of the school population experiencing academic difficulties. Although many of the same ideas are included either implicitly or explicitly, there exists enough variation so that definitional precision is lost. The consequences are found in the lack of a uniform perspective where LD is viewed differently in different contexts. Some 25 years ago, Cruickshank described the variegated picture of LD as students moved from state to state and the situation appears not to have changed appreciably.

A variety of issues remain unresolved, and the notion of specificity provides a number of examples. Many definitions included the adjective specific, which implied that poor academic performance emanates from a limited number of underlying deficits. The purpose was to differentiate LD from conditions where a wide assortment of processes might be depressed, such as MR, which is viewed as a generalized deficit. The idea that LD results from a circumscribed set of problems that interfere selectively with academic functioning is still acknowledged. Assumptions about specificity have, however, been challenged as unrealistic and restrictive. For example, it is suggested that linguistic and memory deficits might conceivably affect adversely a number of abilities (e.g., reading, writing, listening) and that reading and mathematics are not necessarily independent cognitive abilities.

The notion of specificity is also confounded by the myriad catalogue of potential deficits associated with LD. For example, the areas of linguistic and neuromotor functioning are composed of dozens of discrete skills. Although focusing on the same general function, it is difficult to relate each individual deficit to LD. Why do some students with LD manifest one deficit and not another? Are some deficits more associated with LD than another? Can any single deficit be the major contributor to LD?

A problem also emerges when a large majority of the LD population manifest the same deficit as is the case with reading disability (RD). With about 85% of students with LD revealing primary difficulty in reading, differentiating LD and RD becomes problematic. It is not clear whether LD and RD are really similar or whether, because more is known about the established condition, RD, it is easier to explain LD by comparing and contrasting it with RD.

Specificity is also confounded when the basic deficit is termed a "retardation, disorder, or delay," for example, because these imply very different conceptualizations about the nature and origin of LD. For the most part, LD has been viewed as a deficit specifically in the form of a CNS dysfunction intrinsic to the student. This disease model possesses ready appeal but needs to be validated through findings of specific pathology and thus far attempts to specify the neuropathology associated with LD have not received unequivocal support. The disease model emphasizes the primacy of biological over psychological and social explanations, but it is difficult to conceive of a behavioral phenomenon like LD being solely the result of neurophysiological determinants.

An alternative explanation may be found in notions about LD as deficiency, the absence of a critical function. The definition offered by Wepman provides a deficiency explanation of LD in the form of a perceptual deficit. Difficulties are encountered, however, in providing explanations about how a perceptual deficit can result in so specific a problem. For example, the deficiency would have to be selective enough to impair the reading of words, but not the reading of individual letters or numbers. Deficiency explanations fare better with hypotheses linking LD and basic linguistic disorders like phonological awareness or speed of processing. The problem, however, is the large number of possible deficiencies and the way they may be combined to define LD. Deficiency explanations are limited by their specificity, because any particular deficiency can explain LD in particular, rather than LD in general.

Still another explanation is found in LD as difference; basic abilities differ and create a mismatch between student and environment. One difference may be related to normal variation and the possibility that LD problems reflect not specific deficits, but the distribution of abilities along the normal curve. Difference explanations may also emphasize the problem rather than its source. Brown and Campione, for example, perceived the primary difficulty to be the failure to acquire domain-specific knowledge and skills. Difference explanations, however, lack specificity and may result in tautologies. The generalized character of difference hypotheses permit only a global nature for LD and not an adequate level of explanation for LD functioning.

Defining Definition

Many difficulties in defining LD emanate from a failure to understand the nature of definition. A definition represents an attempt to correlate words with a thing. When words have been agreed on in a logical and rational fashion, a definition is achieved but may not be a real and accurate representation of the thing. The "thing" may possess fundamental and basic qualities difficult to capture in words but such qualities are what make the thing real. Aristotle termed these qualities *essence* and, to be attained, must not simply describe a thing's physical properties but also the elements that transcend the physical to make it what it is. Kant made a distinction between "appearance" and "things in themselves." Appearance represents what has come to be perceived about a phenomenon, whereas things in themselves presuppose a more basic level where phenomenon are represented the way they really are. Thus, things in themselves share qualities found in essence and provide a contrast between what we think and what actually is.

Definitions come in many forms. *Real definitions* attempt to correlate things with things in a search for essence, but essence is rarely achieved through words. Real definitions are not often attained and, even though LD has operated as if its definitions are real, they are not real in any significant sense. To think otherwise leads to a false sense of closure. *Conceptual definitions* have been assumed to be represented in the LD field but their formal meaning is often also difficult to achieve. A concept, the basis for conceptual definitions, represents a circumscribed set of characteristics gleaned from the formal activity of concept formation and are theoretically validated. Too many concepts associated with LD have not been theoretically verified and thus not established firmly enough to be included in a "conceptual" definition of LD. For example, Kosc suggested that *LD* need not be defined as such because all that is necessary is "to explain what is to be understood by the component terms 'learning' and 'disabilities'". Kavale and Forness argued that *learning + disability = LD* is too simplistic and disregards the complex and multivariate nature of LD. Furthermore, learning theory is marked by much theoretical) diversity, and *disability* becomes very different as evidenced by the earlier discussion about deficit, deficiency, and difference.

The most common form of definition is *nominal,* whose goal is to correlate words with things. One type is *lexical,* as found in a dictionary and representing the customary meaning at a particular point in time; lexical definitions, however, tend to be too general and not very insightful. Most LD definitions may be termed *stipulative,* an explicit and arbitrary adoption of a meaning relation between words. The passage from Lewis Carroll *Through the Looking Glass* that opened this chapter points to the basic problem with stipulative definitions; they mean whatever a particular individual decide they should mean. Various individuals, groups, and organisations associated with LD have acted like Humpty Dumpty by insisting that *LD* mean what they choose it to mean, based on conventional wisdom about what LD should be.

Stipulative definitions face a fundamental difficulty: They need not be true, only useful. As long as there is consensus about included elements and a perceived heuristic value, the definition is accepted and used. Such definitions never really achieve closure and, as long as consensus is obtained, all theoretical arguments about valid or invalid elements are relative. Stipulative definitions often take the guise of real definitions, but there is no guarantee that they are true; they may be right or wrong but still useful. Most available LD definitions have proven useful, but it is necessary to view them as approximations whose validity still needs to be established.

Operational Definitions

Stipulative definitions are, thus, only of generic usefulness, and require transformation to be applied in practice. The most usual transformation is the operational definition, a rule stipulating that the term is to apply to a particular case if specified operations yield certain characteristic results. Any concept has a set of operations that defines it and knowing these operations is to understand the concept fully.

Although seemingly unobjectionable, operational definitions possess a number of difficulties. First, they do not meet formal definitional criteria because the operations specified do not really define anything, but merely state the operations required to test for the presence of the thing to which operations refer. The meaning can be conveyed in a number of ways, depending on the indicators chosen. For example, the concept of discrepancy is defined as the difference between expected and actual achievement, but any number of IQ measures could be used to "define" expected achievement, and an even greater number might be chosen to "define" actual achievement. It is not clear that different measures are operationally, and thus definitionally, equivalent.

A second problem with operational definitions surrounds the fact that LD concepts relate to experience only indirectly. For example, school frustration in an LD student cannot be measured in a way comparable to the direct measurement of heat with a thermometer. School frustration might be defined operationally, but it would be more indirect and require the use of *symbolic operations* to deal with the open terms (i.e. *school, frustration*); symbolic operations, however, introduce metaphysical. elements that undermine the operationalist approach.

A final problem surrounds the theoretical validity of operations. When based on verified theoretical components, operational definitions may be based on a logical and rational foundation. For example, the motion of mercury molecules in a closed tube permits a mathematical interpretation of heat. When the theoretical structure possesses few validated elements as is the case in LD, operational definitions may not be justified because of the risk of developing spurious procedures. Assume, for example, that there is a proposal for a new *Learning Disability Coefficient* (LDC) defined as the white blood cell count multiplied by body weight in ounces, divided by head circumference in centimeters. Although an LDC could be calculated, it would possess little meaning or significance because a good deal is known about LD and the LDC does not "fit" with any of the existing knowledge. Thus, it is possible to operationalize anything, but whether it "makes sense" is a different matter.

Operational Definitions of LD

The standard definition of LD is the IDEA definition presented earlier and is the official definition under which federal programmes are administered. The definition is essentially the NACHC definition that was adopted because of conflicting opinion delivered during Congressional testimony and the conclusion that there was no consensus about definition. Until more definitive and agreed on parameters are forthcoming, no substantive definitional change would be appropriate.

To be useful for practical purposes, however, formal definitions need to be operationalized. The United States Office of Education, in an effort to guide practice, issued the following guidelines:

> *A specific learning disability may be found if a child has a severe discrepancy between achievement and intellectual ability in one or more of several areas: oral expression, written expression, listening comprehension or reading comprehension, basic reading skills, mathematics calculation, mathematics reasoning, or spelling. A "severe discrepancy" is defined to exist when achievement in one or more of the areas falls at or below 50% of the child's expected achievement level, when age and previous educational experiences are taken into consideration.*

Although appearing to be a useful operational definition, the procedures presented suffer from a fundamental flaw: They bear little resemblance to what was stipulated in the formal definition. Any discussion of operational definition would demand that the proposed operations possess a logical and rational relationship to the elements found in the formal definition in order to avoid meaningless and insignificant procedures. The USOE operational definition focuses on discrepancy, but there is no statement about discrepancy in the formal definition. Conversely, the formal definition talks about psychological process deficits and CNS dysfunction but these ideas are not included in the operational definition. Additionally, although stipulated in the formal definition, the exclusion clause is given no specification in the operational definition. Although the vagueness associated with the phrase "one or more" are not clarified in the operational definition, severity level becomes the single aspect better delineated by the stipulation of a 50% figure to define "severe discrepancy."

The lack of correspondence between the formal and operational definition of LD means that two distinct views of LD are being presented. Ideally, the procedures stated in an operational definition should be used to validate the elements stipulated in the formal definition. When there is no correspondence between formal and operational definitions, theoretical verification is not possible, and what remains is simply a low grade of psychometric engineering.

The problems are further exacerbated by the fact that discrepancy itself is a concept and requires an operational definition for implementation. If discrepancy is formally defined as the difference between expected and actual achievement, then it is necessary to define operationally expected and actual achievement.

The usual solution is to define each term with something readily quantifiable. For expected achievement, the prediction is typically based on an IQ score obtained from an intelligence measure. The IQ score, however, is the operational definition of intelligence, and no consideration is given to how or why intelligence tests measure intelligence; it is sufficient to know that intelligence tests can provide an IQ score. Actual achievement may be obtained from any number of standardized achievement measures. Little consideration is given to the fact that the obtained scores in grade equivalents are problematic, that Kelley's "jingle and jangle" fallacy (i.e., the assumption that tests with the same name measure the same thing or that tests with different names measure different things) may be operating,

Operationally, discrepancy is simply the difference between expected and actual achievement, and, if the difference meets a stipulated, albeit arbitrary, criterion, then a discrepancy is present. Although simple, this view of discrepancy ignores evidence showing difference scores to be notoriously unreliable, to be influenced by the measurement model used, and to remain static with respect to a time dimension that may introduce different levels of experience. Finally, discrepancy itself must be understood as the operational definition of underachievement, not LD. The strongest theoretical link is between underachievement and discrepancy; the linkage between LD and discrepancy is far less robust.

Dilemmas of Definition

Hammill suggested that considerable agreement exists among LD definitions and definers. Although this may be a valid observation, it should provide little comfort. Definitions of LD may show a numbing sameness but do not provide an answer to the question: What is LD? Beyond a vague description about a generalized learning failure, LD definitions are not particularly insightful. To prove this point, it is only necessary to examine actual practice where the primary element for determining eligibility is not even mentioned in the formal definitions. This is not the hallmark of a tightly structured conceptual system surrounding LD.

Definitions of LD evolved from the seminal work of Strauss and Werner and include many of their paradigmatic assumptions. The problem is found in the "softening" of these ideas over time to the point where substantial meaning is lost. The concept of CNS dysfunction provides an example. Brain injury is certainly a valid concept but its modification with adjectives *minimal* and *dysfunction* as well as an emphasis on "soft signs" in diagnosis has made it a behavioral, not physiological, concept with a different meaning. Process deficits share a similar fate. Processes represent hypothetical constructs and, as such, are meaningful only when sufficient construct validity is demonstrated. Generally, the processes associated with LD do not achieve sufficient construct validity to demonstrate an independent reality. Thus, two important core concepts of LD are difficult to measure and substantiate.

The difficulties with CNS dysfunction and process disorders have resulted in a movement away from these stipulated core concepts to other important but more peripheral concepts. Exclusion, for example, is a legitimate element but does not really elucidate what LD is; by emphasizing exclusion, LD becomes a residual disorder. Additionally, exclusion is problematic; at a behavioral level, LD reveals more similarities than differences when compared to MR and BD which has been demonstrated in diagnostic test data not reliably differentiating among LD, MR, and BD. What remained was academic failure, and it became the primary identification criterion. Unlike CNS dysfunction and process deficits that are hypothetical and unobservable constructs, academic failure as defined by discrepancy is a far more tangible criterion that is both efficient and convenient. However, efficiency and convenience are not good reasons for relying on a single factor. The complex nature of LD demands that more than one variable be included to achieve a comprehensive and unified perspective.

The reliance on a single factor, besides offering a limited view of LD, also leads to a situation where other elements are inferred rather than documented. Once a student is classified on the basis of meeting the discrepancy criterion, the presence of CNS dysfunction and processing disorders are often implied. The reason is that these components are explicitly stated in the formal definition and, when designated LD, it is implicitly assumed that a student then meets all the stipulated parameters. Stich an assumption is not justified; you assume something that may not be present and ignore a variety of elements that may be present. Given such circumstances, there is little wonder that LD experiences a "problem of heterogeneity."

Prospects for LD Definition

The definitional problem of LD is genuine. It is unlikely that any tinkering with the available definitions will ever result in "the" definition of LD. The reason is that many of the foundation assumptions included, if not invalid, are, at least, questionable. This problem is exacerbated by the use of operational definitions that exhibit little relationship to whatever is stated in formal definition. The result is a proliferation of LD definitions that have become increasingly obscure and fail to provide insight into the question: What is LD?

Rather than trying to "fix" the present definitions, it seems that resolution can only be achieved if the process starts anew. Kavale and Forness provided an outline for how this process might proceed. A first step would be laying out a set of foundation principles. Through rational and logical debate, propositions about the nature of LD are formulated and serve as a conceptual framework. Next, although problematic, operational definitions may represent the best means of formalizing the LD definition. They, however, must move beyond finely focused attempts at one-to-one correspondence;

LD is too complex to be captured by a single indicator. The solution would be to move beyond the notion of an operational definition as a single statement to include a number of elements that may be defined operationally. Ennis termed these *operational interpretations,* and they would possess the advantage of permitting a number of concepts to be given meaning by describing their individual operational definitions. The operational interpretations would then need to be organized into an ordered and sequenced hierarchical arrangement that essentially defines what LD is. With this process complete, attention can be directed to writing a formal definition that needs only be a descriptive rendering of the process and elements included.

The procedures outlined are a radical departure from the way LD definitions have been developed in the past. This seems absolutely necessary if any substantive change is to be accomplished. Historically, LD came into the special education scene as a full-blown entity. It almost immediately became a popular designation, but the popularization resulted in an unsubstantiated "conventional wisdom" driving the system rather than reasoned, albeit slower, scientific wisdom. The increased popularity was accompanied by increased vagueness. Under these circumstances, changes were difficult to achieve, and the almost endless semantic wrangling over LD definition attests to this fact. If nothing else, the procedures outlined might breathe some fresh air into an increasingly stale debate.

2

DEFICIT DISORDERS

Attention deficit disorder (ADD) is a relatively new diagnostic label for children. ADD constitutes a chronic neurobiological condition characterized by developmentally inappropriate attention skills, impulsivity, and, in some cases, hyperactivity. The term is used by many professionals, such as the U.S. Department of Education, to identify these children. An alternative diagnostic term is recommended by the American Psychiatric Association — namely, *Attention Deficit Hyperactivity Disorder* (ADHD) -and this referent is used in the DSM-IV. In practice, both ADD and ADHD describe the same disability and are frequently used interchangeably. Even though the designations ADD and ADHD are relatively recent, children with the characteristics of ADD have long been recognized and posed a challenge for parents, psychologists, educators, and physicians.

The suspicion that many Americans seem to have ADD may be true. One can speculate that as Americans we inherited the genetic characteristics of our impulsive, hyperactive risk-taking ancestors. After all, we are the descendants of people who made the rash, high-risk decision to leave their native countries and families to start life anew in America. Their peers and family members who remained in the "old country" were the attentive, reflective, conservative people who did not choose to take that impetuous trio to the new world.

Background

A conservative estimate is that 3-5% of our school population, or approximately 2 million children and adolescents, are affected by ADD. Further, studies show that approximately 50% of children with ADD grow up to become adults with ADD.

ADD interferes with many areas of the child's life, disrupting the child's home life, education, behaviour, and social adjustment. At home, children with ADD have difficulty accommodating home routines and parent expectations. They may resist going to bed, refuse to eat, or even break toys during play. At school, they have trouble completing their class work, often missing valuable information because of their underdeveloped attention capacity. They speak aloud out of turn and find themselves in trouble for their behaviour. Their social lives are undermined by inattention, impulsivity and hyperactivity, hampering their ability to make and keep friends. In terms of gender, more boys than girls are diagnosed as having attention deficit disorders; however, research suggests that the prevalence rate is equal for boys and girls. Boys, however, are more likely to be identified.

ADD at Different Stages of Life

Symptoms of ADD change over time, and distinctive behaviours are evident at different developmental stages.

Young Children: Children, ages 2 through 6, who are excessively active, are described as being on the go, or "running like a motor." They exhibit overabundant gross motor activity, with constant running and climbing behaviour, and cannot sit still for more than a few minutes at a time. Parents report that it is particularly trying to take their ADD preschoolers to public places, such as supermarkets or restaurants. Young children with ADD may take toys apart to see how they work, but find that they are unable to put them together and end up by destroying the toy.

Elementary School Age Children: Students with ADD at this age are described as restless, fidgety, poorly organized, and haphazard in their behaviour. They tend to talk too much in class, get into fights with classmates, and their inattention can impede learning to read. If the child has above-average intelligence, the reading problem may not be noticeable at first.

Adolescents: The behavioral problems continue into adolescence. When poor attention and hyperactive behaviour add to the turmoil of adolescence itself, deficiencies in academic skills intensify. Many adolescents with ADD also have coexisting conditions, such as learning disabilities, behaviour disorders, and social problems. Even though adolescents may appear less hyperactive, they develop other symptoms, such as social disabilities, conduct disorders, low self-esteem, inattentiveness, or even depression.

Adults: At one time, ADD was considered a childhood problem; it was thought that ADD symptoms were outgrown when the individual reached adulthood. Now it is recognized that ADD can continue throughout adult life. For many adults, problems related to ADD affect their work and careers, their social lives, marriages, and personal relationships.

Coexisting Disabilities

Frequently, another condition or disability occurs concomitantly with attention deficit disorders. The comorbid or coexisting condition also must be considered in the assessment and treatment. Coexisting conditions are likely to be in the form of learning disabilities, emotional and behavioral disorders, social problems, and traits of gifted/talented children.

Learning Disabilities

ADD is not synonymous with learning disabilities, but many children with attention deficit disorders also display symptoms of learning disabilities, further complicating identification and treatment. Estimates based on research suggest that at least 25% of children with ADD have co-existing learning disabilities. Because many students diagnosed with ADD will also be identified and served under the classification of learning disabilities, it is essential that learning disabilities teachers and regular classroom teachers become knowledgeable about ADD.

Emotional and Behavioral Disorders

Another condition that may coexist with ADD is serious emotional disturbance (SED), an existing category of disability in

IDEA. In the *Diagnostic and Statistical Manual of Mental Disorders*, fourth edition (*DSM-IV*), the diagnostic classifications are identified as *Conduct Disorder* (CD) and *Oppositional Defiant Disorder.*

Children with coexisting ADD and disruptive behaviour disorders often display aggression, oppositional defiance, and conduct problems. It is estimated that 40-60% of elementary-age children with ADD have coexisting oppositional defiance disorders, whereas roughly 20-30% develop conduct disorders.

Social Problems

One of the most consistent findings in the literature on ADD is that children and youth with ADD have significant and persistent problems in social relationships. A social disability is probably the most debilitating problem for a child. Children with ADD often do not relate well to peers and may have few or no friends. Peer rejection can be devastating, leading to feelings of loneliness, poor self-image and low self-esteem. For adolescents, such problems and feelings too often lead to poor school performance, juvenile delinquency, and dropping out of school.

Children with ADD and hyperactivity tend to be aggressive and are rejected more often than comparison subjects. Children with ADD not having hyperactivity are more withdrawn and unpopular but not necessarily rejected.

Gifted/Talented Students With ADD

It has been observed that many of the characteristics of gifted children are also traits of children with ADD. Gifted children are characterized as spontaneous, inquisitive, imaginative, boundlessly enthusiastic, excitable, and emotional-traits that also describe children with ADD.

The nervous system of gifted children seem to require much activity. Gifted children tend to be immovable when engaged in projects, working persistently and passionately. Gifted children also may find regular classroom environments difficult places in which to maintain engagement because of the slow pace. They may respond by becoming fidgety, inattentive, and even disruptive, because their learning needs are not being met. Because of the similarity between these two categories, it is suspected that gifted children are sometimes mislabeled as children with ADD.

Historical Perspective

The concept of ADD has taken a long time to evolve. Although we have long recognized that these children needed help, they have been identified in the past under other labels, including brain injured, MBD, conduct disordered, hyper kinetic, learning disabled, and emotionally disturbed. A number of historical events shaped the field of attention deficit disorders.

1902: Defects in Moral Control

Early in the 1900s, a physician described the symptoms of a group of hyperactive and inattentive children as aggressive, defiant, resistant to discipline, and lawless. Reflecting views of that era, Still believed these children lacked the will to control moral behaviour and characterized them as having "morbid defects in moral control".

1947: Brain Damage Syndrome

Paralleling the history of the field of learning disabilities, influential research in the 1930s and 1940s linked the behavioral and hyperactive symptoms of children to brain damage. The work of Strauss and his colleagues stressed behaviour characteristics more than learning characteristics. Today, many of the behavioral characteristics first identified by Strauss are recognized as key traits of children with attention deficit disorders. There was no vigorous follow-up to this early work, and educators and parents instead turned their attention to learning disabilities, where the focus was on children's learning problems rather than on their behavioral characteristics.

1966: Minimal Brain Dysfunction

The term *brain damage* proved to be troublesome for professionals and parents for several reasons, including that it did not differentiate between gross and less severe brain damage. A new term, *minimal brain dysfunction* (MBD), was recommended in a report sponsored by the National Institutes of Health. The symptoms of MBD included specific learning deficits, hyperkinesis, impulsivity, and short attention span.

1968: Hyperkinetic Reaction of Childhood

A significant historical event was the publication of the *Diagnostic and Statistical Manual of Mental Disorders*, second edition. The DSM publications provide diagnostic criteria for various mental disorders. In the *DSM-II*, the phrase hyperkinetic reaction of childhood was first used to describe the hyperactive child.

1980: Attention Deficit Disorder: ADDH and ADD

In 1980, diagnostic guidelines were revised in the third edition of the *Diagnostic and Statistical Manual of Mental Disorders*. The focus shifted to attention problems rather than hyperactive behaviour. The *DSM-III* established the term *attention deficit disorder*, classifying two types: (a) ADD with hyperactivity (ADDH), and (b) ADD without hyperactivity (ADD/noH). In addition, the *DSM-III* established criteria of onset prior to age 7 and duration of the behaviour for at least 6 months.

1987: Attention Deficit Hyperactivity Disorder (ADHD)

Further modification appeared in 1987, with the publication of the *Diagnostic and Statistical Manual of Mental Disorders*, third edition-revised. In the *DSM-III-R*, the term attention deficit hyperactivity disorder (ADHD) was recommended. The criteria for the diagnosis of ADHD required that the child exhibit 8 of 14 symptomatic behaviours. In addition, the *DSM-III-R* described a condition referred to as *undifferentiated attention deficit disorder* (U-ADD), which roughly corresponds to the earlier ADD/noH designation.

1994: Attention-Deficit Hyperactivity Disorder (ADHD)

The fourth edition of the *Diagnostic and Statistical Manual of Mental Disorders* (*DSM-IV*) revised the diagnostic criteria for ADHD. Because *DSM-IV* criteria is the basis for the diagnosis of ADHD by psychologists, psychiatrists, and other professionals, the *DSM-IV* is discussed in greater detail.

Attention Deficit Hyperactivity Disorder

The *DSM-IV*, published in 1994, contained new diagnostic criteria for *attention deficit hyperactivity disorder* and has substantial implications for school assessment and for instruction of children with ADD or ADHD. The individual is judged on specific symptomatic behaviours obtained through observation or from informants. The DSM-IV continues the terminology of ADHD, but designates three subtypes of ADHD.

ADHD-I: Primarily Inattentive Subtype

In the ADHD-I subtype, the primary problem is that of attention. This subtype is familiar to clinicians as a variant of ADD without hyperactivity. The criteria for the diagnosis of ADHD-I requires that the individual display at least six attention symptoms, but fewer than six hyperactivity-impulsivity symptoms.

ADHD-IH: Primarily Hyperactive-Impulsive Subtype

The ADHD-IH subtype is new, as these individuals display behaviours of hyperactivity and impulsivity, but they do not manifest problems with attention. The criteria for the diagnosis of ADHD-IH requires that the individual display at least six hyperactivity-impulsivity symptoms, but fewer than six inattention symptoms.

ADHD-C: A Combination of ADHD-I and ADHD-IH

The ADHD-C subtype refers to individuals who have both attention problems and display symptoms of hyperactivity and impulsivity. These individuals have at least six inattention symptoms and six hyperactivity-impulsivity symptoms.

In developing these new criteria for ADHD, researchers conducted field trials with 380 children who were referred to clinics. The study found that 27% of the ADHD population were identified with the subtype ADHD-I, 18% were identified under the subtype ADHD-HI, and 55% were identified under the subtype ADHD-C.

Education Clarification Memorandum on ADD

A major step in the recognition of attention deficit disorders in the public schools occurred in 1991, when the U.S. Department of Education issued a memorandum clarifying its policy with regard to eligibility for services for children with ADD. The Department of Education's policy memorandum on ADD was a response to the vigorous lobbying effort of concerned parent groups, particularly CH.A.D.D., and by practitioners and researchers in education, medicine, and psychology. This significant policy memorandum was signed jointly by representatives of three offices in the Department of Education: The Office of Special Education and Rehabilitative Services, the Office for Civil Rights, and the Office of Elementary and Secondary Education.

Eligibility Under IDEA

The U.S. Department of Education's memorandum on ADD states that a child with ADD may qualify for special education and related services under Part B of IDEA, within the category of "other health impaired" if the ADD constitutes "a chronic or acute health problem that results in limited alertness," thus adversely affecting educational performance. As defined in IDEA:

> Other health impaired *is having limited strength, vitality, or alertness, as a result of chronic or acute health problems, such as heart conditions, tuberculosis, rheumatic fever, nephritis, asthma, sickle cell anemia, hemophilia, epilepsy, lead poisoning, leukemia, or diabetes, that adversely affects educational performance.*

The memorandum further states that children with ADD may be eligible for services under Part B of IDEA if they satisfy the criteria applicable to other disability categories, such as learning disabilities or serious emotional disturbance. Thus, children with ADD may be eligible for services under three categories of disability in IDEA: other health impaired, learning disabilities, and seriously emotional disturbance.

Eligibility Under Section 504 of the Rehabilitation Act of 1973

The U.S. Department of Education policy memorandum on ADD also states that a child with ADD may be eligible for services in the general education classroom under Section 504 of the Rehabilitation Act of 1973, even if that child does not qualify for special education and related services under Part B of IDEA. Under Section 504, if the child is found to have "a physical or mental impairment which substantially limits a major life activity", then the school must make an "individualized determination of the child's education needs for regular or special education or related aids and services". For the student identified as having ADD under Section 504, "reasonable accommodations" must be provided within the general education classroom. Section 504 states: "No otherwise qualified handicapped individual shall, solely by reason of his/her handicap, be excluded from participation in, be denied the benefits of, or be subject to discrimination under any programme or activity receiving federal financial assistance."

School Placement for Instruction

Most students with ADD are served in the general education classroom under the rules and regulations of either IDEA or Section 504. IDEA's provisions for the *least restrictive environment and a continuum of alternative placements* mean that many children with ADD who are eligible under IDEA for special education services receive instruction in the regular classroom, with support and collaboration of special education teachers. With the current inclusion movement, even more children with ADD are likely to be placed in general education classrooms. Some students with ADD need other placement options and should receive services in resource rooms or special classrooms. Children with ADD who are eligible for services under Section 504 are served in the regular classroom through appropriate modifications and accommodations. A.D.D. estimates that about 50% of students with ADD can be appropriately served within the regular classroom, about 35% need resource services, and 15% have severe ADD disabilities and need a special education classroom. Thus, most children with ADD (85%) will be in general education classrooms. Over half will be served solely in general education classrooms. The 35% of the children in resource rooms will be in the general education classroom for a large portion of the day; therefore, the need to offer training for elementary and secondary teachers to work with students with ADD is tremendous.

A recent survey of classroom teachers shows that teachers receive virtually no training for working with students with ADD.

General Education Classrooms

Because most children with ADD will be served in the general education classroom, it is important to know about (a) accommodations and modifications in the general education classroom, and (b) promising classroom intervention programmes for students with ADD.

Accommodations and Modifications in the General Education Classroom: A number of ways to modify the classroom for children with attention deficit disorders are described in this section.

Improving Organizational Skills: Students with ADD have difficulty in organizing their lives, and their lack of organisation results in uncompleted assignments. The following suggestions are designed to help students learn how to plan ahead, how to gather appropriate materials for school tasks, how to prioritize the steps to complete an assignment, and how to keep track of their work:

1. Provide clear classroom rules to add structure and communicate teacher expectations.
2. Establish routines for placing objects – especially routinely used objects (such as books, assignments, and outdoor clothes) – in designated places so that they can be found easily.
3. Provide the students with a list of materials needed for the task. Limit the list to only those materials necessary to complete the task.
4. Provide a schedule so that the students know exactly what to do for each class period.
5. Make sure the students have all homework assignments before leaving school. Write each assignment on the board and have the student copy it, or write the assignment for a student in a pocket notebook.
6. Provide students with pocket folders to organize materials. For example, place new work on one side and completed work in chronological order on the other.
7. Use a different color folder for each subject.

Increasing Attention: Inattention is a primary characteristic of children with ADD. Because of their short attention span, they may initially attend but their attention soon wanders. The following activities are designed to help students attend and prolong their concentration:

1. Shorten the task by breaking a long task into smaller parts. Assign fewer problems; for example, fewer spelling words or mathematics problems.
2. Shorten the homework assignment by giving fewer problems.
3. Use distributed practice. Instead of a few, long, and concentrated practice sessions, set up more short, spaced, and frequent practice sessions.
4. Make tasks more interesting to keep the student's interest. Encourage children to work with partners, in small groups, or in interest centers.
5. Alternate highly interesting and less interesting tasks.
6. Increase the novelty of the task. Tasks that are new or unique are more appealing and will increase attention.

Improving Ability to Listen: Students with ADD frequently miss important instructions and information because they are not actively listening. They may even be unaware that a message is being given. Listening means more than hearing or recognizing the words that are spoken; it means comprehending the message. The following strategies can help students acquire better listening skills:

1. Make instruction simple by using short, direct sentences. Give one instruction at a time. Repeat as often as necessary. Make sure students know the vocabulary being used.
2. Prompt student to repeat instructions after listening to them, then have the students repeat to themselves information they have just heard to build listening and memory skills.
3. Alert the student by using key phrases, such as "this is important" and "listen carefully." (For college students, the phrase "this will be on the exam" is very effective.) Some teachers use prearranged signals, such as hand signals or switching the lights on before giving directions.

4. Use visual aids (such as charts, pictures, graphics, or written key points on a chalkboard or overhead transparencies) to illustrate and support verbal information.

Adapting the Curriculum: Often the curriculum can be changed, modified, or adapted without sacrificing the integrity of the basic curriculum. Even a small change can be beneficial for students with ADD:

1. Select high interest materials to reinforce the basic curriculum.
2. Use manipulable, hands-on materials whenever possible. Create activities that require active participation, such as talking through problems and acting out steps. Many students learn better when they actually do something in addition to just listening and observing.
3. Use visual aids to supplement oral and written information. Use learning aids, such as computers, calculators, and tape recorders to increase motivation.
4. Modify tests, allowing the student to take tests orally instead of writing the answers. Teach students how to cross out incorrect answers on multiple-choice tests.

Helping Students Manage Time: A common problem area for many students with ADD is the management of time. They get pulled away from the task at hand and become involved with new challenges and tend to become procrastinators, a trait they retain into their adult lives. The following activities are designed to help students with time management:

1. Set up a specific routine and adhere to it. When disruptions occur, explain the situation to the students and appropriate ways to respond.
2. During the school day, alternate activities that are done while sitting and those that involve standing and moving about.
3. Make lists that will help students organize their tasks. Have them check off tasks as they complete them.
4. Use behavioral contracts that specify the amount of time allotted for specific activities.

Classroom Intervention Programmes for Students With ADD

The U.S. Department of Education funded a research team at the Research Triangle Institute to conduct an extensive study of effective school-based interventions that teachers can employ in regular classrooms for teaching students with attention deficit disorders. Although their search found limited studies on teaching students with ADD in school settings, the researchers extrapolated from programmes for other difficult-to teach students. Eight intervention programmes are described, which the researchers consider to be promising classroom interventions for students with attention deficit disorder. The promising programmes, which include academic, affect, study skills, behaviour, and career programmes, are: (a) Class-wise Peer Tutoring, (b) Early Literacy Programme, (c) Tribes, (d) Self-Regulated Strategy Developing in Writing, (e) Early Science Videodisc Programme, (f) Skills for School Success, (g) Aggression Replacement Training, and (h) Life-Centered Career Education. Each is briefly described here.

Class-wise Peer Tutoring (CWPT): This is a system in which tutor-tutee pairs work together on a class-wise basis. The CWPT research was conducted at schools in Juniper Gardens, a housing project in Kansas City, KS.

In the CWPT programme, at the beginning of each week, all students in a class are paired for tutoring, and these tutor-tutee pairs are then assigned to one of two competing teams. Tutees earn points for their team by responding to the tasks presented to them by the tutors. The winning team is determined on the basis of the highest team's point total.

Fuchs, Fuchs, Hamlett, Phillips, and Bentz enhanced CWPT by combining the procedure of classwide curriculum-based measurement with classwide peer tutoring. The researchers report positive results for children with special needs in regular classrooms.

Early Literacy Programme (ELP): This programme is a curriculum that promotes student metacognitive awareness of themselves as readers and writers, and promotes students' abilities to self-regulate literacy performance. The students engage in literacy activities that support four literacy principles: (a) literacy instruction must be embedded in meaningful and purposeful activities; (b) instruction should be responsive to the needs, capabilities, and interests of learners and should reflect their zone of proximal development; (c) instruction should promote self-regulated learning; and (d) instruction should be designed to foster student membership in a literacy community. All of the reading and writing activities are interrelated in thematic units. Students are taught to brainstorm ideas; organize ideas into maps or webs; gather related ideas for expository or narrative texts and revise their maps; read, comprehend, and monitor texts; and use their maps to write, monitor, revise, and publish expository reports using comprehension-monitoring and editing strategies. Activities include choral reading of poems, using predictable texts and other texts related to the thematic units, engaging in sustained silent reading, using partner reading/writing, sharing the chair, having morning news, setting up an author's center, and using story response. The programme is designed for nonreaders as well as children who have some reading skills.

Tribes: It is a programme that sets up a positive classroom climate. The tribe is a group of five or six children who work together throughout each day throughout the school year. They are seated together in a circle of desks or at the same table in their classroom and each classroom has four to five tribes. The teacher acts as a facilitator, giving time limits and intervening only when necessary. The teacher transfers management responsibilities to the students within the tribes. The programme uses cooperative learning, Tribe norms, and group process. The tribe activities fall into three general categories: (a) sharing personal concerns, feelings, and positive regard for one another; (b) planning, problem solving, and maintaining an environment of positive support for all members; and (c) working cooperatively on curriculum as assigned by the teacher.

Self-Regulated Strategy Development in Writing (SRSD): This intervention combines elements of self-regulation with dynamic stages of instruction in order to effectively teach strategies for writing in general, and for writing in different genres. Teaching students to self-regulate their behaviour helps them become more independent, increases task engagement, and helps students monitor and regulate their own academic performance. The SRSD programme teaches students to write through the following stages:

1. Pre-skill development (the teacher helps the student develop prerequisite skills).
2. Initial conference — Instructional goals and significance (the teacher and student discuss past performance and goals).
3. Discussion of the strategy (teacher and student discuss the strategy).
4. Modeling (the teacher models the strategy).
5. Memorization of the strategy (the student memorizes the steps of the strategy).
6. Collaborative practice (the student practices the strategy with teacher support).
7. Independent performance (the student performs the strategy independently).

Earth Science Videodisc Programme: This is a videodisc-based science programme for middle- and high-school students. Emphasizing the teaching of science concepts, rather than facts, the visual presentation keeps the attention of the students. The programme is based on effective teaching principles: (a) begin each lesson with a review, (b) begin each lesson by stating the goal, (c) present new material in small steps, (d) give clear instructions, (e) provide active practice, (f) ask many questions, (g) guide students during practice, (h) provide systematic feedback, (i) provide explicit instruction and practice for seatwork.

Skills for School Success: This programme addresses the organisation needs of all students, but especially those with mild disabilities who are being educated in mainstream classroom. The programme is designed to teach critical organisation skills and study skills systematically to students in grades three through six. *Advanced Skills for School Success* is a similar programme for junior-high and middle-school students. This programme teaches appropriate school behaviours, organisation skills, specific learning strategies, textbook reference skills, graphics skills, and use of classroom reference materials.

Aggression Replacement Training (ART): This programme teaches prosocial skills to aggressive adolescents or juvenile delinquents who exhibit acting-out behaviours and have severe problems with prosocial behaviours. There are three components:

1. *Structured learning.* Students learn behaviours such as how to express a complaint, how to respond to anger, how to keep out of fights.
2. *Anger control training.* Students learn how to inhibit anger aggression, and antisocial behaviour.
3. *Moral reasoning.* A set of procedures designed to raise the student's level of moral reasoning and have concern with the needs and rights of others.

Life-Centered Career Education (LCCE): This curriculum is designed to promote the development of skills that students will need to succeed in life after graduation. LCCE instruction is divided into three instruction domains that include 22 competencies in all: daily living skills, personal-social skills, and occupational skills. Daily living skills refers to learning how to manage a home, family, and finances as effectively as possible. Personal-social skills involves developing independence, self-confidence, socially acceptable behaviours, and maintaining friendships. Occupational guidance and preparation involves becoming aware of diverse job opportunities, developing the necessary skills, and learning to make logical and viable job choices.

Summary

The number of children in our schools who are identified as having attention deficit disorders is rising. The challenge of teaching children with attention deficit disorders and serving them appropriately in schools is increasingly recognized by all who come in contact with these children. Significant issues related to attention deficit disorders from a school perspective reviewed in this chapter include: the characteristics of ADD at difference stages of life, prevalence, coexisting conditions, historical evolution of the field, the *DSMIV*, the U.S. Department of Education Memorandum on ADD, school placement for students with ADD, accommodations in the general education classroom, and promising programmes for intervention.

3

Deaf Child in the Family

Parents of a deaf child, like the parents of any child who has special needs, want answers to what seem to be some simple and straightforward questions — questions like: What kind of language experience is best for my child, speech or sign language? Will my child ever learn to speak normally? Does being deaf affect how smart a child is? What kind of school is best? Will my child be able to get a good job? Regrettably, these questions are not as simple as they might appear, and parents may sometimes get contradictory information from professionals who are supposed to have the answers. Great strides have been made over the last twenty years in psychological and educational investigations relating to children who are deaf, but sincere differences of opinion still exist, just as they do in education generally and in various guides to "good parenting." Physicians, school officials, and counselors thus may have different responses to the same questions — differences that also will be affected by whether they, themselves, are deaf or hearing. In other cases, there simply will be no right answers.

These cautions notwithstanding, deaf children will be as happy, smart, and successful as hearing children, as long as they are given equal opportunities. It is true that every child is different, every family is different, and every school is different. Nevertheless, there is enough good information available about the growth and education of deaf children to allow parents to make enlightened decisions. Not all of those decisions will be easy, and some of them may turn out to have been wrong. Hearing parents unfamiliar with deafness will have some particular challenges with regard to raising their deaf children, especially if a child has multiple handicaps, and they will vary widely in how they respond to the situation. Some will take the initiative and become active in fostering their children's development, spending extra time with them on school work, language skills, and in play. Those parents also will probably learn sign language if their children's hearing losses prevent early learning of spoken language. Eventually, their deaf children will be involved in all of the normal activities of young kids, from dinner-table conversation to Girl Scouts. As a result, those children will have essentially all of the learning opportunities of their hearing peers in both social and academic areas.

Other parents will leave the initiative up to schools and to others "who should know." They will follow available advice for the most part, but they will be hesitant or unable to seek out new information and new strategies. Either they will fear that they might make matters worse, or they will not be able to imagine that they could do much to make matters better. Those parents typically will find it much harder to make the time to learn *and use* sign language, even when it is clearly appropriate, or to make other modifications to day-to-day family life such as installing visual doorbells or television caption decoders. They simply will not realize how much more they could do to help their children succeed.

Being the parent of a deaf child is even more challenging when the child has multiple handicaps. Recent estimates suggest that over 20 percent of all deaf children have one or more handicaps beyond their hearing losses. Those handicaps include both physical challenges and impediments to normal cognitive development. In decreasing order of their frequency, the most common physical challenges accompanying severe hearing loss in children are vision problems (including blindness), cerebral palsy, orthopedic problems, epilepsy, and heart disorders. The most common intellectual challenges are learning disabilities, mental retardation, and emotional or behavioral problems This is not to say that those conditions are particularly frequent; they occur in only about 1 to 10 percent of children who are deaf. Because they are receiving medical care for those conditions, children with multiple handicaps tend to have their hearing losses diagnosed earlier than children without other challenges. Often, however, hearing loss is considered secondary while parents and doctors deal with more immediate medical problems. It is only after doctors turn out to be unhelpful in dealing with their child's behaviour that many parents seek help from organisations that understand and specialize in the problems of deaf children. Everyone involved may overlook the fact that without access to language, multiple handicapped deaf children cannot understand what is happening to them and what others want from them. Establishing an effective means of communication should be a first priority with such children, not something to take care of later. Otherwise, medical issues may be resolved, but behavioral difficulties will remain and perhaps increase.

Part of the difficulty is that what most hearing people know about being deaf and about deaf people is limited to what they have seen in movies like The Miracle Worker and Children of a Lesser God or what they have gleaned from popular television shows. Other people have had personal contact with someone who is deaf — either a member of their extended family or, more likely, a child in the neighborhood. When I meet hearing people who say they "know" a deaf person, however, I am struck by the fact that regardless of the closeness of the relationship, the hearing person rarely seems to know any sign language. Often, they say that they can **fingerspell** a little — a form of communication that plays a relatively small role in communication among deaf people but adds to the erroneous assumption that **American Sign Language (ASL)** is somehow related to English. Some of those well-meaning individuals do know a few basic signs, typically less than a dozen, but they readily admit that they never have actually carried on any kind of a normal dialogue with their deaf "friend." What kind of friend can that be? What kind of relationship can you have with someone when you do not share a common language? What must it be like to grow up unable to have regular conversations with your parents not to be able to talk to them about school, about love, or about God?

Certainly there are language and cultural differences to be surmounted by anyone who really wants to understand what it means to be deaf, but if we are willing to expend the time and energy; most deaf people are willing to aid in our education. There is also a wealth of literature about deaf children and about the Deaf community, much of it published very recently. For parents in need of "hard data," the task is somewhat more difficult. Some of the information they need is published in places and in jargon not easily accessible to the public and, to be honest, some of it is biased and poorly researched. The goal of this book, therefore, is to provide a description of recent advances in research and practice that is both objective and understandable. In so doing, its aim is to help readers gain a better understanding of the context, abilities, and needs of deaf children, with an eye toward improving their opportunities and the likelihood of their success.

The chapters will provide several different perspectives on the development of deaf children, no one of which will give a complete view of the whole story. Taken together, however, they will provide a broad view of what we know about the growth and education of deaf children and what parents and teachers can do to optimize them.

View from within

Before I talk about what it is like to grow up deaf, it is important to clarify some basic terminology and issues as they are perceived from both Deaf and hearing communities. Only then can we avoid the kinds of overgeneralization and faulty assumptions that have plagued the field in the past.

Big D and Little d

Let's start with the fact that the word *deaf* appeared in both capitalized and uncapitalized form in the preceding paragraph. Most commonly, *Deaf* is used as an adjective, referring to deaf people who see themselves as part of a community bound together by a common culture and, most often, a common language — ASL. That community has a rich history of art, humor, literature, and customs in addition to sharing most of those enjoyed by hearing people. In this sense, it offers the same kind of cultural enhancement available to African-American, Hispanic, or Jewish families who can appreciate both mainstream American culture and a link to a special heritage. Although *deaf* is sometimes used as a generic adjective, many people now use it to refer only to lack of hearing, preferring to use *Deaf* as a more restricted socio-cultural term.

Part of the reason for this attention to the word *deaf* comes from the fact that people who are deaf have long been described in medical terms rather than as a people with a rich tradition and cultural pride. For similar reasons, the term *deafness* is frowned upon by some Deaf people who argue that it carries a connotation of pathology, although the National Association of the Deaf uses the term quite freely in its publications. It is difficult to talk about the field without a noun, however, as can be seen by the fact that the word has slipped into this book occasionally despite my efforts to use alternatives.

Meaning of Deaf

Hearing losses are not all-or-none, but there is a continuum of hearing loss from those so subtle that they might not be noticed to losses so severe that hearing aids and other amplification devices are essentially worthless. In this book, I will not use the word *deaf* to refer either to people who have lost some of their hearing as a normal part of growing older or to people who have slight hearing losses, perhaps from ear infections as toddlers. Consistent with my primary focus, I will apply it only to those children and adults with hearing losses that are classified as severe to profound — hearing losses that eliminate the use of speech and hearing for all of the practical purposes of day-to-day life.

Hearing Losses *vs.* Hearing Impairments

For most hearing parents of deaf children, their child's hearing loss is at first seen as a major problem that will interfere with family life, education, and potential success. While family life certainly is different when hearing parents have a deaf child, there is no reason why hearing loss should create any insurmountable obstacles to either education or career success. Some parents of deaf children will be told about all the things their child supposedly cannot do, but as the quote at the start of this chapter indicates, most educators of deaf children and deaf people themselves do not see hearing loss in the same light. To people who understand Deaf culture, hearing loss is a sign of community membership rather than a limiting characteristic. Admittedly, this perspective has created some discussion within the Deaf community concerning its apparent conflict with the demands of deaf people for special consideration under the **Americans with Disabilities Act (ADA)** and other legal safeguards. This issue will be addressed later in several contexts. For now, we will focus on the practical issue: Most parents of deaf children will need to seek advice and assistance from government and educational agencies charged with supporting children with special needs. Therefore, parents and practitioners need to be aware of the several terminological categories that might be used to describe a child in any particular situation.

The term *hearing impaired* is one that is used frequently. According to the World Health Organisation, an impairment is any loss of physiological or psychological structure or function considered normal for human beings, a disability is any restriction or lack of ability to perform "normally" due to an impairment, and a handicap is a disadvantage for a particular individual, resulting from an impairment or disability, that limits or prevents that person's full functioning in appropriate social and career roles. By these medical definitions, all deaf children have impairments, those with hearing parents have disabilities, and in the reality of today's world, most will be handicapped. An alternative and more accurate description, however, is that because of their hearing losses, deaf children lack full access to information and opportunities normally available to hearing children. Some of those experiences can be made available through sign language, but not all. To the extent that the absence of particular kinds of experience affects deaf children's learning or behaviour, there may be consequences for other aspects of development. Nevertheless, whether or not such differences make any difference in the grand scheme of growing up is separate from the terms we use to describe them. In other words, differences between deaf and hearing children need not imply deficiencies.

Although the above definitions are intended as medical descriptions, they have become generic labels that are applied widely to deaf children and deaf people. With their own language, culture, and traditions, members of the Deaf community resent those labels, and the community prides itself as unique among groups who would normally be considered handicapped. Consistent with this community self-image, studies involving deaf children have indicated that the best way to optimize their academic, career, and social success is to consider them a linguistic and cultural minority that deserves appropriate educational considerations. Deaf children can be members of multiple cultures, but their development and education clearly depend on experiences that may not be available to them from hearing environments. The reasons for this situation and its implications will require several more chapters. Meanwhile, my goal is to emphasize the potential of deaf children, not traditional labels.

Sign Language

One final terminological distinction we have to make is that between sign language and American Sign Language or ASL. The issue will be discussed in depth later, but for the moment we can use the term *sign language* to refer to any language that makes primary use of the hands and face to communicate **grammatically** through visual-spatial means. *American Sign Language,* in contrast, refers to a specific sign language used in the United States and in English-speaking parts of Canada. There is no universal sign language any more than there is a universal spoken language, and attempts in this regard have little more use than Esperanto. Knowing ASL myself, and having experienced both British Sign Language (BSL) and Italian Sign Language (LIS), I can confirm that there is no more carry-over from ASL to BSL or LIS than there is from English to French or Italian.

In the following sections, I will remain true to the above terminology in the hope of keeping some difficult issues from becoming confused. Rest assured that the distinctions are important and will surface again later. Meanwhile, I will choose my words carefully.

Deaf Child in the Family

Imagine for the moment a hearing American couple adopting an eighteen month-old hearing toddler from a non-English-speaking country. Bridging the language gap seems like it would be relatively easy: The child will have some words and a few simple sentences in her native language, but not too many. The new family and the community then flood the child with language, both intentionally and unintentionally, and eventually she becomes fluent in English rather than the language of her native country. At the same time, of course, she learns more than just a particular language. Through the speech that she hears, the child also learns who people are, about social rules and customs, about objects and events in the world, and about the uses of communication. This same process occurs quite naturally for the vast majority of young children in essentially all cultures. Language learning in more "natural" situations may be a bit less contrived and explicit than in the case of an international adoption – after all, most parent-child interactions involve language, regardless of which one it is – but the process is fundamentally the same.

Now consider the situation of a child who cannot hear. In the United States alone, there are close to a million children who have some degree of hearing loss, and one in a thousand babies is born with a hearing loss sufficient to prevent the hearing and understanding normal speech. Some people are surprised to learn that over 90 percent of those children are born into hearing families. Hearing parents who discover that they have a deaf child are probably the most surprised of all! The diagnosis of a hearing loss is so unexpected for children who are not multi handicapped that it typically is not made until a deaf child is between two and three years of age, when his language has fallen noticeably behind his playmates or when the preschool teacher suggests that something might be wrong. Boys are only slightly more likely to have serious hearing losses than girls, but the warning signs of hearing loss are often recognized later for them, because boys are notorious as slower language learners.

The relatively late diagnoses of hearing loss, on average, might be viewed two ways. From one perspective, if it takes two to three years to discover that a child is deaf, perhaps hearing loss does not have much of an impact during the first months of life. After all, how much hearing does a child need at that age? From another perspective, and the one that turns out to be correct, the late discovery of a hearing loss can have significant and far reaching consequences. Late diagnoses mean that for the first months of life, when most infants are hearing and beginning to learn the sounds of their native language, deaf children are not. Deaf infants do not hear their mothers coming down the hall nor do they turn to look when she enters the room. They are not soothed by their parents' voices and do not respond their to parents' attempts to have "baby talk" conversations. While these might seem like relatively minor problems to some people, they will have a lasting impact on the children, their parents, and on the relationships between them.

There are, of course, ways other than speech in which parents can communicate with their deaf children, just as they do with their hearing children: by touching, holding, and even through smell. Within the first twenty-four hours after birth, for example, babies can distinguish their mothers from other women by how they smell, and by three days after birth, they can recognize their mothers by sight. On the mother's side, several investigations have found that hearing mothers with deaf babies touch them more than do mothers with hearing infants. They also use more frequent and more exaggerated facial expressions with their deaf infants, and they bring more things into their babies' lines-of-sight so that they can share experiences and play together. But our knowledge about this apparent compensation for the lack of hearing in mother-child interactions comes from observing mothers who already know that their infants are deaf and therefore recognize the need to do something more than talk to their babies.

Our naive assumption might be that hearing parents who unexpectedly have a deaf baby go through a fairly long period of unintentionally treating him as though he could hear. They would talk to him and expect him to respond with attention, smiling, and his own share of gurgling and cooing. Hearing parents might also touch and cuddle their deaf babies more than they would hearing babies, even before they suspect that their babies could be deaf. It likely would not take most of these parents very long to discover that talking to their babies was not as soothing as holding and stroking them, and those parents might be quickly "trained" by their babies to use more physical contact and face-to-face communication, even if they are unaware of it. Unfortunately, there is no way to evaluate this possibility, because as soon as a baby is identified as deaf, parents are likely to change their behaviour.

During the first year or so of life, babies normally experience a variety of things that will have important consequences for language, social, and cognitive development. In the case of deaf babies of hearing parents, their early understanding of the world will be somewhat different from hearing babies and different from other deaf babies who have deaf parents. Later chapters will consider some specific consequences of a deaf child being born into a hearing family. First, however, it will be worthwhile to consider several different perspectives on deaf children and to get some background on issues relevant to deaf people. Throughout this discussion and the coming chapters, it is important to keep in mind that perspective is everything for the deaf child and for his parents, just as it is for educators and others who are interested in the welfare of deaf children. One memorable reminder of this came in a March 11, 1990, 60 Minutes television interview with Dr. I. King Jordan, president of Gallaudet University, who became deaf as a young adult. During the discussion, the woman interviewing Jordan asked him if he would want to take a "miracle pill" that would allow him to hear. Jordan countered by asking the interviewer whether she would want to take a pill that would make her into a man. His point was clear: Being Deaf is his identity, and he is quite comfortable with who he is.

Importance of Language

For those children whose hearing losses are sufficient to prevent their efficiently learning an oral (speaking) and aural (hearing) language, sign language can provide a viable alternative method for communication — the advice of out-of-date grandmothers and pediatricians notwithstanding. The dilemma for many parents is deciding when hearing losses are sufficiently severe. For many, learning sign language seems a drastic step. Perhaps it is not quite as drastic as it would be if they were told they had to learn Chinese and use it all of the time, because you cannot speak Chinese and English at the same time. However, learning to sign and using it *all the time* is not an easy feat, and even those parents who sign and speak simultaneously have no guarantees that their children will be either fluent signers or fluent users of English.

The question To sign or not to sign? is just one of many issues facing the family of a deaf child, but it is perhaps the most central one. From soon after birth, and maybe even before, language plays an essential role in parent-child relationships. Contrary to some popular beliefs, sign language works every bit as well as spoken language in educational settings and social relationships. Parents need to recognize that the majority of children who have greater hearing losses are unlikely ever to learn language through oral-aural means alone. It is true that about 25 percent of deaf children have some understandable speech, and **speechreading** or lipreading is certainly helpful to those children who have partial hearing losses. Nevertheless, many people are surprised to learn that the average deaf adult with years of speechreading practice does not read lips any better than the average hearing adult.

I know that this is counterintuitive. I once described this finding to a class of Italian special education students who would eventually have deaf children in their classes. My interpreter, an Italian educator familiar with deaf children in that country, was so convinced of the effectiveness of speech reading that she refused to translate my assertion to the contrary. She could not bring herself to tell those future teachers of deaf children something she "knew" was false. After finishing the lecture on my own in my poor Italian, I suggested that anyone who wanted to see how difficult it is to read lips should try a very simple experiment: Down the hall, we found a television set. We watched it first with normal volume, then with very low volume, and then with the volume off. While comprehension was still perfect at low volume, everyone was startled when it suddenly became impossible when the volume was turned off. My colleague never brought up the topic again.

The presence or absence of communication in early and later childhood has broad consequences for development. For deaf children with greater hearing losses, this most often translates into a signing (communication) versus speaking (no communication) dichotomy. As we will see later, those deaf children who learn to sign at a young age also tend to be better adjusted emotionally, tend to do better in school, and tend to have better social relationships with their signing parents and peers relative to children raised in speech-only environments. The situation is more cloudy for children with mild to moderate hearing losses, who may learn spoken language more easily. In any case, the most important thing is full access to *some* language — and the earlier the better.

Regrettably, many parents still complain that they have trouble getting information and advice about the pros and cons of sign language, therefore is intended to give them all of the information they need. Some of this difficulty might result from their being understandably sensitive and confused when they first learn that their child is deaf. Still, I have heard too many stories of audiologists leaving parents standing in clinic hallways with mouths open and heads buzzing, and too many accounts of misdiagnoses or denials of early hearing losses by trusted pediatricians to consider professionals guiltless in this failure to convey the necessary information about dealing with childhood hearing loss. An excellent example of this was recounted recently by two of my colleagues. When they noticed that their three year old son was not playing with other children, and his teacher reported that he was not talking to anyone in school, they had his hearing tested by an audiologist in an otolaryngology practice. They described what happened:

> *During the visit, the audiologist took Bernard to his office, while we waited in the waiting room. Approximately 15 minutes later, the audiologist came back dragging Bernard, who was crying. He told us that he could do nothing for Bernard, as he was not cooperative during the test. He told us to bring him back when he was good and ready. We were furious at the way he had handled our son and demanded that he do the test again in our presence and with our assistance. At first he was hesitant to comply, but we were persistent in our demand.*
>
> *In the testing room, the audiologist handed Bernard an abacus with colored beads for him to move from one side to the other each time he heard a sound. There was no communication or explanation on the part of the audiologist to Bernard, and it was clear that Bernard was tentative and frightened with not knowing what was expected of him.*

At this point, Bernard's father intervened, and turned the testing session into a game which his son clearly enjoyed. To the surprise of the audiologist, the test was now completed smoothly. It showed that Bernard had a significant hearing loss. Then, the doctor appeared on the scene.

The otolaryngologist told us that Bernard had "inner ear deafness." We asked for further explanation about the nature of the deafness and what recourse, if any, we had. He told us that he couldn't explain any more about it, and at that point a hearing aid dealer came into the office to talk with the otolaryngologist. After the hearing aid dealer left, the otolaryngologist told us he had to leave for lunch. We were dumbfounded at his rudeness in leaving us hanging and demanded time to speak to him. We proceeded to ask him what we should do to help Bernard and he simply told us to go to a hearing and speech clinic. Then he left the office.

This kind of experience is not unusual, and you can imagine the hurt and anger experienced by parents in such situations. Actually, *these* parents are deaf! Imagine what the experience would have been like for hearing parents who would have had almost no idea what the audiologist and otolaryngologist were talking about!

Hearing Loss as Pathology

Family doctors are most accustomed to dealing with hearing children. The frequency of severe to profound hearing loss in the general population is so low that most pediatricians encounter deaf children only rarely, if ever. Moreover, **congenital** and early onset hearing losses are not so easily noticed unless one is looking for them. When physicians do encounter young children with serious hearing losses, they tend to view them in terms of the pathology model acquired during their medical school training. From their perspective, being deaf is considered a serious handicap and an impediment to normal development. True, being deaf, like having any other impairment, deprives deaf children of some of the experiences available to normally hearing children. Other experiences may simply be different than they would be if their hearing were intact. Anyone who has ever watched a basketball game between two deaf schools or the enthusiasm fostered by their cheerleaders, however, knows that some things never change.

The different experiences of hearing and deaf children will affect how they view and interact with the world in a variety of subtle and not-sosubtle ways. In the case of deaf children of deaf parents, their full range of natural experiences will lead to their passing through the various developmental stages at the same rate as hearing children. For deaf children of hearing parents, early experiences may not blend so readily into the background of family and community life. For them, the potentially limited or atypical nature of their experiences are more likely to lead to differences in their social, language, and perhaps their intellectual functioning relative to hearing children. My primary reason for emphasizing differences between deaf and hearing children at this point is a practical one. There is an understandable impulse on the part of many of us to deny or minimize handicaps that are not visible. A Deaf man once told me that deaf people do not receive as much understanding or consideration as those with other handicaps because deaf people "look too normal." Indeed, it is easier for most people to accept the obstacles faced by someone in a wheelchair than those faced by someone with a learning disability, easier to recognize the challenges encountered by someone who is blind than those of someone who is deaf. But denying a child's hearing loss, no matter how stress-reducing to parents or grandparents in the short run, does no one any good in the long run. Eventually, overlooking children's difficulties catches up with them, with their parents, and with society. Sometimes the realization comes too late; it always comes at a higher price.

Let us return to the language-learning issue as an example. It is easy enough to understand the desire of most hearing parents to have a child who speaks and acts normally. The truth is, however, that most deaf children will never sound like their hearing brothers and sisters. Delaying the learning of sign language in the hope of developing better speaking skills in deaf children simply does not work in most cases. In fact, such delays can make matters more difficult for both children and their parents. The first years of life are when basic language skills develop, and the first two to three years are generally recognized as a critical period for language learning. There is no substitute for natural language learning, and language acquisition that begins at age three or four is not natural.

It should be apparent by this point that the necessity of early language — any language — is an assumption that guides most of our thinking about the normal development of both deaf and hearing children. For centuries, philosophers and scientists have sought to understand the relation between language and thinking. Although the language we use does not *determine* the way we think, as was once believed, the language that children learn and the context in which they learn it will affect the way that they view the world. It is not just the explicit teaching in the classroom that requires and contributes to fluency in language. In addition, the vast majority of most children's experience comes in the form of language or accompanied by language. Our perceptions and conceptions of the world will be colored as much by the way something is described as by its factual content. Most of young children's experiences in the world will be shaped by the language of parents who are communicating with a particular purpose in mind. It does not matter much if the parents are using English, Japanese, ASL, or BSL; the content and effects of that communication are always present. Therefore, if a child does not receive any language, an essential component of development will be missing. Parents of deaf children with greater hearing losses can compensate for their children's lack of hearing if they are aware of the loss and are willing and able to learn sign language, but early awareness by hearing parents that their child is deaf is the exception. The primary issues we need to consider thus will concern how parents normally interact with their deaf infants, both before and after the diagnoses of their hearing losses, and the consequences of those interactions for a happy and healthy childhood.

Early Childhood Hearing Loss

The diagnosis of a significant hearing loss in a young child and a hearing family's adjustment to its new situation have a variety of ramifications. The most important thing to keep in mind is that the entire family is affected by having a deaf child. Although mothers tend to take the greater share of responsibility for dealing with the added necessities of a deaf child, the effects of such changes are felt by each member of the family. Frequently forgotten in the new and sometimes stressful situation are the older children, who now are likely to receive relatively less attention than they did prior to their sibling's diagnosis. One couple I know avoided this problem by putting a note on their door requesting visitors to remember to pay attention to the hearing four year-old sister of a deaf toddler. Whatever the methods, the goal of parents and children alike in this situation is to maintain comfortable and "normal" interactions within the home. In this, the whole family is involved and has to work together with patience and understanding.

It is well worth emphasizing that no matter how upset a hearing couple may be when they discover that their child is deaf, those feelings do pass. Any stress between the parents because of their different ways of responding to the situation also will dissipate, and there is no evidence that having a deaf child influences marriages in any way that affects their success or failure. Once the initial surprise passes, parents start to collect useful information on what it means to be deaf and about accommodating their child's hearing loss. Things that initially may have seemed overwhelming are recognized as less burdensome than they originally appeared. Not surprisingly, research has shown that those mothers who receive emotional and practical support from their family and friends are best able to cope with the demands of having a deaf child. This finding reinforces the impression that support groups consisting of other parents and professionals involved with young deaf children can be invaluable resources.

Down the road, mothers' abilities to function and deal with their children's being deaf will affect the child in a variety of ways. Mothers who are more secure and confident about themselves tend to treat their deaf children in ways that lead to better social and emotional adjustment in childhood and eventually better performance in school. Findings of this sort clearly indicate the need for greater support and training for hearing parents throughout their deaf children's childhood. Parents need to be educated about childhood deafness and its consequences, about the possible special needs of deaf children that must be addressed to ensure normal development, and about the educational alternatives open to deaf children and their families.

Just as the causes and characteristics of childhood deafness vary widely, so do the early experiences of deaf children and the abilities of parents and families to adapt to the changes that accompany having a deaf child. These changes are not always dramatic and need not be negative. Nevertheless, parental acceptance of children's hearing losses and adjustment to their needs are essential for a normal childhood. Therefore, this book is not a how-to guide to raising a deaf child, but a guide to understanding the implications of being deaf and of having a deaf child in the family or in a classroom. This understanding has implications not only for parents and teachers of deaf children, but for anyone who has contact with deaf children or with children who are academically or emotionally challenged for any reason. It is essential to remember that as with most generalities, those that are applied to deaf children in this book are rarely accurate in individual cases. The strengths and weaknesses of each child must be considered, and we must be aware that deaf children may be even more variable than hearing children. Perhaps most importantly, parents should be wary of taking advice about deaf children from people who are not knowledgeable about deafness or do not have first-hand experience. In this situation, *knowledgeable* does not necessarily refer to those of us who are trained in a relevant field and have diplomas or certificates hanging on the office wall. Professionals will be able to provide important information related to language, hearing aids, and so on. We often have our own biases, however, usually based on where and how we were trained. I therefore believe that because we are seen as authorities, parents and teachers sometimes may be too quick to accept our advice as necessarily the only true path. To really understand what it means to have a deaf child, there is no substitute for chatting with other parents who have been or are currently working their ways through similar issues. At this juncture, local groups or national organisations like the American Society for Deaf Children can be important sources of information and support. In the spirit of avoiding some of the common overgeneralizations about early childhood hearing loss, let us look at some of them. Most of these are discussed at various places later in this book. Just to clear up some of the inaccurate claims at the outset, however, it is generally *not* true that:

- Deaf children who learn to sign will not learn to speak.
- Deaf children and adults are very quiet.
- Hearing aids enable deaf children to understand speech (by amplifying sound, they do help to hear speech, but understanding it is a different matter.
- Cochlear implants are a very effective kind of hearing aid.
- All deaf children can be taught to "read lips".
- Deaf children are less intelligent than hearing children.
- Deaf children have more emotional difficulties than hearing children.

- **Mainstreaming** is the best way to educate all deaf children.
- Deaf children will not have many friends.
- American Sign Language is a form of English.
- All deaf people know sign language.
- Deaf people all wish that they could hear and seek hearing friends.
- Deaf people cannot drive cars because they cannot hear.

It is generally true that:

- Deaf children cannot hear how much noise they are making.
- Hearing aids may enable some deaf children with partial hearing losses to understand speech.
- Cochlear implants are not yet as helpful as many people claim.
- Speech reading is very difficult, especially in English.
- Deaf children tend to have more academic difficulty than hearing children, especially in learning to read and write.
- Deaf children may have behavioral problems in school that are traceable to home environments.
- Mainstreaming in public schools may work for some deaf children but has drawbacks for others.
- Many deaf adults are members of Deaf social groups.
- American Sign Language is a language in its own right and differs from English in grammar and vocabulary.
- Most deaf people hold regular jobs and are fully functioning members of society.
- Most deaf people resent the patronizing attitudes of hearing people.

Summary

Most deaf children have hearing parents, and those parents often are unprepared to deal with the emotional and practical issues related to having a deaf child. Whether due to denial or misunderstanding, diagnoses of hearing losses in children who are not multi handicapped typically are not made until between two and three years of age. Many parents then strive to have their child learn spoken language. Earlier chapters will discuss the fact that educating deaf children in spoken language only works for a minority of children, particularly those with lesser hearing losses, while children with greater hearing losses typically do not benefit significantly from such experience. Delays in deaf children's access to language during the most critical stages of development have a variety of consequences in social, language, and academic areas.

Sign language can provide deaf children with access to the information flow of people around them, provided that their parents and teachers are competent and consistent signers. Learning to sign as an adult is as difficult as learning any foreign language, however, and many people have considerable difficulty in learning a second language, whether spoken or signed. This situation may be even more complex for hearing parents who have discovered that their child is deaf and may be receiving conflicting and incomplete advice. Although many hearing parents will view their deaf child as disabled, the vast majority of deaf people are fully normal contributing members of the community. Within the Deaf community, art, Deaf history, and Deaf culture provide deaf people with a unique identity and a large network of friends. Therefore, most deaf people resent patronizing attitudes that suggest that their lives are any less full or important than those of hearing people.

In most respects, then, deaf and hearing children are the same. Like hearing children, deaf children's success begins with acceptance and communication at home. Attention to their special needs acknowledges that deaf children may be different from hearing peers, but those differences should not be taken to mean that deaf children are in any way defective. Instead, it is essential that we recognize that deaf children vary greatly — just like hearing children — and we have to treat them as individuals. Optimizing their opportunities in school and the social world requires a more complete understanding of deaf people and deaf issues than most hearing people will ever obtain in their own communities. The remainder of this book therefore will provide a survey of what we currently know about the language, social, and intellectual development of deaf children and will extensively consider the educational and practical issues confronting them and their families. First, we will consider characteristics of deaf children-and of the deaf population in general — as well as the importance of communication and language, whether signed or spoken.

4

Communication with Deaf Children

Deaf children are not "broken" hearing children, and trying to make them more like hearing children is unlikely to be the best way to support their development. Instead, we have to accommodate to their needs and perhaps alter our approaches to education and child rearing. In this regard, it would not be an exaggeration to suggest that most of the ways in which deaf and hearing children are different and the factors on which their success depend revolve around the availability and effectiveness of early communication.

Language is an essential component of normal development for all humans. Unfortunately, exposure exclusively to spoken language usually is not very successful for deaf children who have more severe prelingual hearing losses. While it is important for parents to strongly support deaf children's spoken language, it should not be to the exclusion of sign language. Similarly, while it is important for parents to strongly support deaf children's sign language, I do not believe that this should be done to the exclusion of spoken language. The important thing is to establish an effective mode of parent-child communication as early as possible. Postponing the beginning of sign language learning until they have given up on speech training is a common pitfall for parents of deaf children. It is also one to avoid unless you want to put all of your eggs into one very precarious basket. After exploring all of the available evidence, we will see that it clearly points to three conclusions: (1) There is no single, correct answer to the language question that applies to all or even most deaf children, (2) there are places for both signed and spoken language in the lives of many deaf children, and (3) sign language will play a vital role in the lives of most deaf children and its value should not be underestimated.

Language for Deaf Children

In the 1960s, about 90 percent of hearing parents used only spoken language with their deaf children, while the remainder used one or more of the forms of manual communication described below. Since that time, American Sign Language (ASL) has been on the rise, and recent surveys indicate that most deaf students sign at least some of the time. Still, fewer than half of the children who use sign language in school also sign when they are with their families, and only a small fraction of those are able to carry on normal, everyday conversations with their parents. This situation does not mean that signing is really unnecessary; in most cases, it means that children and parents are being short-changed in their interactions.

Despite occasional claims to the contrary, there is no evidence at all to suggest that the early use of manual communication by deaf children hampers their development of skills in spoken language or in any other area. Gestures, in fact, appear to be an essential prelude to language development, establishing the rules and contexts of interpersonal communication for both deaf and hearing children. Denying the use of gestures to deaf children, as is done in many programmes emphasizing spoken language, thus seems more likely to hurt them than to help them.

Moreover, the available evidence clearly indicates that, on average, deaf children who learn sign language as preschoolers show better academic achievement and social adjustment during the school years, and they also show superior gains in learning to read and write in English. Children of hearing parents who become deaf after learning language also tend to exhibit better academic and social abilities than children who became deaf prior to learning language. Thus, the important factor is not necessarily the ability to speak, but the ability to communicate through language, whatever its form, from an early age.

Also contrary to popular claims, spoken language skills in deaf children usually do not result in their full assimilation into hearing society. In this case, it is important to distinguish between those deaf children who have greater hearing losses and those children with enough residual hearing to benefit from speech training. This latter group is not *deaf* in the sense of being unable to use and understand speech for the purposes of day-to-day living, even though their hearing losses may have some effect on their development and academic achievement. Many children who are truly deaf eventually will find themselves with friends, dates, and spouses who are deaf. They eventually will become involved in Deaf social clubs and other Deaf organisations that play an important role in the Deaf community and Deaf culture. They do not give up roles in the hearing community and hearing culture, but rather they are able to draw from both groups.

Over 80 percent of American schoolchildren with severe to profound hearing losses now receive some kind of sign language education in school. Because most hearing parents cannot communicate effectively with their deaf children, residential schools and other special programmes are important environments where they learn a large part of their social skills and social roles as well as academic subjects. Deaf children born to deaf parents who use sign language, in contrast, will be exposed to language from the beginning of their lives — a language that serves both social and educational functions. Most deaf children of deaf parents thus learn more about life and about who they are at home, in the context of the supportive Deaf community.

Before describing sign language as it is taught and used by deaf children, two important distinctions should be noted. The first concerns what we mean by manual communication and sign language, and how they relate to the language actually experienced by deaf children. *Manual communication* is now recognized as somewhat of a misnomer, even though it is often used in contrast to *spoken communication*. The error here is that although many people who learn to sign use only their hands, true sign languages like ASL include a variety of other features as well. Facial expression is particularly important, for example, in the way it carries grammatical information. Emotion is communicated by signing rate and size as well as by facial expression and sign selection. Even talking about deaf children learning sign language rather than manual communication is somewhat misleading, because it is extremely rare that deaf children are exposed *exclusively* to sign language. Many deaf adults rely solely on ASL in communication among themselves, but their communication with deaf children and hearing individuals frequently includes mouth movements and sign modifications which increase the number of "comprehension cues" available to the receiver. Some of these are actually part of ASL, but others are included to ensure communication with less-than-fluent language users.

In educational settings, a multiplicity of language cues for deaf children is made quite explicit through artificial means, and most sign-language oriented schools for deaf children actually employ either **Simultaneous Communication** (SC) or Total Communication (TC). **Simultaneous Communication** refers to the concurrent production of both sign and speech and is the most common means of educational communication between deaf children and hearing individuals who can sign. Within the classroom, many schools make use of Total Communication, a method which utilizes all potentially available sources of linguistic communication, including sign, speech, and amplification through the use of hearing aids. While such methods are designed to give deaf children access to as much information as possible, it should not be assumed that they result in deaf children who are fluent in both ASL and English. SC and TC are not the same as ASL, any more than they are the same as English. Fluency in each of those "real" languages will require exposure to them and considerable instruction if they are not learned naturally.

A second important distinction to keep in mind is that between real languages, such as English or ASL, and the gestures and pantomime that accompany them both. Gestures and body language are normally used to facilitate both signed and spoken communication. Complex gesture and pantomime also have been shown to develop out of necessity when deaf children grow up in hearing families without the benefit of exposure to sign language, although they are insufficient to communicate more than the most basic information between child and parent.

Looking ahead, deaf and hearing children tend to use many of the same gestures, both before they actually learn a signed or spoken language and in their day to-day use of language as they get older. If these gestures are common to speakers of both sign language and English, clearly they cannot be said to be part of ASL any more than they are part of English. It just happens that hearing people tend not to notice how frequently they use gestures — an oversight that can be remedied by careful observation during any five minute conversation.

Knowing about Sign Language

Like a spoken language, a signed language consists of a large vocabulary of arbitrary signs, together with a set of rules, or a grammar, that governs both the formation of individual signs and combinations of signs into phrases and sentences. In addition to the repertoire of formalized signs, a variety of which are found at the end of the book, signed languages contain a set of number signs and a manual alphabet.

Number signs are used just as they are in spoken language: The signs represent number concepts just as the words ten and *ten million* do. Spelling also fills the same function in sign language as it does in spoken language, at least in part. We can spell words in English when they are new or when we do not know how to pronounce them, but we normally do not use spelling in our everyday conversations. Finger spelling is used primarily in cases where there are no conventional signs for particular ideas or where a sign is obscure or unknown, but for a variety of reasons it also occurs in conversational signing even when there is an available sign. Finger spelling thus does not replace signing, but supplements it. In fact, the manual alphabet used in the United States cannot correctly be called English, because the two-handed manual alphabet of British Sign Language (BSL) is quite different.

As in the case of spoken languages, ASL and other sign languages are quite distinct from each other. Signers of ASL and BSL, for example, are no more likely to understand each other than are speakers of English and Chinese. What is called Signed English (or Sign English) should not be confused with any of the naturally occurring sign languages like ASL. Signed English is actually an artificial signing system combining the signs of ASL and the grammatical structure of English. Although it is taught to deaf children around the country, Signed English is not normally used in day-to-day conversations among deaf adults. It is possible that with improvements in the reading and writing skills of deaf children, the mingling of English and ASL someday might make Signed English far more conventional and accepted than it is now, but that remains to be seen.

The goal of Signed English and other hybridized forms of English/sign language is clear enough: They seek to facilitate signed communication for deaf children while also encouraging acquisition of the English structure necessary for reading, writing, and possibly speech. After many years of debate concerning whether deaf children should be taught signed or spoken communication, a new educational debate is whether deaf students should continue to be taught using systems like Signed English or taught in ASL instead. Teaching ASL would contribute to the preservation and extension of Deaf culture, and some authors claim that learning ASL can also facilitate deaf children's learning to read and write. This argument may seem to have some credibility, because sign language is more accessible to young deaf children than spoken language if their parents know it and use it consistently. Because ASL bears no resemblance to English or any other written language, however, it should not contribute to reading English any more than would the learning any other language. At the same time, the artificial nature of Signed English may make it less effective than other alternatives as a foundation for natural language development. While the jury is still out on this issue, normal development clearly demands the availability of some early language. ASL and similar sign languages clearly are excellent alternatives to spoken language, even if they do not contribute directly to children's English literacy skills. At the same time, early learning of ASL provides deaf children with proficiency in at least one language, and with that comes access to information that will contribute to subsequent development. Acquisition of ASL or another natural sign language also gives children a sense of mastery and control that is important to subsequent academic success.

History of Sign Language

From both practical and educational perspectives, it is difficult to understand how any informed observer could claim that a sign language like ASL is anything but a true language. Historically, extensive vocabularies of signs appear to have existed in Spain as early as the sixteenth century, but it was not until two hundred years later that signs were combined with grammars, and sign language moved into the classroom. This shift, and the accompanying changes within the Deaf community, also moved signing from a gestural system to a full-fledged language.

The distinction of being the first to take the important step of combining signs with a signing grammar is usually ascribed to the French educator Abbé Charles Michel de l'Epée (1712-89). Some years later, it was Thomas Hopkins Gallaudet (1787-1851) and Laurent Clerc (1786-1869) who brought Abbé de l'Epée's sign language to America and opened the first public school for deaf children, in Hartford, Connecticut. At that point, de l'Epée's sign system was blended with many of the signs that were already in common usage by American deaf people, and ASL was born. One suspects that the resulting change in education of the deaf and in the communication between deaf children and their parents must have opened new horizons of interpersonal contact not much less dramatic than the classic scene in *The Miracle Worker* in which the deaf and blind Helen Keller first grasps the meaningfulness of finger spelling.

Although ASL is sometimes compared to Native American "sign languages," the comparison is a faulty one. The truly *manual* communication systems of Native Americans did not replace spoken language, and as far as we know there were no silent tribes. Rather, Native American signs were used primarily to allow communication among different tribes having different spoken languages when they gathered for festive, political, or commercial purposes. Over the last two hundred years, signed languages have become both more conventional and more rule-governed in their use by deaf people and more accepted by hearing educators. Until the late 1960s, however, signing was still thought by many hearing people to be a relatively primitive communication system that lacked extensive vocabulary and the means to express subtle or abstract concepts.

This impression remains in some countries, but in North America the language status of ASL and other signed languages has been well documented by linguists, psychologists, and educators. Beyond naturally occurring sign languages, several alternative systems have been developed, and these will be described after considering some of the mechanics of sign language. Those readers not interested in the linguistic details of ASL might want to skip directly to the section on artificial speech and sign systems.

Components of Signs

Modification and Inflection

A glance at the Everyday Signs section at the back of the book will reveal that signs can be described in terms of three primary characteristics: the shape of the hand or hands, the place at which the sign is made or where it begins, and the movements involved in making a sign. Signs also can be distinguished by whether they are made with one or two hands, by the orientation of the hands relative to the signer, and whether they involve a stable "base" hand or not. Most signs, in fact, can be defined in terms of a combination of components from a set of eighteen hand shapes, twelve places of articulation, and twenty-five different movements. By comparison, there are forty four different sounds and twenty-six letters that make up all English words.

Changes in the movement, place of articulation, or hand shape of a particular sign also can be used to modify the number or tense of a sign, just as words in English can be inflected by adding particular beginnings or endings: *dog* to *dogs, jump* to *jumped, important* to *unimportant* and so on. In ASL, the sign DOGS is made by repeated signing of DOG, and JUMPED is made by adding a FINISH past-marker to JUMP or letting context specify the past. Only the sign UNIMPORTANT is made by the addition of a simple NOT marker, although there are other ways to sign the concept as well. More extensive inflections also occur in ASL. For example, the movement in the sign COMPLAIN can change to communicate COMPLAIN CONSTANTLY or COMPLAIN VEHEMENTLY, and the sign CHAIR can be altered to mean COUCH or ROW OF CHAIRS. The ability to make such changes, represents one of the properties that distinguishes sign language from gesture. A true language must have a mechanism for modifications of this sort in order to be efficient and allow a full range of communication. Similarly, new signs, like new words, are constantly being invented, and signs can be used in metaphorical ways or as puns.

Classifiers

One central component of signs is what is referred to as a **classifier.** Most simply, classifiers in sign language are particular hand shapes that have general-purpose meanings. For example, rather than using the normal, literal signs in the context of a sentence, an upright 1-hand can be used to indicate a person; a bent, downward V-hand can be used to indicate an animal; and a rotated 3-hand can be used to indicate a car or other vehicle. Classifiers typically are first assigned to a particular person or thing and then are used to indicate actions or directions taken within an episode. More complex uses of classifiers also occur, and one can easily imagine classifiers used to describe a person (1-hand) who gets into a car (horizontal 3-hand) and weaves down a hill before hitting an animal (bent V-hand) which dies, with "feet" turned upward (two inverted, bent V-hands).

There is also a class of less specific classifiers that function more like adjectives than nouns. These are most often used for indicating either shape or size. For example, F-hands or C-hands moved vertically or horizontally are used to denote the size of cylindrical objects, and I-hands can denote thin filaments or lines (the I-hand also is involved in signs like STRING and SPAGHETTI — see Everyday Signs). Note that although both these general classifiers and the more specific nounlike classifiers make use of alphabetic and numerical hand shapes, their meanings are completely arbitrary and are not tied to the letter-meaning of the hand shape. Similar characteristics are found in spoken classifier languages like Japanese and Thai.

As one might suspect by this point, sign languages have their own accents, dialects, and idiosyncratic signs. Signs can be limited to particular regions, schools, or even individual families. **Home signs,** for example, are signs used in much the same way as some special words and names are used in hearing families. Both are most common in homes with small children, often originating from mispronunciations or missing. Some such words seem to live on into adulthood, like the words *grabbers* and *bazuter* in my family. Dialectical differences in sign language, like some differences in spoken language, can make for some difficulty in communication. These differences also can make for some funny incidents, as when I first discovered that one commonly used sign I had learned in Canada was indistinguishable from a common four-letter signed profanity in North Carolina.

Combining Signs

Sign language sometimes gives the impression of not having very strong requirements about the order of signs within sentences, occasionally leading people to assume that it has no grammar. This appearance occurs primarily because of the contrast with English, which happens to be a language with relatively rigid word-order rules. Other spoken languages, like Italian or Japanese, have more flexibility in word order and are closer in this respect to ASL.

There are a variety of grammatical rules within sign languages operating at several different levels. Most signs, for example, must be made within a particular **signing space,** a roughly square area from the top of the head to the waist and about one foot to either side of the body. Signs made outside of this space might be seen as ungrammatical or as having some kind of special extended or metaphorical meaning. There are also rules about the positioning of "base" hands, the ways in which signs and classifiers are combined, and symmetry of movement. Because the two hands have the same movement but different hand shape, the sign is technically ungrammatical even though it has been used for years. SAME-TIME COMMUNICATION , thus has replaced the old sign for SIMULTANEOUS COMMUNICATION. As in English, however, some ungrammatical forms continue to stay in the language despite our best attempts to purge them. When I recently took a sign language examination, I made sure that I used the sign SAME-TIME COMMUNICATION. But when I used the same sign later that week in a meeting of deaf and hearing colleagues, one of the deaf people said "huh?" Luckily, another deaf person interjected, "Oh, he means SIMULTANEOUS COMMUNICATION," using the more common sign.

Using Space

One of the most salient grammatical characteristics of signed languages is their use of the signing space to communicate both time and location. Time is indicated by positions moving from behind the signer (the PAST), through the here and NOW, and out in front of the signer (the FUTURE). The sign WEEK (see Everyday Signs), for example, is normally made out in front of the body. When the basic sign is finished by moving the right hand backward toward the right shoulder, it means LAST-WEEK; finishing it with a forward arc means NEXT-WEEK. Signs for YEAR and MONTH can be similarly modified.

The space in front of a signer also is used to establish the location of people, objects, and places that are part of an ongoing conversation. When first mentioning particular individuals in an event, usually via a name-sign or finger spelled name, those people can be placed in different locations in the signing space, to the right, to the left or in front of the signer. Later, they can be referred to just by pointing at the location in which they were put, without having to rename them. Sign language novices might have some difficulty keeping their signing spaces organized, but it is only a matter of practice before the utility of locating signs is appreciated, and both production and comprehension are made much easier. As with any language, regular use in many contexts is essential for the acquisition of the signs and rules of sign language. Being hearing does not make sign language any easier or harder to learn. As a second language, it takes just as much effort as any foreign language. You do not have to learn to read and write it, but most signers will tell you that good finger spelling is a real challenge.

Beyond constraints on the form of individual signs, sign languages like ASL have rich varieties of rules for sign combination that had gone unnoticed until relatively recently. For example, although ASL has considerable flexibility in sign order, the subject-verb-object ordering of English is most frequently used, probably because of the immersion of ASL within a culture in which the host language is English. Still, the fact that all of the rules and structures of signed language's do not necessarily conform to those of their host languages should not be surprising. That lack of correspondence would only be worthy of wonder if signed languages mapped directly onto their host spoken languages, and we have already seen that this is not the case.

Artificial Speech and Sign Systems

In addition to ASL and Signed English, there are several other communication systems for deaf children that have been around for some time. These language alternatives fall into two categories: modifications to sign communication, typically intended to make it more English-like, and modifications to spoken communication. None of these formally developed systems has caught on to the degree of Signed English, primarily because no one has provided any firm evidence about their effectiveness. Nonetheless, each alternative has its proponents, and anecdotal evidence concerning the successes of particular children with particular systems is not hard to find. This is not to say that one of these alternatives, or another yet to be invented, might not prove effective in facilitating the education and interpersonal communication of deaf children as a group or for particular deaf children. As with ASL and Signed English, however, we will not be in a position to decide which way of expressing language is best for which children until appropriate, scientific evaluations have been made. Meanwhile, there seems no reason why any one mode of language need be used in isolation, and various combined methods are possible. Most importantly, it is essential that deaf children begin to be exposed to language as early as possible and that parents and other family members be fully involved partners. If there is no one to communicate with outside of the classroom, language experience in any mode does little good. With this in mind, let us briefly survey some of the available language alternatives for deaf children.

Cued Speech

The primary reason for this approach is that the focus here is on deaf children with greater hearing losses, those who are less likely to benefit from exposure to spoken language. The claim is not that these deaf children cannot learn to speak; surely some of them can. Rather, the point is that in the absence of hearing (especially during the critical periods of language learning), spoken communication is rarely viable as the primary means of communication for deaf children or deaf adults. With extensive speech training, some deaf children reach the point where family members can understand some of their speech, but that does not mean that they will be understood by others outside the family or that they will be able to understand the speech of others.

Still, there are exceptions. We have all seen deaf people on television or elsewhere who appear to have excellent, or at least pretty good speech. In many cases, these are individuals with lesser hearing losses or people who had better hearing when they learned to speak and then experienced progressive or acute hearing losses. Others have improved their speech as older children or as adults. Often, this shift occurs only after using sign language early in life, at the point where an individual has the motivation and ability to benefit from spoken language methods. And still, there are exceptions like several of my deaf colleagues and Heather Whitestone, Miss America 1994, who were raised with intensive speech therapy and have very good speech. There are several schools and programmes in this country offering education exclusively in spoken language and claiming varying degrees of success. Still to be determined is whether the children who succeed in such programmes are representative of all deaf children or whether they have particular characteristics that make them most likely to benefit from such exposure in the first place. In any case, the argument for exclusive exposure to spoken language has never been supported in any broad sense and thus, for the present, spoken language seems most likely to be effective when combined with ASL.

Cued Speech

One increasingly popular supplement to spoken language is **Cued Speech,** which supports spoken language with a set of sound-related hand shapes. The motivation for the invention of Cued Speech lay in the fact that many speech sounds look the same on the lips when they are pronounced, especially in English, making speech reading difficult. For example, if you look in the mirror, and pronounce the names of letters c, e, g, and z, they look very similar on the lips. Speech reading of some other languages, like Italian, is somewhat easier because of greater regularity in the way in which sounds are combined and their unambiguous correspondence to writing. More of the language therefore can be "seen on the lips," and one therefore might expect that deaf children in such countries would have relatively better speech skills, and perhaps reading skills, than deaf children in the United States. Preliminary findings appear to support this prediction.

The idea behind Cued Speech is that if deaf children could be given cues sufficient to distinguish sounds that look alike on the lips in English, they would be better able to learn to lip read and reproduce those lip movements, themselves, in spoken communication. Cued speech thus maintains an "oralist" approach to language, while providing a manual means of overcoming the limitations of oral ambiguity. Overall, it uses thirty-six different cues to clarify the forty-four different sounds in English. Cues for vowel sounds are produced by placing the hand at one of four different locations on the face in the area of the mouth (plus two location combinations). Cues for consonant sounds are provided by making one of eight alternative hand shapes and combining them with the vowel locations. The hand shapes of Cued Speech thus play a very different role from the hand shapes of ASL, which carry information about meaning rather than about sound. Accordingly, Cued Speech is not technically a language, but is a support for spoken English – providing, of course, that everyone involved in a conversation knows how to read and produce the cues.

Although the effectiveness of Cued Speech is still under investigation, there are some encouraging research findings related to its effects on reading ability. Dr. Jacqueline Leybaert and her colleagues in Belgium have shown that deaf children who are consistently exposed to French Cued Speech during the preschool years *both at home and at school* learn to read faster and show enhanced subskills in reading relative to deaf children exposed only to spoken language. Still to be determined is how reading skills of children learning Cued Speech compare to children learning sign language or some hybrid, like Signed English. Meanwhile, we need to recognize that Cued Speech alone will not give younger deaf children access to speech. Some parents have found it effective to expose their children to ASL first, and then bring in Cued Speech during the school years. One former colleague of mine followed this route, teaching her son Cued Speech when he was about eight years old.

The problem, of course, is that if you are using your hands for vowel and consonant cues, you cannot be signing at the same time. Therefore, Cued Speech may be most effective in situations where a story or situation is first described in sign language and then, when it is fully understood, retold with Cued Speech. This combination may help to convey the link between speech and the printed word, but the necessary research has yet to be done.

Alternative Forms of Sign Communication

These combination forms of signing are collectively known as manually coded English, because they present English on the hands rather than the lips.

Pidgin Signed English

Most people who learn to sign as adults do not really use either ASL or Signed English (for which we have little need). I was in that situation myself when I started learning to sign in North Carolina. My sign teacher there was the son of Deaf parents (or a **CODA,** a child of deaf adults) who insisted that ASL could not be taught, only learned naturalistically. What he taught, therefore, was a hybrid sign language known as **Pidgin Signed English** or PSE. Pidgin languages, in general, are those that develop when different languages mix together, typically through the immigration of language groups into new locations. In this manner, English mixed together with French in Louisiana to produce Cajun, and English mixed with several African languages in South Carolina to produce Gullah. When a pidgin is passed on to a second generation as their first language, it evolves into a more rich, complex language called a *creole.* It is via this mechanism that a more complex form of Signed English may become more common in the future. PSE combines the signs of ASL with a mixed grammar of English and ASL. It also includes a variety of initialized signs. Initialized signs typically involve a single sign made with various letter hand shapes that give it several different but related meanings. Examples include a cluster of signs containing SITUATION, CONTEXT, ENVIRONMENT, and CULTURE and one containing GROUP, CLASS, DEPARTMENT, and TEAM. In ASL, all four signs in each group are made with the same hand shape, and the precise meaning must be derived from context. In PSE, like other forms of manually coded English, they are all different.

Signed English

As noted earlier, Signed English is the form of signing most frequently taught to deaf children in the United States. Like PSE, Signed English combines English grammar with the signs of ASL, but it goes beyond the use of initialized signs and English word order. Signed English also includes a set of fourteen markers that are combined with signs to communicate English structure. Consistent with its purpose of helping deaf children learn to read and write, these structural markers refer to important grammatical features of English. The fourteen markers correspond to the following structures, all but one occurring at the end of a sign:

- regular noun plural (ducks)
- irregular noun plural (children)
- possessive (Simon's)
- regular past tense verb (jumped)
- irregular past tense verb (wrote)
- third person singular (written)
- present progressive (jumping)
- past participle (gone)
- adverbial -ly (slowly)
- adjectival -y (funny)
- comparative (fannier)
- superlative (funniest)
- agent (person or thing)
- opposition: not, un-, im-, in- (impolite)

Although potentially an important aspect of language used in the classroom, the grammatical markers of Signed English are unnecessary when signing is in the hands of an expert.

Seeing Essential English (SEE1)

SEE1 was developed during the early 1960s as a way to express English literally using the hands. Every English word is supposed to have a basic (ASL) sign in SEE1, and signs are produced in English word order. Additional signs are used to represent English grammatical structures, as in Signed English, but SEE1 goes farther, using a different sign for each meaningful unit of English rather than for each concept. Thus, for example, while ASL and Signed English use single signs for compound English words that represent a single concept *(butterfly* or *sweetheart)*, SEE1 uses two signs, one for each component unit. *Butterfly* is thus signed by combining the signs BUTTER and FLY, and *sweetheart* is signed by combining the signs SWEET and HEART — combinations that make spelling sense but not conceptual sense.

SEE1 retains those ASL signs that conform to a "two-out-of-three" rule. A single sign is used for an English word with two or more uses, as long as each pair shares two of the following: sound, meaning, or spelling. Thus *bow* as in *bow and arrow* can have the same sign as *bow* as in *tie a bow* or *violin bow* because they share sound and spelling. *Bow* as in *bow from the waist,* however, would have to have a different sign because it shares only spelling with the previous two *bows.*

Signing Exact English (SEE2)

SEE2 was a spinoff from SEE1, the consequence of a difference of opinions among the developers of SEE1 about their goals rather than any agreed upon improvement in the system. SEE2 uses the same general rules as SEE1, but has a one-to-one correspondence between signs and meanings. In SEE2, therefore, the word *bow* has four different signs, and SEE2 thus has more signs than SEE1. SEE2 also makes considerable use of initialized signs.

Among the several alternative communication systems available for deaf children, it would seem that the systems that are likely to be most effective are those that combine as many sources of information as possible. Indeed, this is precisely the philosophy behind Simultaneous Communication and Total Communication. These artificial sign systems, however, do not lead deaf children to fluency in either sign language or in English. If they do not facilitate learning to read and write, there does not seem any good reason to use them. At present, it is unclear whether the limited benefits to deaf children's English skills after learning a hybrid sign system are significant enough to offset their failure to become fluent in ASL. Until more work has been done, this issue will continue to be a problem.

Speech Training and Speech Assessment

Speech training and speech assessment should be thought of as a whole, not as two different endeavors. Assessment of a child's skills and needs are essential to effective teaching of spoken language, and the progress of teaching requires regular assessments both of progress in speech skill acquisition and possible changes in young children's hearing. Both assessment and training therefore have to take into consideration the goals and capabilities of the children and their families, not just abstract principles about the importance of spoken language. Indeed, it is the intense adherence to the primacy of speech by some advocates of oral approaches to education that drives many deaf individuals away from its potential benefits.

The goal of speech and speech reading training should be to allow deaf children to take advantage of the most information possible and have access to the full range of opportunities offered to hearing children. As indicated in the quote by Robert Davila at the beginning of this chapter, the ultimate decision to use speech, sign, or some combination of them rests with the individual. Parents and educators will find themselves — and their children -best positioned if they make all resources available to children until such time as the children themselves are able to make their own decisions.

Speech training can take a variety of forms, depending on the needs of the individual child. Different programmes focus on different levels of spoken language, from individual letter sounds, through syllables, to whole word pronunciation methods. Syllable methods, for example, involve repeated practice with single consonant-vowel pairs such as *pa, pa, pa* or sets of pairs that vary in the vowel's place of articulation, such as the set that would sound like *pee, pa, peh, po, pu,* where you can feel the tongue moving farther and farther back in the mouth. Examples like this are not visible on the mouth and are extremely difficult for deaf children to learn; hence the potential usefulness of Cued Speech. Alternatively, speech training can focus on the pronunciation of whole words. This is often done with words in isolation, although their presentation within meaningful contexts can also contribute to reading as well as speech reading skill.

Regardless of its level, speech training usually involves one-on-one interaction with trained speech therapists over relatively long and repetitive sessions in which student model therapists' behaviour. Parents are given exercises to work on at home with their child when the therapist is not around, but this is rarely sufficient. There are also a variety of technological tools available for professional and home use for speech training. Several computer software companies, for example, market interactive computer software in which young children's productions of correct sounds lead to interesting visual events, such as a monkey climbing a tree. Older children might be shown speech patterns on the computer screen and work to match them with their own productions. These and other methods serve to help coordinate motor movements of the tongue and mouth and appropriate inflow and outflow of air as well as establishing rapport and comfort between the child and the speech training enterprise.

As with speech training, speech assessment can take various forms. At the level of individual sounds, speech therapists evaluate vocal intensity, duration, and pitch, in addition to the correctness of the articulation. As individual speech sounds come into a child's repertoire, they have to be expanded, combined, and regularly maintained or they frequently will "degrade." Some speech skills that are acquired at the level of individual sounds are not easily integrated into syllables and words, so that there must be a constant monitoring and correction of the fall repertoire. Clearly, this relatively intense focus can be difficult for younger deaf children, many of whom will never master the basics well enough to engage in spoken conversation outside of the family. At the same time, because of positive responses from many hearing adults, spoken communication successes can add to a child's feelings of accomplishment, as well as facilitating communication within the home and school.

Speech training must be coupled with appropriate amplification, so that children can receive some feedback in addition to what they can see on the lips. If they also have sufficient residual hearing and speech reading skills to comprehend the spoken language of others, spoken language can be a valuable tool. Unfortunately, there is relatively little research available to parents and professionals on the effectiveness of different speech training methods, and each method has its own adherents and success stories. Without good information on which to evaluate the appropriateness for any given child, parents may be at a loss in deciding how to proceed. In such cases, information can be obtained from *experienced* speech pathologists and audiologists within the school system, avoiding, perhaps, new graduates who may not have had as much experience with diverse methodologies or others who have entrenched biases.

Summary

Language is an essential component of normal development. Because the vast majority of deaf children are born to non-signing hearing parents, however, most of them will be denied access to many parts of the world until they have passed the most critical ages for language acquisition, the first three to four years. All available research indicates that for children with greater hearing losses, exposure only to spoken language usually fails to give children all of the linguistic tools they need for academic and social purposes, although some children will benefit. While access to English may be essential for English literacy, it is most important that deaf children, like hearing children, be able to communicate with their parents from the beginning. Following chapters will show the various ways that early communication affects social and cognitive development, while the present chapter has focused on demonstrating that signed languages are as complete and rich as spoken languages and can fill all of the same roles.

Almost every country has its own sign language, and some countries have more than one, corresponding to their multiple spoken languages. Parts of American Sign Language, especially the grammar, actually came from France, but ASL differs dramatically from the sign languages used in Quebec and England. True sign languages are characterized by the same kinds of features as spoken languages, including rules for formation, modification, and combination of signs. Signs are generally characterized by several clearly defined characteristics such as hand shape and movement. They are combined in grammatically defined ways using three-dimensional space and a variety of grammatical devices such as classifiers, used like pronouns, and linking movements. Like spoken words, most signs are arbitrary and combine with a manual alphabet, facial expression, and body movement to yield a full and natural language taught by deaf parents to their deaf children.

A variety of hybrid systems have been developed in an effort to provide deaf children with early access to language via signing while simultaneously giving them access to English. Some of these, such as Cued Speech, are spoken language systems that include manual movements that disambiguate sounds (and hence words) that are made similarly on the lips. Other systems, such as Signed English, include ASL signs combined through English grammar. Research to date suggests that such artificial combinations do not result in children being fluent in two languages, and most often they are fluent in neither. The variety of difficulties encountered by children who learn artificial sign systems may be offset by advantages in learning to read, at least relative to children who are exposed only to spoken language, but research on this point is not conclusive.

Regardless of its method — signed or spoken — consistent access to a natural language is essential to deaf and hearing children if they are to have the tools they need to become literate and get a comprehensive education. Whatever system a deaf child might experience at school, language learning cannot stop there. Unless deaf children can bring language home with them and use it during play, to get help with schoolwork, and to communicate with their families, they cannot be expected to reach their full potentials. If deaf education is not yet producing high school graduates who are fully literate, the blame cannot be placed wholly on the schools. The basic underpinnings of learning and education begin at home, years before the young deaf or hearing child goes off to school. We therefore now turn to consideration of deaf children's development from birth through adolescence. By this point, the reader should have some understanding of deafness, which will help us to examine social, language, and cognitive development more closely. Thus armed, we will be able to see the implications of early hearing losses for growth throughout childhood and make some fairly good predictions about how and when we will need to compensate for those losses.

5

Classification for Children

In this chapter we examine how disability classifications are constructed from the perspectives of society and science. The social and scientific approaches to the construction of disability are not often considered simultaneously, but we believe these perspectives make more understandable the systems used to classify children. We seek to understand the contributions of these approaches to the education of children. The latter point, educating children, is central to our concern in this chapter. That is, the educational and scientific communities often discuss classification of children. We propose that another, perhaps more appropriate, emphasis is classification for children. This distinction provides a different window from which to view and evaluate classification systems. When classification activities are reified without reference to the original purpose of educating children, it is time to revisit the basis of the system.

Social Construction of Disability

The notion that disability is socially constructed is not new. The process of social construction means that members of a society identify a point at which an unusual pattern of behaviour is seen to be deviant, or beyond acceptable boundaries. Thus, the concept of disability represents a decision made by the society regarding a form of physical or mental deviance, usually thought to be caused by some deficit within the individual. To speak of social construction is not necessarily to argue that the condition does not exist, but to observe that there is a shared understanding that the condition falls outside the norm of what is expected or acceptable.

There is one central question and one subsidiary question relevant to decisions about what constitutes deviance on any particular dimension. The primary question is at what point will a difference in behaviour or development be designated as deviant? Secondarily, how will the designated deviance be valued or not valued?

On the first question: Because deviance exists on a spectrum in relation to some accepted norm, the range of what is considered "normal" is decided on either explicitly, by a body given the responsibility for defining deviance, or implicitly, by some mutually arrived at consensus within the community. In either case, it is reasonable to assume that the condition must relate to a human aspect that is seen as important in that society. If the feature were not of importance, it probably would not be noticed or investigated.

Dexter offered the example of a hypothetical society in which physical awkwardness was seen as a point of deviance, and for which a scale of "normal" to "deviant" was established. A more familiar version of this is the value placed on literacy skills in technological societies where educational equity is a goal. Failing to attain literacy may, thereby, be deviant and certain criteria may be established for the determination of the presence of a "disability" thought to be causing the deviance. We emphasize "where literacy is highly valued" because it is possible to value literacy while expecting it to be the property of a small elite. In such cases, the failure to attain literacy would not be unusual, nor would it be cause for investigation or for the designation "disability."

It is evident, therefore, that if literacy is not an important or expected skill for the majority of a population, it is unlikely that explanations for difficulty in attaining this skill will be sought. Indeed, the concept of a learning disability related to literacy attainment is but a few decades old. This fact could be attributed to previous lack of scientific or pedagogical interest in the question of why some individuals may experience difficulties in this area which may, in turn, relate to the increasing demands of technology. Without such demands, individual variations in literacy acquisition would be of no importance.

Research on culturally diverse parents of children with disabilities indicates how the meaning of disability may vary with culture and acculturation. There is a clear pattern that parents from some minority or working class backgrounds within the United States, or from less technologically developed societies, seem to hold broader parameters of what is normal or acceptable with respect to cognitive development, the attainment of literacy, or both. This has implications for the classifications *mild mental retardation* and *learning disability*. For example, working-class Puerto Rican parents in a study by Harry did not share the U.S. school system's notion of either of these categories. With regard to mental retardation, a child's daily mental functioning had to be seriously impaired for the term to be used whereas, for learning disability, difficulty in learning to read was seen as a matter for concern "but not necessarily a disability".

In another study by Harry, the following excerpt from an interview with a couple from the Dominican Republic illustrates how the definition of disability differed according to each parent's level of acculturation to U.S. norms. These parents had been asked whether they would use the word "handicapped" or "disabled" to refer to their 13-year-old son who had Down syndrome. Mother and Father replied simultaneously and respectively "Yes/No!" The father applies the Dominican understanding of "disability," which is used only to refer to the most severe disabilities. On the other hand, the mother uses the U.S. version, explaining that you can be called disabled if you just have "a limp."

Consensus on what constitutes a disability may also vary within a community, according to the acculturation status of an individual belonging to a minority group within that society. This may be particularly so when the condition is perceived as relatively mild and its impact on individual functioning slight. For example, the following excerpt from an interview with a working-class, African American father of a preschooler labeled mildly mentally retarded shows how the view of mental retardation can differ from that of the school: " to me it means like they're slow; I mean very slow, to the point where they really need some heavy duty attention. But in the school, I guess they use it for any little difference".

It seems the point of view here is affected by the individual's expectations of what is needed for effective and independent functioning. It is likely that people of working-class status and minority groups who have, traditionally, been accustomed to fewer opportunities for advancement, may hold expectations that do not require advanced education and skills. Therefore, like people from less technological cultures, they define the parameters of normalcy more broadly.

It is important to note that cultural change also occurs within a society over time. This is evident in the previously observed point that the concept of learning disability is a recent phenomenon. However, in a matter of 25 years the percentage of school-age children identified as learning disabled grew nearly 300%: from 1.8% in 1976-1977 to 5.2% in 1992-1993. On the topic of mental retardation, cultural change has wrought equally dramatic effects. The initiation of psychometric measurement coincided with this society's intense concern with eugenics in the early to midyears of this century.

During that period, fear of the mentally retarded was reflected in stringent parameters of normal cognitive functioning, by which an IQ of 85 was the definitive cut-off point for mental retardation. In the 1960s, a relaxation of these views, and increasing concerns regarding treatment of persons with retardation, resulted in the American Association on Mental Retardation's change in the criterion for intelligence scores from an IQ of 85 to one of 70. This decision by the official defining body for mental retardation indicates that the cut-off points are entirely up to society and may, in fact, be quite arbitrary. Obviously, there was no change in the approximately 14% of the population previously defined as mentally retarded, yet they were no longer so classified.

The secondary question identified at the beginning of this section was how an identified disability was valued by the society. There are many societies in which certain physically or mentally handicapping conditions are interpreted in a positive light. In the United States, it is fair to say that the notion of disability has traditionally connoted deficit and is therefore interpreted negatively. The increasing efforts to diminish this trend and to treat people with disabilities with equity has not yet succeeded in relinquishing stigma. However, not all disabilities are created equal with respect to stigma as seen in the decrease in diagnoses of mental retardation and the corresponding increase in diagnoses of learning disabilities. In documenting this point, MacMillan commented that this situation is not the result of "mental retardation somehow being cured while an epidemic in learning disabilities occurs", but rather it is due to system identification factors and sociopolitical issues. These factors, of course, pertain to the social construction of disability.

Scientific Construction of Disability

American society has agreed, through legislation and litigation, that there are types of children in school whose behaviour does fall outside the bounds of acceptability. This agreement gives license to the scientific study of these types. From perspective of science, classification is regarded as a basic scientific activity that serves to promote understanding of the phenomenon under investigation. Gould captured the importance of classification in science:

> *Taxonomy is often undervalued as a glorified form of filing, but taxonomy is a fundamental and dynamic science, dedicated to exploring the causes of relationships and similarities among organisms. Classifications are theories about the basis of natural order, not dull categories compiled only to avoid chaos.*

To address the contribution of science to classification for children, it is necessary to (a) understand terminology, (b) differentiate the purposes of classification, and (c) examine the reciprocal influences between scientific classification and practice. With respect to terminology, it is useful to distinguish the terms *typology* and *taxonomy* as presented by Bailey. Both are classification activities. Construction of typologies is conceptual, whereas taxonomies are empirical. In special education, the typology of children is reflected in concepts such as mental retardation, learning disabilities, and behavioral disorders. Numbers are not required to develop a typology, but they may be required to identify members of the type. Taxonomies, on the other hand, require empirical data and the process of defining "taxons" and their members is simultaneous. Readers familiar with the classification research in special education will recognize that the statistical methods of cluster analysis are associated with the development of taxonomies. Examples are most evident in the field of learning disabilities, as researchers attempt to address the acknowledged heterogeneity of skills in this population of learners.

The distinction between typologies and taxonomies is not trivial in special education. Whereas professionals agree, at some level, on the typology, the development of taxonomies is more problematic. Because taxonomies require data, the investigator must select and measure the critical variables as part and parcel of developing a classification. There is little agreement on what the defining variables are (e.g., learning disabilities) leading some to relegate the empirical approach to the back burner until there is consensus on the definition. However, Speece and Cooper argued that the development of taxonomies can assist the definitional problem through careful analysis of multiple variables and rigorous testing of the validity of the resulting taxonomy. This work has proceeded on a domain by domain basis and a single taxonomy of learning disabilities has yet to emerge. It is also true that the typology of atypical learners across the broader spectrum of disability has more conceptual than empirical support. That is, more effort has been placed on classification within a disability category (e.g., mental retardation, learning disabilities) than on distinguishing among the conceptual categories. This brief review of scientific progress indicates that classification of children is the prominent orientation of researchers and that there is still more work to be done in this arena.

The almost exclusive focus on definitional issues, however, need not be the case in scientific classification when we examine the purposes of classification, the second issue to be addressed in this section. The purposes of classification in the social sciences are to enhance prediction and communication. Prediction carries a developmental connotation (e.g., longitudinal outcomes, the stability of a type or taxon) whereas communication is associated with clinical concerns (e.g., response to intervention, enhancing understanding among practitioners). In either case a "good" classification system is one that possesses clear definitional criteria and distinguishes definitional criteria from correlates of the class, leading to reliable identification of entities. Given reliable identification, one assumes homogeneity in which members of the type or taxon resemble each other more than those who are not members. It is at this point that questions concerning long-term outcomes and effectiveness of interventions can be entertained. Answering these types of questions provides the basis for determining the validity of the classification scheme. For example, in the realm of prediction, Feagans and Appelbaum demonstrated that oral language subtypes of children with learning disabilities had differential academic outcomes over a 3-year period such that children with stronger narrative skills outperformed children with stronger semantic and syntactic skills. Cross and Paris showed, in the domain of meta-cognition, that subtypes of children with different strengths and weaknesses benefited from different reading instruction. The latter study demonstrates validation from the perspective of communication.

From a scientific perspective, then, a worthwhile classification system must pass the tests of reliability and validity. This is true regardless of whether the purpose is prediction or communication. Both purposes are worthy goals in the study of classification in special education. The problem is one of emphasis when we consider this chapter's theme of classification for children. That is, if one is concerned with developing a system that leads to better outcomes for children, then the communication value of the classification is paramount. It is fair to say that the development of taxonomies more often has focused on prediction rather than communication. Validation studies have more often addressed naturally occurring outcomes and not the effects of interventions or the value of a particular classification to practitioners. Thus, classification researchers have little to say to practicing professionals when the issue is educating children.

This state of affairs is troubling, but it is not to say that researchers and practitioners have not influenced each other. This is the third point of this section. Practitioners, valuing the reliability and validity criteria of scientists, proceed as though we have the means of valid classification. In the field of learning disabilities this classification is operationalized primarily through an aptitude-achievement discrepancy. Although this criterion has a scientific "ring," it is rarely noted that discrepancy has its basis in federal regulations rather than science. The resulting muddle between science and practice can be observed either by perusing the description of samples in research studies on "LD" or attending eligibility team meetings in the schools. In the former case, children identified by the schools are used as research subjects with investigators paying scant attention to the tremendous variability across classification systems, thus producing results that are applicable to unknown populations. In the latter case, evaluation teams rely on a standard of aptitude-achievement discrepancy that has uneven scientific support.

What is wrong with this picture? In our view, the fundamental problem on both ends is the *assumption* of validity of classification where none exists. Because there is societal agreement that a type exists (e.g., learning disabilities, mental retardation), there is the assumption of validity or simply ignorance of its importance. An examination of statistics on identification rates for each handicapping condition by State shows the folly of this assumption. For example, if classification criteria were valid, why would New York identify 60% of its disabled, school-age population as learning disabled but Georgia identify only 32%.

A second issue is the acceptance by both researchers and practitioners that the disability is the property of the child being classified and that they have no hand in this development other than to apply the "rules." We do not argue that individual differences are unimportant. Rather, we argue that classification efforts for children have lost their way by being overly enamored of quantitative over qualitative data and by focusing on the individual to the exclusion of ecological factors. This situation has produced a culture of classification where a score on an intelligence test has more meaning than a child's classroom performance. Gerber and Semmel captured this phenomenon in the phrase "teacher as imperfect test". That is, when classification decisions are made, a teacher's observations of a child are given less weight than the results of published, standardized tests.

Thus, the science of classification and the practice of classification in the schools have little in common save for a shared but absent value of validity and the assumption that the disability is the property of the child. Professional judgment, not discrepancy formulas, is the legal cornerstone of learning disabilities identification, but scientific study of disability has rarely acknowledged this and it is difficult for practitioners to articulate the multiple variables that lead to an eligibility decision. Any serious attempt to understand classification wreaks havoc with the underlying need for objectivity. To understand disability classifications, one must stir in the context in which scientific and educational classification decisions get made. This is true even in epidemiological studies where unselected samples of children are studied to understand the expression and development of disabilities. Although these types of studies are not "tainted" at the outset by murky professional criteria, someone must decide who has the condition and who does not and, ultimately, the study of children must address the fact that they are in schools, a critical context. Despite what we would like to believe, learning disability and mental retardation are relative conditions: relative to the community (including scientists), relative to who else is in the classroom, relative to the teacher's skills and beliefs, relative to other services in the schools, relative to the school's approach to exclusionary criteria, and relative to researchers' theoretical assumptions. Any discussion of classification needs to confront this messy but fundamental truth.

Summary

We have sketched how classifications are constructed from both social and scientific perspectives. Neither approach appears to serve the goal of providing better educational services for children even though we value the contributions of each perspective in understanding how we go about the business of classification. We are reminded of Annie Mae's response to Heath in elaborating on why interpersonal relationships and linkages between concepts were more important than knowing a label in the poor, Black community of Trackton:

What Annie Mae suggests and what we wish to elaborate is the relative importance of classification. There seems to be no way around the fact that humans, by their very nature, need to classify. Life is too complex to hold in mind all of the individual elements of phenomena. Indeed, when we try to rid ourselves of one classification, another will take its place. A colleague recounted a school-related example: In attempting to implement inclusion practices, children formerly referred to as "LD" or "BD" became the "inclusion kids." No amount of exhortation will reduce our need to classify and we will not argue that classification is unnecessary. The very real dilemma is that there are scarce resources which need to be appropriated and uncertainty in both science and society about who should be served.

The point that we believe requires elaboration is the process by which classification takes place. Both the social and scientific construction of disability classifications reify the condition such that the child *becomes* the condition, as in "He is LD." This reification can be mitigated by changing the classification focus from the child to the nature of instructional interactions and their outcomes. Instead of a preoccupation with measuring individual differences, more effort is devoted to understanding the content and method and response to instruction. As it now stands, instruction is more of an afterthought that follows designation as handicapped rather than a driving force that explicates learning difficulties. We suggest that eligibility discussions take instruction as the primary issue, relegating measurement of a host of individual differences and the naming of the condition to secondary status.

Fuchs has clearly articulated how this can be accomplished. Thus, our desire to change the focus of classification has empirical backing and does not represent an admirable but unattainable goal. Fuchs proposed that eligibility be approached through a treatment validation framework. Her three-phase model that emphasizes collection of curriculum-based data requires (a) documentation of achievement discrepancies relative to local norms that addresses both absolute performance and growth, (b) documentation that instructional changes in the general education setting do not produce adequate growth, and (c) documentation that instruction in a special education setting does result in academic growth. Only when these three requirements are met is a child found eligible for services. That special education services would be provided only if a trial period in special education demonstrated progress is revolutionary in our history of classification. Fuchs carefully detailed feasibility issues and required research, but it is clear that there is both a research and a practice base for implementing these ideas.

A focus on the interactions between children and teachers addresses a number of problems with current classification practices. From the perspective of social construction, emphasis on response to instruction reframe the parent-professional interaction. Instead of discussing labels that have different interpretations among participants, discussion can revolve around what works and what does not. Our prediction is that this type of conversation is both more useful and understandable and does not require professional jargon. From a scientific perspective, valid information is used to identify children who are not progressing, paving the way for the design and implementation of interventions that will accelerate the communicative value of classification. This does not negate the importance of understanding children's characteristics. However, this is a side issue to developing classification practices that serve children.

Finally, and perhaps most importantly, the onus of the problem is shifted from the child to the nature and outcomes of instructional interaction that necessarily involve the child *and* the teacher. We are not so naive as to think this shift will be easy to attain. As Schulte documented, nativist beliefs about the locus of disability run deep in our culture and teachers may hold these beliefs. We do believe, however, that the shift can occur and that the result will address the issue of classification *for* children.

6

Defining Emotional or Behavioural Disorders

In special education, the field of emotional or behavioral disorders seems to have considerably more problems in definition than other major categories such as learning disabilities or mental retardation. Although some disagreement remains, both these latter disorders have a much greater consensus as to definitional and diagnostic criteria, not only within special education, but in other related professions such as psychology, pediatrics, or psychiatry. Emotional or behavioral disorders is a subspecialty that, like mental retardation and learning disabilities, has focused on developmental and academic issues yet, at the same time, must give a certain priority to social or emotional issues as well. These are less well understood and enjoy less agreement as to definition, cause, and treatment, both within special education and in its related professional fields. It is also a specialty whose treatments are increasingly seen as dependent on interdisciplinary or interagency services in which a wide variety of professionals must agree on need for service. There has thus been an understandable tendency to identify only the most obviously or seriously disturbed children in this category. The outcomes for children with emotional or behavioral disorders are therefore understandably less optimistic than for children in almost any other category of special education.

This chapter focuses on the current definition of serious emotional disturbance (SED) used to determine eligibility for special education and on a definition of emotional or behavioral disorders that will replace it in federal law. Because school is not the only agency providing services for such children and eligibility for related services is often largely dependent on other agencies, other definitions of emotional or behavioral disorders are also reviewed briefly. These include a definition used in Head Start programmes, an NIMH definition used in a generic sense to determine Baseness, a definition of eligibility used to determine disability in this area under the Social Security administration, the definition used by the American Psychiatric Association, and the definition used in Section 504 of the Rehabilitation Act . The chapter concludes with a discussion of issues related to eligibility under these various definitions.

Sed Definition

For nearly two decades, the terminology that has been used to determine eligibility of children with emotional or behavioral disorders for special education is serious emotional disturbance (SED). SED is defined in federal law as a:

> *Condition exhibiting one or more of the following characteristics over a long period of time or to a marked degree which adversely affects school performance: (a) an inability to learn which cannot be explained by intellectual, sensory, or health factors; (b) an inability to build or maintain satisfactory relationships with peers and teachers (c) inappropriate types of behaviour or feelings under normal circumstances (d) a general pervasive mood of unhappiness or depression; or (e) a tendency to develop physical symptoms or fears associated with personal or school problems.*

The definition continues by indicating that the term does include children who are schizophrenic, but does not include children who are "socially maladjusted, unless it is determined that they are seriously emotionally disturbed". Thus, to qualify, a youngster must have a problem in at least one of the five areas listed here that must further meet all three limiting criteria; that is, severity, duration, and impact on school performance.

Most professionals in special education consider both the term itself and its definition not only problematic but also a primary source of difficulty in under identification. The principal division of the Council for Exceptional Children, which represents nationally over 9,000 special educators involved in education of children with behavioral or emotional disorders, has published position papers attacking both the terminology and definition. Similar criticism has come from the National Mental Health and Special Education Coalition organized to address the problem of inadequate service delivery for emotionally disturbed children and youth. A disclaimer has even come from the person from whose early research the five definitional criteria were adopted.

Use of this particular terminology and definition has led to several problems. For example, the term *seriously* makes this the one special education category in which only the most impaired tend to be considered for eligibility. Of the five criteria, the first, "inability to learn," is often confused with the learning disability (LD) definition. The second, "inability to build or maintain satisfactory relationships with teachers or peers" (i.e., social adjustment problems), confuses matters because children are excluded if their problems are considered merely "social maladjustment." Many children are also excluded because their problems are considered to be "merely" conduct disorders or discipline problems; however, their actual underlying emotional disorders, such as depression or anxiety, are not recognized or identified as such because "social maladjustment" problems become automatic exclusions. Epidemiologic studies also suggest that symptoms of conduct disorders are inextricably woven into symptoms of other psychiatric disorders, such that very few children are referred to special education with "pure" conduct disorders. The vast majority of states do not exclude children with "social maladjustment," as this definition requires, presumably because of the impossibility of reliably distinguishing "social" from "emotional" maladjustment.

The EBD Definition

Responding to these issues, the Council for Children with Behavioral Disorders drafted a substitute terminology and definition. This draft was submitted to the National Mental Health and Special

Education Coalition, which was composed at the time of 30 different education, mental health, advocacy, and parent associations. The Coalition task force on definition further reviewed and revised the draft.

This draft terminology and definition was also submitted to relevant House and Senate subcommittees of the U.S. Congress. There were simultaneous contacts with a wide range of other stakeholders in education and mental health, including members from associations or groups representing ethnically diverse populations such as the NAACP and La Raza. Although the terminology and definition change was originally scheduled as an amendment to pending legislation in the summer of 1992 and quick passage was expected, many individuals representing state and local school boards objected at the last minute. This was mainly because of fears that large numbers of children previously unserved in this category would now have to be included in special education at great cost to states and local districts.

It was clear, however, that the newly proposed terminology and definition had nonetheless been "vetted" in a historically unique process and that it enjoyed widespread support in the special education and mental health communities. It was also clear that families of children with this disorder had both been included in this process and were supportive of its outcome. For this reason, Congress compromised by directing the U.S. Department of Education to publish a "notice of inquiry" in the *Federal Register* asking for comments on the advisability of changing to the new definition and terminology in IDEA. Approximately 1,200 responses were received, among the largest number of responses ever received from such a notice of inquiry. Although the terminology was originally proposed as "emotional or behavioral disorders" or EBD, the terminology currently proposed in the latest House of Representatives proposal to reauthorize IDEA is "emotional disturbance". The definition may thus be linked to this terminology, but this is yet be determined. The text of the new definition as published in the *Federal Register* is:

> *The term means a disability that is characterized by behavioral or emotional response in school programmes that is significantly different from appropriate age, cultural, or ethnic norms to the extent that the responses adversely affect educational performance,*

> *including academic, social or vocational skills; more than temporary, expected response to stressful events in the environment; consistently exhibited in two different settings, at least one of which is school related; and unresponsive to direct intervention applied by general education, or the condition of a child is such that general education interventions would be insufficient.*
>
> *The term includes such a disability that coexists with other disabilities. The term includes a schizophrenic disorder, affective disorder, anxiety disorder, or other mental disorder, affecting a child if the disorder affects educational performance.*

There are a number of major advantages and improvements in this new terminology and definition. The core of the definition stresses that emotional or behavioral problems must exist and must have an impact on adaptive behaviour, broadly defined. It not only focuses directly on the child's responses in school settings and places these responses in the context of appropriate age and cultural norms but also has several qualifying statements that insure that only children who appropriately qualify will be eligible. The additional qualifying statements indicate that emotional disorder (a) is more than a temporary, expected response to stress; (b) should be based on data gathered in more than one setting; (c) would persist even with prereferral interventions; (d) can coexist with other disabilities; and (e) is referenced to a listing of examples of current mental health diagnoses that *could* make a student eligible, *if* educational performance is also impaired, thus allowing for greater coordination with other agencies that can provide related services in addition to the school. In contrast to the current definition, the definition does not require meaningless distinctions between social and emotional maladjustment, distinctions that often waste diagnostic resources when it is already clear that serious problems exist. It is not at all clear at the time of this writing, however, that the new EBD terminology or definition will be incorporated into IDEA. They have nonetheless been widely accepted as a generic terminology definition for the field.

The Head Start Definition

Even before the first draft of the EBD definition was formally considered in the U.S. Department of Education notice of inquiry, the U.S. Administration on Children, Youth, and Families adopted a version of it for Head Start programmes. The Head Start version was used as part of its revised disability regulations and is as follows:

(a) An emotional/behavioral disorder is a condition in which a child's behavioral or emotional responses are so different from those of the generally accepted, age-appropriate norms of children with the same ethnic or cultural background as to result in significant impairment in social relationships, self-care, educational progress or classroom behaviour. A child is classified as having an emotional/behavioral disorder who exhibits one or more of the following characteristics with such frequency, intensity, or duration as to require intervention:

1. Seriously delayed social development including an inability to build or maintain satisfactory interpersonal relationships with peers or adults (e.g., avoids playing with peers);
2. Inappropriate behaviour (e.g., dangerously aggressive towards others, self-destructive, severely withdrawn, noncommunicative);
3. A general pervasive mood of unhappiness or depression, or evidence of excessive anxiety or fears (e.g., frequent crying episodes, constant need for reassurance); or
4. Has a professional diagnosis of serious emotional disturbance.

(b) The eligibility decision must be based on multiple sources of data, including assessment of the child's behaviour or emotional functioning in multiple settings.

(c) The evaluation process must include a review of the child's regular Head Start physical examination to eliminate the possibility of misdiagnosis due to an underlying physical condition.

As can be seen, the Head Start definition is an amalgamation of the two previous definitions. It borrows the core of the EBD definition and some of its qualifying statements along with considerably revised versions of the SED subtype categories. It adds a provision for medical screening in order to rule out other conditions that might be causing emotional or behavioral symptoms. Because Head Start is perhaps the largest single referral source for children identified for special education in the early years, this represented a significant attempt to make the two agencies more compatible in their eligibility requirements.

The CMHS Definition

At about the same time that the EBD definition was proposed to Congress, the National Institute of Mental Health (NIMH) reorganized its applied epidemiologic and mental health service efforts into a new Center for Mental Health Services (CMHS). It became clear that several issues in child mental health in particular could not be effectively addressed without a functional definition of childhood emotional or behavioral disorders. CMHS commissioned a panel of experts to draft a definition of caseness that could not only be used in epidemiologic studies but could also be used in planning for child mental health services. The text of this definition became part of the reorganization of child mental health services under the Alcohol, Drug Abuse, and Mental Health Administration as follows:

Children with serious emotional disturbance are persons:

- from birth up to age 18
- who currently or at any time during the past year
- have had a diagnosable mental, behavioral or emotional disorder of sufficient duration to meet diagnostic criteria specified with *DSM-III-R*, that resulted in functional impairment which substantially interferes with or limits the child's role or functioning in family, school or community activities.

These disorders include any mental disorder listed in DSM-III-R *or their* ICD-9-CM *equivalent, with the exception of* DSM-III-R *"V" codes, substance use, and developmental disorders, which are excluded, unless they co-occur with another diagnosable serious emotional disturbance. All of these disorders have episodic, recurrent or persistent features; however, they vary in terms of severity and disabling effects.*

Functional impairment is defined as difficulties that substantially interfere with or limit a child or adolescent from achieving or maintaining one or more developmentally appropriate social, behavioral, cognitive, communicative, or adaptive skills. Functional impairments of episodic, recurrent and continuous duration are included unless they are temporary and expected responses to stressful events in the environment. Children who would have met functional impairment criteria during the referenced year without the benefit of treatment or other support services are included in this definition.

It should be noted that explanatory footnotes are included in the text of this definition. These note (a) that the definition normally applies up to age 19, but some states currently extend the range to age 22; (b) that the reference to a 1-year period is commonly used both in epidemiologic research and in service planning cycles; (c) that the publication of the *DSM-IV* would cause this to be updated accordingly; and (d) that substantial functional impairment would subsequently be operationally defined as standardized methods are developed.

Beyond the issues of determining prevalence and state planning for Community Mental Health Services Block Grant Awards, it is not yet clear what impact the CMHS definition will have. Perhaps like the proposed school definition of emotional or behavioral disorders, it may only be destined to become a generic definition in the mental health field. Although its dual emphasis on presence of a disorder and on functional impairment render it somewhat compatible with the EBD definition, the SED terminology may continue to pose problems in that only the most severe or obvious cases may be eligible for consideration in service planning.

SSI Definition

Within the U.S. Social Security Administration, the Supplemental Security Income (SSI) programme provides funds for people at any age who have severe disabilities and meet requirements for limited income. Most states have a disability determination service that reviews decisions on each child made by a disability examiner and a medical or psychological specialist. This team develops a care record of each child applicant's medical and functional history from a wide variety of sources including parents, caregivers, school staff, and other practitioners as needed. The team uses a sequential evaluation process in which it considers in turn whether the child is not able to engage in gainful activity, whether the child has a severe impairment, and whether the child's impairment meets an official listing of impairments, or, if not, whether the impairment is comparable in severity to that which would disable an adult.

The childhood mental disorders in which a child might qualify for SSI were first listed in the *Federal Register* in 1990 as follows:

112.02 Organic Mental Disorders: Abnormalities in perception, cognition, affect or behaviour associated with dysfunction of the brain. History and physical examination or laboratory tests, including psychological or neuropsychological tests, demonstrate or support the presence of an organic factor judged to be etiologically related to the abnormal mental state and associated deficit or loss of specific cognitive abilities, affective changes, or loss of previously acquired functional abilities.

112.03 Schizophrenic, Delusional (Paranoid), Schizo affective and Other Psychotic Disorders: Onset of psychotic features, characterized by marked disturbance of thinking, feeling, and behaviour, with deterioration from previous level of functioning or failure to achieve the expected level of social functioning.

112.04 Mood Disorders: Characterized by a disturbance of mood (referring to a prolonged emotion that colors the whole psychic life, generally involving either depression or elation), accompanied by a full or partial manic or depressive syndrome.

112.05 Mental Retardation: Characterized by significantly sub-average general intellectual functioning with deficits in adaptive functioning.

112.06 Anxiety Disorders: In these disorders, anxiety is either the predominant disturbance or is experienced if the individual attempts to master symptoms, e.g., confronting the dreaded object or situation in a phobic disorder, attempting to go to school in a separation anxiety disorder, resisting the obsessions or compulsions in an obsessive compulsive disorder or confronting strangers or peers in avoid disorders.

112.07 Somatoform, Eating and Tic Disorders: Manifested by physical symptoms for which there are no demonstrable organic findings or known physiologic mechanisms, or eating or tic disorders with physical manifestations. The required level of severity for these disorders is met when functional requirements are satisfied.

112.08 Personality Disorders: Manifested by pervasive, inflexible, and maladaptive personality traits, which are typical of the child's long term functioning and not limited to discrete episodes of illness.

112.09 Psychoactive Substance Dependence Disorders: Manifested by a cluster of cognitive, behavioral, and physiologic symptoms that indicate impaired control of psychoactive substance use with continued use of the substance despite adverse consequences.

112.10 Autistic Disorder and Other Pervasive Developmental Disorders: Characterized by qualitative deficits in the development of reciprocal social interaction, in the development of verbal and nonverbal communication skills, and in imaginative activity. Often, there is a markedly restricted repertoire of activities and interests, which frequently are stereotyped and repetitive.

112.11 Attention Deficit Hyperactivity Disorders: Manifested by developmentally inappropriate degrees of inattention, impulsiveness, and hyperactivity.

112.13 Developmental and Emotional Disorders of Newborn: and Younger Infants (Birth to Attainment of Age 1). Developmental or emotional disorders of infancy are evidenced by a deficit or lag in the areas of motor, cognitive/communicative or social functioning. These disorders may be related either to organic or functional factors, or to a combination of these factors.

As indicated earlier, each of the listings includes not only a detailed description of various criteria for each disorder but a detailed description of various criteria for functional impairment associated with it, Currently, there would appear to be more than a quarter of a million children or adolescents receiving SSI under these listings. The three most common listings used were ADHD (29.5%), personality disorders (21%), and mood disorders (12%). All the remaining disorders were each less than 10%. From the criteria listed in "Personality Disorders," it is possible to conclude that social or conduct disturbances may have accounted for a large proportion of the 21% listed. There is currently no way of determining the extent to which the approximately quarter of a million cases eligible for SSI overlap the approximately 400,000 cases identified as eligible for special education in the SED category.

The DSM-IV Definition

Underlying nearly each of the previous definitions is the spectre of psychiatric diagnosis and classification as determined in the current *Diagnostic and Statistical Manual of Mental Disorders*, or *DSM-IV*. At least some of the subtypes of the school SED definition appear to correspond with certain psychiatric diagnoses. The EBD definition lists some of the major diagnostic categories. The SED definition used by CMHS refers directly to the *DSM*, and the SSI listings correspond at least approximately to major *DSM-IV* categories. The primary definition of "mental disorder" is not given particular prominence in the *DSM-IV*, but is presented here in order to help define the parameters by which a particular diagnosis is included:

> *In the* DSM-IV, *each of the mental disorders is conceptualized as a clinically significant behavioral or psychological syndrome or pattern that occurs in an individual and that is associated with present distress or disability (i.e., impairment in one or more important areas of functioning) or with a significantly increased risk of suffering death, pain, disability, or an important loss of freedom. In addition, this syndrome or pattern must not be merely an expectable and culturally sanctioned response to a particular event, for example, the death of a loved one. Whatever its original cause, it must currently be considered a manifestation of a behavioral, psychological, or biological dysfunction in the individual. Neither deviant behaviour nor conflicts that are primarily between the individual and society are mental disorders unless the deviance or conflict is a symptom of a dysfunction in the individual, as described earlier. The core of the* DSM-IV *is a multiaxial system in which various primary and secondary diagnoses are listed on the first axis, presence of personality disorders or mental retardation on the second axis, general medical conditions that may be relevant to understanding a disorder on the third axis, psychosocial and environmental problems that may affect diagnosis or treatment on the fourth axis, and a global assessment of functioning rated from 1 to 100 on the fifth axis.*

There are approximately 40 different disorders usually first diagnosed in infancy, childhood, or adolescence and at least 100 other primary disorders with which children or adolescents could be diagnosed, not counting each of the various subtypes of these disorders, substance abuse disorders, dementias, sexual or gender identity disorders, or other conditions that do not constitute a disorder but might be a focus of attention. Examples of major categories include pervasive developmental disorders, schizophrenia and other psychotic disorders, mood disorders (major depressive disorder, dysthymic disorder, bipolar disorder, cyclothymic disorder), anxiety disorders, personality disorders (antisocial personality disorder, schizoid personality disorder, schizotypal personality disorder, borderline personality disorder), feeding and eating disorders (pica, anorexia nervosa, bulimia nervosa), tic disorders, and attention deficit and disruptive behaviour disorders (attention-deficit/hyperactivity disorder, conduct disorder, oppositional defiant disorder). Mental retardation, learning disorders, and communication disorders are also listed, although these each comprise separate categories in special education.

The types of information contained in each listing include primary diagnostic features (usually a minimum threshold number of symptoms chosen from among a list of several that might comprise the disorder); subtypes or specifiers that provide further classification (for example, schizophrenia, paranoid type, or major depressive disorder, single episode); associated features or disorders; specific culture, age or gender features; prevalence; expected course of the disorder; familial pattern; and any differential diagnoses that should be considered.

It should be noted that enormous effort was expended by the American Psychiatric Association in development of the *DSM-IV*. Work groups were assigned to 13 major categories, and the work of each was critiqued by as many as 100 professionals for each group. One of the authors served on the learning disorders subgroup, composed of eight psychiatrists, psychologists, or special educators, and wrote seven different drafts of that section over a 6-year period. Some two dozen other professionals provided specific written or oral input on one or more of the drafts. This was for only one of the 40 disorders assigned to the workgroup on disorders with child or adolescent onset. On a dozen of the more prominent disorders, year-long field trials were conducted at 70 sites involving over 6,000 subjects. Psychiatric diagnoses under such a system nonetheless continue to be plagued by problems of validity, reliability, and relevance to treatment.

The 504 Definition

Under Section 504 of the Rehabilitation Act of 1973, discrimination against individuals with handicaps is prohibited by any agency receiving federal financial assistance which obviously includes public schools. Thus schools are required to make necessary accommodations for any pupils meeting 504 criteria, even if these pupils do not meet criteria for special education under IDEA. Procedures have been outlined suggesting how 504 accommodations can be made.

Unlike previous definitions, however, the 504 definition is rather broadly defined to refer to any and all conditions of disability. Under this law, an individual with handicaps is defined as "any individual who (a) has a physical or mental impairment which substantially limits one or more of such person's major life activities, (b) has a record of such impairment, or (c) is regarded as having such an impairment".

These terms are further defined in the law. Mental impairment is defined as "any mental or psychological disorder, such as mental retardation, organic brain syndrome, emotional or mental illness, and specific learning disabilities." Major life activities include "functions such as caring for one's self, performing manual tasks, walking, hearing, speaking, breathing, learning and working".

In effect, any of the disorders in the *DSM-IV* as listed earlier could qualify a pupil for accommodations in the school or classroom. ADHD and even conduct disorders could indeed fall under the purview of these 504 regulations. It is clear, however, that unlike most of the previous definitions for eligibility, 504 does not necessarily bring guaranteed programmes, funding, or even, in many cases, substantial accommodations once an individual qualifies. The Council for Administrators of Special Education mentioned such areas as communication, organisation, alternative teaching strategies, or pupil precautions as accommodations in the regular classroom environment. In many cases, these adaptations are relatively minor such as scheduling periodic parent-teacher meetings, networking with other staff, reducing external stimuli in the classroom, individualizing classroom assignments, adjusting level of reading materials, administering medications, and the like. Few accommodations appear to go beyond what one might consider effective teaching or prereferral interventions of mild or moderate intensity.

Most school districts, however, have developed procedures to meet 504 regulations. These usually include a written individual plan, at least some parental input, procedure for both initial and subsequent evaluations, progress monitoring, and procedural safeguards. Prior notice is required if there is any "significant change" in educational placement, but the law remains relatively vague as to how substantial these procedures must be. Although increased emphasis on 504 definitions and accommodations became apparent largely as a result of increasing attention to children with ADHD, there is considerable evidence that any child with disruptive or troubling behaviour could be seen as eligible under this law, especially if he or she fails to qualify under IDEA .

Summary

There are, of course, other definitions under which children with emotional or behavioral disorders could conceivably receive services. The definition of developmental disability in federal law not only encompasses children with coexisting developmental disabilities and mental health disorders, but the state system of protection and advocacy services for persons with developmental disabilities is also responsible for children with mental health needs even when other developmental disabilities are not present .

Various textbook and research definitions have also been used to define eligibility for services in university-based clinics or in the private sector. Other systems used in classification of medical disorders have sections defining various mental illnesses.

It is quite clear from the aforementioned that a child might be found eligible in one system yet not meet criteria given the definition in another. As noted previously, the SED definition appears to require deficits in academic performance, whereas other definitions tend to define education or adaptive skills much more broadly. Only two definitions, EBD and 504, would seem to target vocational skills as significant determinants of eligibility, an area that becomes increasingly critical as children move into their adolescent years. Most definitions tend specifically to mention social skills among their listings of adaptive skills that could be affected, yet criteria for several *DSM-IV* diagnoses are vague in this area. Relatively few definitions tend to require expression of a disorder across more than one setting. Only the EBD, Head Start, and CMHS definitions mention such a requirement specifically. The EBD, Head Start and *DSM-IV* definitions are the only ones that appear to mention ethnic or cultural considerations.

Only one definition, SED, has a substantial exclusion clause. As noted earlier, this definition excludes children or adolescents with "social maladjustment" unless other emotional disorders are present. Much has been made of this exclusion by proponents who seek to exclude children with oppositional or conduct disorders from receiving special education services under the SED label. Nonetheless, it is clear that a variety of disorders may underlie symptoms of social maladjustment or conduct disturbance and that these may require and indeed deserve, both in a legal and a professional sense, special education services. The problem of single eligibility in dual systems is especially significant in the field of emotional or behavioral disorders. It has been demonstrated repeatedly that mental health and special education diagnostic categories are not concordant. This lack of concordance has led to a variety of difficulties both in service delivery and in applied research on collaborative treatment systems. Even by conservative estimates in well designed, epidemiologic studies, as many as 1 in 7 children or adolescents may have an emotional or behavioral disorder that both meets a diagnostic threshold and is in need of treatment. Estimates are that fewer than one third of those needing treatment are actually receiving it, and far fewer than that are receiving the interdisciplinary or interagency services that are considered critical to successful outcome. There are a variety of reasons for lack of collaboration among professionals, including disagreement on the nature of emotional or behavioral disorders, different treatment goals or modalities, lack of interdisciplinary training, and lack of resources or systems for coordination.

Lack of definitional concordance, however, is clearly a primary cause of under identification. In a recent study, Duncan, Forness and Hartsough demonstrated that parents were aware of their child's emotional or behavioral disorders in the preschool years but that initial services were not provided until early elementary years. Special education within the SED category was not begun until late in the elementary grades. In many cases, services begun in one system such as mental health were inadequate, of and by themselves, without simultaneous efforts in another system such as special education. Although this initial service might have been initiated early enough in some cases, the treatment was clearly inadequate for the problem because collaborative efforts were not simultaneously begun in other systems. It is clear that definitional issues, especially in the school system, were at the root of this problem.

For better or worse, school is the one agency that serves as a mental health screening system. Teachers in general education classrooms may not recognize a bona fide emotional or behavioral disorder for what it is, but they do have a built-in normative sample of children against which to measure deviance. It is this system that inevitably sets into motion a chain of events that leads to formal or informal prereferral interventions, referral for special education, and ultimately referral procedures for services in other related agencies. This referral process is by no means completely systematic. Walker and his colleagues have developed early identification systems to make school screening much more systematic, with relatively little effort on the part of teachers. Such a system is much more compatible with the EBD and Head Start definitions than it is with the SED definition. It is nonetheless a decided improvement, under any definition, than the relatively haphazard system that we now have.

School is also the one agency with the bulk of responsibility for children with emotional or behavioral disorders because it is the only agency currently with a continuous mandate to serve children regardless of budget cuts, lack of resources, or problems in training personnel. Lack of resources and diminished federal mandates may soon force professionals in this area into a very different mode. Rather than being the lead agency as it now seems to be for children in the school years, school may well begin to assume a role as but one of many collaborating agencies. This school-age model may become similar to that of interagency collaboration under Public Law 99-457 for infants, toddlers, and preschoolers. Instead of an individual family service plan for preschool, an individual educational plan for school, an individual treatment plan for mental health, an individual habilitation plan for employment training, and the like, there may very likely be a comprehensive individual plan that all involved agencies will develop collaboratively. This plan might follow the child not just from agency to agency but from one developmental stage to the next. As these new developments begin to take hold, it seems clear that the school will continue to be an important link in the service system but that other agencies may assume a much greater share in the collaborative network of care for children with mental health needs. This may in turn lead to a generic definition of emotional or behavioral disorders in which a core component defines the disorder and is used throughout every agency, but a list of related skill deficits also becomes part of the definition and triggers the need for services from a particular agency or set of professionals.

7

LANGUAGE DEVELOPMENT

As a starting point, let us consider the very beginnings of communication, when a child's spoken, signed, or gestural productions first begin to have what I call "communicative consequences" for mothers and fathers. This is the point, during the first year of life, when both deaf and hearing children are beginning to make regular vocal sounds and are using simple gestures.

With both hands and voices available to young children, many researchers believe they should be equally able to learn either a signed or a spoken language. Although both kinds of language require small but accurate muscle movements, such agility develops at different rates in different parts of the body. In particular, coordinated hand movements generally develop before coordinated mouth movements. This manual priority has been taken to indicate that children should be able to produce sign language earlier than they can produce spoken language, a possibility that we will consider later. At this point, it is sufficient to note that a biological preference for signed over spoken language is also consistent with the belief that in the history of humankind, manual communication was used before spoken communication.

Most of the evidence concerning the development of spoken communication in humans, as a species, comes from historical studies of brain development and anthropological findings concerning our distant ancestors. Closer to home, some relevant evidence comes from studies concerning the early use of signs and words by young hearing children of deaf parents and some hearing children of hearing parents who use sign language with their children for other reasons. Although these findings are far from conclusive, they suggest that sign languages can be acquired just as early as spoken languages, and perhaps somewhat earlier. In order to set the stage for discussions of the emergence of the first words and the first signs, let us consider what often appears — at least to parents — to be even earlier approximations to communication.

Do Deaf Babies Babble

Babies come into the world with the potential to learn any human language. Not all languages, however, consist of the same basic elements. In Italian, for example, the pronunciation of a longer or shorter's sound can make for two different words. I discovered this fact — to the delight of my Italian audience-when I once confused the word for "to marry" with the word for "to be worn out" in describing my relationship with the woman who is now my wife. This difference is one that native English speakers do not hear without considerable practice, just as native Japanese speakers cannot easily hear the difference between rice and lice and hearing students of American Sign Language (ASL) initially are unable to see the difference between I AM ALWAYS SICK and I FREQUENTLY GET SICK . It is only with time and exposure to many examples that children learn the range of elements, either sounds or sign components, in their native language. Meanwhile, they gradually lose the ability to discriminate and produce language elements with which they have no practice. This process may explain, in part, why it is easier to learn a second language in early childhood than in adulthood, regardless of whether that language is spoken or signed: Children's "sensory software" has not yet become exclusively tuned to the repertoire of only a single language.

Infants who can hear appear to start homing in on the sounds relevant to their native language during the first few weeks or months of life, when they start producing the simple sounds we call babbling. There are at least two ways in which the babbling of young infants might be related to later language acquisition. One possibility is that babbling actually is a direct precursor to language. From this perspective, babbling is seen as babies' exercising their language production equipment in preparation for language, even though they are not really trying to talk. A second possibility is less concerned with the particular sounds or gestures that an infant might produce than the effects of those productions on other people, and especially the parents. We will consider both of these possibilities in asking two related questions: Do deaf babies vocally babble in ways similar to hearing babies and Do deaf babies do anything with their hands that resembles the babbling that hearing babies do with their voices?

Vocal Babbling by Deaf Infants

Although it might not seem that way to an untrained ear, hearing children's babbling actually follows a fairly regular course of development. During the first two months of life, for example, infants produce what appear to be simple vowel sounds: *ah, ee,* and *oo.* From two to three months of age, these vowel-like sounds are joined by consonant-like sounds, made for the most part in the back of the mouth, producing sounds like *ka, coo,* and *goo.* This stage is thus called the cooing stage, although it usually sounds more like a "gooing" stage. Over the next three months or so, these vocal sounds are further expanded to include a variety of other sounds like grunts, growls, and squeals, as well as clearer vowels and consonant-vowel combinations. Typically, it is not until seven to eleven months that hearing infants start to produce the well-formed syllables needed for babbling. This is the stage in which sounds are repeated to form the first vocalizations that excited parents might interpret as words: *mama, dada, kaka,* and so on. This type of babbling is important for two reasons. On the technical side, such repetitive babbling is the first time that infants produce the syllabus, which will be the building blocks of words. On the social side, it is at this point that parents start responding to their children's apparent attempts at communication, leading to a new form of parent-child interaction and reciprocity.

In many books and articles written about deaf children, the question of whether deaf babies babble *vocally* appears very complicated. The confusion arises for the most part from informal observations of deaf babies made by parents and other untrained baby watchers. That is, it seems to make sense for deaf babies to babble early on, perhaps up to the point when hearing babies start to produce words, even if they cannot hear what they babble. This pattern of early vocalization would suggest that babbling is an innate, natural behaviour that occurs regardless of a baby's early environment or hearing status. However, this sequence is not what generally occurs. When it comes to early vocalizations like crying, fussing, grunting and cooing, deaf babies really do sound much the same as hearing babies of hearing parents. Then, after the first few months, their vocal babbling usually shows a steady decrease both in frequency and variety. These declines contrast with the babbling of hearing babies, which increases steadily in both quantity and variability over the first year of life. Even when hearing losses are discovered early and children have received hearing aids and intensive early speech therapy, deaf children's vocal babbling diverges from that of hearing children. Repetitive babbling may still occur; but it appears later and less frequently than in hearing children. Some investigators have reported vocal babbling in two- to five-year-old deaf children, but these vocalizations clearly differ from the babbling of hearing children, who would have moved on to using words and phrases at that age.

The lack of complex early babbling by deaf children means that at the age when parents and siblings should be beginning to respond to their grunts and babbles, deaf babies already may be at a disadvantage both socially and communicatively relative to hearing children. As we will see in the next section, deaf and hearing children of deaf parents at this stage will be making and seeing signs and gestures that may function in the same ways as vocalizing and hearing do for hearing babies. For the vast majority of deaf children, however, it is still too early for their hearing parents to suspect their hearing losses. It will be one to two more years, on average, before those children are recognized as deaf and some form of early language intervention can begin. The lack of spoken communication between hearing parents and their deaf children is thus a real and potentially important factor in development, with implications even at this early age for later cognitive and social development as well as for language development and day to-day functioning. There are, of course, other modes of communication available for hearing families with deaf children. Hearing mothers and their deaf infants presumably have developed regular patterns of interaction through physical contact at this point, and they soon will begin to use gestures and body language to communicate just as deaf mothers do with their deaf and hearing infants. Often overlooked by hearing parents are the beginnings of non vocal communication, beginnings at least as important as vocal babbling is for hearing infants. This topic has received far less attention than has vocal babbling, but it is an exciting one that may hold considerable promise for understanding and facilitating language development in deaf children.

Manual Babbling

Whereas vocal babbling consists of the combined vowel and consonant sounds that make up language, there are various forms that manual babbling could take. One of these would be the simple production or repetition of components of signs, such as isolated hand shapes or movements. Some of those movements actually will constitute complete signs that are made by repeating simple hand shapes and movements. For example, the sign MILK is made by opening and closing of the hand into a fist, as in milking a cow, and the sign MOTHER or MAMA is made by touching an open hand to the chin. Mabbling of this sort is likely have social consequences when seen by deaf parents, just as babbling by hearing infants ("mama") might get reactions from hearing parents. Another form of mabbling would resemble the combination of sounds seen in babbling. Some young deaf children of deaf parents, for example, produce individual and repeated sign components without any apparent attempt at communication. This form of mabbling has only been documented in a few children, but it may well be a more general phenomenon. There is a relatively small set of about a half dozen hand configurations that frequently are seen in deaf infants who are learning sign language as a first language. These handshapes comprise the primary stuff of later signs and, like the basic vowel and consonant sounds in spoken language, are general enough to be found across all documented sign languages.

Just as importantly, mabbling provides a motivation for deaf parents or signing hearing parents to engage in "conversations" with their deaf infants in the same way that babbling prompts hearing parents to talk to their hearing infants. Eventually, the language-relevant parts of mabbling will become incorporated into communication along with meaningful gestures, and deaf children will be well on the way to acquiring language. Mabbling is thus different from gesturing, because gestures are meaningful while mabbling is not. Nonetheless, early gestures play a vital role in early learning and communication and are worthy of consideration in their own right.

Gestures and Signs

The focus of most research on deaf children's early manual behaviour has been on their use of meaningful gestures. My own research has shown that gestures accompany the speech of hearing children in much the same way as they accompany the signs of deaf children. When hearing children use gestures, however, we can easily distinguish them from words. The distinction is somewhat harder to make when deaf children mix gestures with their signs, because the two forms of communication share the same channel of communication — from hand to eye. Deaf children's gestures nonetheless may give us some insight into their language development and, later, into their cognitive development and the thoughts that underlie their behaviour. We therefore need to look more closely at the relations among early gestures, early words or signs, and children's knowledge of the things to which they refer.

Observers and investigators of young children's early gestures generally assume that their use paves the way for hearing and deaf children's eventual use of words and signs, respectively. When children are at the point of using only single words or signs and also when they move to using combinations of two words or signs, gestures continue to play an important role in the language development of hearing children. I argued that this fact makes it odd and likely disruptive for language development to deny deaf children the opportunity to use gestures in interpersonal communication. Of course, we would not want deaf children to depend on gestures to the exclusion of signed or spoken communication, but there is no evidence that this ever occurs when a more regular form of communication is available. Rather, for both deaf and hearing individuals, gestures are an essential component of communication from the first year of life through adulthood. The questions of interest are how deaf and hearing children use gestures and how they eventually come to be supplemented by language. In fact, there appear to be several shifts in the frequency and purpose of gestures at various points of development. Among young deaf children of deaf parents, for example, there is a noticeable change in use of pointing from its immature use as a gesture showing or requesting something to a mature form in the personal pronouns of ASL like ME, HER, and YOU. At around nine months of age, both deaf and hearing children use pointing as a showing or requesting gesture. Then, at around twelve months, deaf children stop using pointing to refer to people, although it still can refer to things and places. Six to twelve months later, person-pointing comes back into use, but this time, those motions are used in the context of sign as personal pronouns. Such shifts indicate that gestures and signs are distinct, even if they look the same.

In terms of their form and frequency, most of the gestures of young deaf and hearing children appear to be the same until about age two. During the school years, deaf children tend to use more gestures with their sign language than hearing children use with their speech, although my own research has shown that this difference disappears by the time they reach adulthood. In terms of their function, it is during the earliest stages of parent-child communication that gestures are particularly important because of the role they play in social interactions. That is, both gesture and language initially develop in children largely because of the need to communicate their wants, needs, and desires. Even deaf children who do not have the benefits of early language input therefore show spontaneous and regular use of gestures to communicate with those around them.

Initial Signs and Words

The ages at which deaf children first begin to use signs and words vary considerably. There have been occasional claims of deaf children using simple signs like MILK and MAMA as early as five or six months of age. One problem with such observations is that they almost always have been made by parents, who might read more into their child's behaviour than would unbiased witnesses. Several investigators, meanwhile, have reported that deaf and hearing children who learn sign language naturally from their deaf parents produce their first recognizable signs at around nine months of age. Hearing children, by contrast, tend to produce their first words around their first birthdays, regardless of whether they have hearing or deaf parents and regardless of whether they are already using some simple signs. That is, signs do *not* slow the emergence of speech.

Deciding when the first words occur has never been easy, even with hearing children. Between nine and twelve months of age, hearing children make some sounds that are similar to adult words. These protowords often, but not always, are produced in the correct context and so they tend to sound like real words, at least to parents' ears. At the same time, the fact that protowords are also produced in contexts that are not correct, in which case they are less likely to be noticed by parents, suggests that children in this stage do not understand the "language" they are producing. Protowords simply may be attempts to imitate sounds made by adults and may have no more meaning for the child than babbling.

In the context of dealing with a young child at home, as opposed to in a research study, it probably is not too important to decide which early sounds are protowords and which are true words. What is important is that whateve they are, these vocalizations lead to responses from listeners. As a result, protowords either get used more often and more correctly, gradually becoming or being replaced by real words, or they drop out of a child's vocabulary. For this to occur, it does not matter whether the "words" are real, baby talk, or even babbles, as long as there is some kind of social agreement between the child and her listeners that particular sounds have particular meanings. Some of these baby words will remain with children if they continue to be used in the family. Such home words are paralleled by home signs in deaf families.

A parallel scenario presumably develops for deaf children who are ready to produce their first signs. As with the appearance of the first words, it is difficult to know how seriously to take reports by parents of signs being made as early as six months of age. Like first words, first signs tend to be rather simple approximations that, at least initially, could be entirely unintended by the child. The sign MILK is a good example, here. Is it because milk is so important for infants (from whose point of view?) that MILK is most frequently reported as children's first sign? Or is it because the sign is so simple, being made by the simple opening and closing of a 5-hand.

Flexing of the unformed hand occurs frequently in both deaf and hearing infants, and it seems only a matter of time before it is produced in an appropriate context and interpreted as a sign by enthusiastic parents. Similarly, the signs MAMA and DADA or some simplified version of them seem likely to occur occasionally just by chance. As it happens, MAMA generally occurs earlier and more frequently than DADA. Is this because mama is more important to the child than dada? Is it because mama is more likely to be around and see early MAMA signs? Or is it because DADA is made on the forehead, outside of the infant's line-of-sight, and thus is more difficult to repeat correctly once it has been seen by an excited father? Probably it is some combination of all of these factors.

Examples of this sort suggest some caution in attributing intention or meaning to the very early signs produced by young deaf children. Nevertheless, the social implications of those early signs and protosigns are exactly the same as those created by the first words and protowords of hearing children. Once again, it seems that deciding exactly when early spoken or signed productions should be considered language may be less important than identifying their roles in social communication. The earlier appearance of signing over speech by up to three months does seem to be a real phenomenon, however, regardless of how long it lasts. This early sign advantage is seen in both deaf and hearing children who are learning to sign and is consistent with what we know about the maturation of the hands before the vocal system. Whether or not this early advantage gives deaf children who sign a long-term edge over nonsigning, deaf or hearing peers remains at issue.

Growing Vocabularies

Consider now the relation between the number of words a young hearing child knows at any particular age and the number of signs that a young deaf child knows at the same age. Some children learning to sign have been reported to have larger vocabularies during the first year or two than hearing children learning spoken language only. This finding could be taken as support for the suggestion that signed languages can be acquired earlier than spoken languages, but in almost all cases where such advantages have been documented, the children have been hearing rather than deaf. Hearing children of deaf parents who use ASL are able to benefit from a much wider range of language experience than deaf or hearing children who have only spoken language available to them. It thus is unclear whether the advantage in early vocabulary size should be attributed to the language or to the context in which these bilingual children are learning language.

In any case, the difference does not last long. Typically, any sign language advantage disappears by age two, when the ability to combine signs and words becomes important in the two-word, **telegraphic speech** stage (e.g., "want milk"). In other words, when we remove the head start that signing (deaf or hearing) children have over speaking (hearing) children, signs and words appear to be learned at about the same rate. As far as I can tell, the spectacular exceptions in this regard — children who have been reported to have vocabularies that increase much faster than is normal — have not only been hearing, but they also have been children of university professors who are fluent in ASL and specialists in language development, which is why they are studying their children in the first place! This observation suggests that under special circumstances signs *can* be acquired at a faster rate than words, but this does not seem to be the case under more natural circumstances (but see the last two paragraphs of this section).

Hearing children of hearing parents generally use about ten different words when they are fifteen months of age and fifty words and about ten phrases at around 20 months. Of course, these numbers are rough averages, and particular children may be faster or slower in their rates of vocabulary growth. Those averages, however, also appear to hold for the sign vocabularies of deaf children with deaf parents learning ASL in the U.S. and Canada as well as those learning La Langue des Signes Quebecoise (LSQ), the sign language of French-speaking Canada. Children learning to sign and those learning to speak also seem to have a lot of overlap in the particular words and signs that they use. This consistency makes some intuitive sense in that we would expect that regardless of their language, deaf and hearing children likely would have similar things to talk about.

One aspect of signed languages that people expect to affect early learning is the fact that some signs look like what they mean. As mentioned signs actually fall along a continuum, from looking very much like what they mean (GOLF, BOWL), to having some association with what they mean (BOY, DOG), to being completely arbitrary (NUT, CHURCH). It would not be surprising to find that the signs acquired earliest are those falling toward the "obvious" end of the continuum, and naive observers, including both parents and scientists who are unfamiliar with sign language, often claim that this is the case. But those observers are wrong. Such claims frequently are based on the incorrect interpretation of signs: The observer thinks that a sign means what it looks like, when it actually means something quite different. Alternatively, they may only notice the few obvious signs that occur in a signed conversation and assume that most of the language is like that.

More important than the fact that there are not really very many transparent or iconic signs is the fact that the obviousness of a sign actually has no effect on how likely it is to be learned by young children. Transparent signs are easier for hearing adults to remember when they take sign language classes, but that is a function of experience and learning strategies that young children do not yet have. Either deaf children do not understand the "obvious" bases of such signs (any more than they understand words like *submarine* or *antiseptic* from analyzing their component parts) or they may have less use for them. If you look at the list of Everyday Signs at the back of the book, it should be apparent that most of the signs likely to be important for young deaf children bear little resemblance to their meanings.

Before moving on to more complex language, a note seems in order concerning the early language of deaf children in speech-only programmes. Regardless of the rate of early sign acquisition by young deaf children in sign language settings and hearing children in spoken language settings, there is little doubt of the contrast they provide with the rates of language learning by deaf children exposed to spoken language. Among children with severe to profound hearing losses, even the best pupils of the best spoken language programmes have extremely limited early vocabularies, rarely beyond ten words at two-and-a-half years of age. The language of deaf preschoolers in speech-only programmes generally is at least two to three years behind the language of hearing children, even after more than a year of intensive speech therapy as part of early intervention programmes. Beyond the extent of their hearing losses, part of the difference in language development by deaf children in speech-and sign-oriented programmes may be related to differences in the ages at which their parents become aware of those losses. Recent surveys indicate that children who attend speech-oriented programmes generally have had their hearing losses discovered considerably later than children who attend sign-oriented programmes. Further, parents who notice their children's hearing losses very early may have been initially more sensitive to their children's language needs or might have less time and emotion invested in attempting exclusively spoken language instruction before trying the route of Total Communication. Whatever the reasons, most severely and profoundly deaf children who receive early exposure to sign communication are more competent in their early language development than those children who receive only exposure to spoken language.

Learning to Sign Affect and Learning to Speak

One of the longest-running debates within deaf education has been whether teaching young deaf children sign language will impair their ability or motivation to acquire spoken language. As I indicated earlier, there is no evidence to support that claim. Although it has been observed that ASL grammar sometimes intrudes into deaf children's speech and writing, this phenomenon is a common one among children and adults learning a second language, and it has nothing at all to do with sign language per se. What seems to be neglected in most prospeech arguments is the importance of early linguistic stimulation of children, in any mode. Regardless of how language acquisition occurs, it requires regular input and feedback during the first two to three years of life. Spoken language communication does not work well for very young deaf children because they lack the abilities and motivation available to older children and adults, not because spoken language is in any way inferior to sign language. Later, some deaf children will develop speech that is well enough understood by others and sufficient for the practical purposes of day-to-day life. Other children will not reach those levels of proficiency. Most importantly, speech ability does not confer any advantage on the receptive part of language — speech and speech reading are not the same skill. I do not mean to suggest that language learning in sign language is a cure-all, but the consistency of the available evidence clearly tells us that it is potentially an important tool in childhood as well as later.

Signs and Words in the Same Child

During the first two years of life, young hearing children, as a group, tend to have considerable overlap in the ideas that they express, although some children communicate them via gesture and others via words. Looking at individual children, however, we see that any particular child generally has either a gesture or a word for a thing, but not both. Similarly, it appears that deaf children either have a gesture or a sign for a thing, but not both, even though their gestures and signs are in the same modality. One family I know, for example, includes a mother who is deaf and a father and one child who both have normal hearing. As in many such families, the hearing daughter has grown up a bilingual, using both spoken English and ASL. This girl started signing before she started talking. During her early childhood, when her parents kept careful records of her language progress, the girl acquired signs and words at about the same rate. In this natural setting, well over three-quarters of all of the signs and words she used occurred in only one of her two languages. That is, she had either a sign or word for a concept, but not both. Only about 15 percent of the concepts in her vocabulary were expressed in both signs and words (although not necessarily at the same time).

Beyond this frequently reported tendency to have a label for a thing in only one language at a time, there is also an inclination in later childhood to use only one mode of communication at a time, that is, not to use Simultaneous Communication. Deaf preschoolers, for example, tend to prefer signed communication over spoken communication even when both languages are available. This preference results from the simple fact that signed communication is more likely than spoken communication to be successful for these children, independent of the extent of their exposure to speech. In both later childhood and adulthood, some deaf individuals are more comfortable with spoken language than others, and some are more comfortably and competently bilingual than others. Deaf children's bilingual balance — that is, their relative fluencies in the two languages — will depend in part on the age of onset and degree of their hearing losses. Other factors, such as parental language abilities and the quality of early education and exposure to language (for example, in a **bilingual-bicultural** programme) also will make a difference.

Finally, for children who are initially exposed only to spoken language, later learning of sign language does not affect how often they use their voices, and parental concerns that sign language will replace early speech are unfounded. Rather, speech and sign skills may become increasingly intertwined in these children, improving both speech production and comprehension.

Putting it all Together

The preceding sections have focused on young children's use of single signs, words, and gestures. We now move beyond those early vocabularies to the ways in which signs and words are put together into what really looks like, and is, language. In considering the learning of sign language and spoken language, we need to recognize that languages vary in the ways that particular ideas are expressed, and one cannot always translate word-for-word from one spoken language to another, even though we can translate the meaning of what is said. This situation also holds when it comes to ASL and English, and that is why ASL and Signed English are not identical.

The ability to translate fully between signed and spoken languages is important to note because some observers of deaf children's early language learning have claimed that their signing tends to be more concrete and more tied to the "here and now" than the speech of hearing age-mates. We have seen that deaf and hearing children follow essentially the same course of early language learning in terms of their ability to express various meanings, but this claim concerns *what* young deaf and hearing children talk about. For example, the vocabularies of deaf children of hearing parents generally have a greater percentage of words that refer to people, places, and things as compared to hearing children of hearing parents or deaf children of deaf parents. At the same time, their vocabularies have fewer signs or words that allow them to refer to more abstract concepts like time or the existence of things. A major contributor to this difference is undoubtedly that their parents differ in what *they* talk about. The majority of deaf children learn to sign from hearing parents who themselves are only beginning signers and thus are less able to communicate at a complex or abstract level. To make this more obvious, we need only think back to the ways in which we were taught foreign language in school: Generally, we learned about practical things, about going to a restaurant or to the doctor, about travelling on a train, and about visiting museums or other historical places. I do not ever recall having learned how to talk about abstract things like religion, politics, or the meaning of life in a foreign language. If parents are able to sign or speak only about food, toys, and simple social situations, their children are likely to have similar limitations, at least early on. At the same time, as noted above, parents' imperfect use of ASL is not an impediment to their children's eventual ASL fluency.

To the extent that slow growth in deaf children's vocabularies is a consequence of the context of their early language learning, we would not attribute the observed lags to anything inherent in the children. After all, deaf children of deaf parents have no trouble becoming fluent in ASL and have vocabularies just as large (or larger) and just as abstract as hearing children of the same age. Rather, parents' shortcomings in the language domain are often passed on to their children, who may not yet have sufficient vocabulary to function in social and academic settings. Unless deaf children *and* their hearing parents receive additional language instruction, the children will continue to fall behind hearing age-mates. That is why deaf children of hearing parents often enter school already at a language disadvantage relative to hearing age-mates, and some may never overcome that lag.

As deaf children move into preschool and other settings outside of the home, they usually have more varied sign language experiences with more signing partners, and the language learning context becomes more complex. One interesting aspect of this situation is that young deaf children of hearing parents often learn sign language at a faster rate than their parents. There are at least two factors that contribute to this situation. One of these is the fact that once they enter a preschool programme, those youngsters are exposed to far more sign language, and more natural sign language, than are their parents. It would be a rare parent indeed who had the time to spend four to six hours a day in a room where signing was the primary means of communication.

A second factor affecting the rate of sign language learning is that deaf children are far more dependent on signing than are their parents. For many deaf children, sign communication is essentially the only way to express their needs, desires, curiosity, and creativity. Their parents, in contrast, have a full range of spoken language at their disposal. This situation is unfortunate in some ways, because parents and teachers of deaf children often do not realize that they are saying far more in their speech than in their signing. The problem is not that the signs cannot express the same information. It is just that greater fluency in speaking seems to overpower one's signing ability. It therefore is not at all unusual to see people who think that they are using Simultaneous Communication (SC) omitting signs from over half of their sentences. One of the more glaring examples of this I have seen occurred when I introduced an older deaf gentleman to a hearing friend who worked at a school for the deaf. Although I had signed my introduction, my friend began an animated conversation with the man in spoken English. When I interrupted and pointed out that the fellow was deaf, my friend paused and then said, "So you're deaf are you?" while signing only "YOU." He then waited for an answer, while the deaf man walked away, unaware that he had been asked anything, and it was probably just as well that way.

Language ability varies, of course, but the available evidence indicates that even in the classroom, at least one-quarter of a spoken message may be omitted from the signed message by teachers who honestly believe that they are using SC. Even more troubling are cases in which people say one thing and incorrectly sign something else. Not only is there no real communication, but the child is faced with erroneous information about which signs mean what. Many deaf children thus not only start learning language later than peers who share a language with their parents, but they are confronted with less consistent and less useful language experience when they do start. Is it any wonder that they often lag behind those other children in the quality and complexity of their language skills?

Learning to Use Sign Efficiently

During the preschool years, ages two to five, deaf children who are naturally exposed to signing in the home rapidly increase the frequency with which they use conventional signs to communicate about objects and actions. When signs begin to fill out the vocabulary, they do not necessarily replace gestures. As with the words of hearing children, they often fill other roles in communication instead. In addition to the accumulation of new signs, modifications of existing signs also enhance the preschooler's ability to communicate with others. Deaf two-year-olds exposed to ASL, for example, appear to understand conventional sign modifications, such as verb inflections, and by age three they are modifying signs themselves. The early modifications produced by those children generally do not conform fully to the rules of ASL until they are closer to five years old. Nevertheless, deaf three- and four-year-olds clearly know that signs can be altered to modify their meanings. Most of their invented modifications make sense, and, like the spoken modifications of words produced by hearing children, there is remarkable consistency across children.

One common example of such approximations to ASL occurs with directional signs. **Directional signs** (LOOK-AT, GIVE, INFORM, and so on) are those signs that include a movement component that indicates the *from* and to of the action. Prior to their understanding of the directional quality of signs, deaf children often use sequences of several signs linked together to communicate the same information. For example, because GIVE is a directional sign, an older child can sign YOUGIVE-ME as a single sign. Two-year-olds in contrast are more likely to use the three sign sequence YOU GIVE ME containing two personal pronouns and a verb. From about two-and-a half to four years of age, pointing and other gestures are used together with signs instead of using more grammatically complex, if formationally simpler, verb inflections. These replacements are most common during the latter half of that period, although many deaf children continue to use them occasionally until they are near five years old. Interestingly, this seems to be a common phenomenon in language learning, and I still find myself doing exactly the same thing in Italian, even though I have all of the pronoun forms in my repertoire.

During the second half of their fourth year, when deaf three-year-olds begin to modify verb signs, they tend to use them first to communicate directions and locations. They begin to include qualitative and quantitative information in their signs, indicating how big, how good, how bad, or how fast something is. They also modify signs and their meanings through conventional ASL facial expression to indicate subjective meaning. For example, I WANT THAT becomes I REALLY WANT THAT A LOT. When signed with vigor and appropriate expression and THERE'S A WORM similarly becomes THERE'S A YUKKY WORM with correct changes to the face and orientation of the head. By the time they are four, deaf children exposed to sign language are able to express how things occur, why things occur, and their intentions.

As with hearing children, deaf three- and four-year-olds, also use some signs incorrectly in what are called overgeneralizations. Hearing children of this age, frequently overgeneralize irregular verbs and nouns that they previously used correctly. Thus, *fell* becomes *falled* and *children* becomes *childrens,* presumably because they have learned the general rule (for the past tense and the plural in these examples) and attempt to make all similar words conform to that rule. Deaf children similarly are seen to overgeneralize, for example, by adding direction to nondirectional verbs such as TOUCH or DRINK, giving them understandable points of origin and conclusion. Overgeneralizations of this sort are as well understood by others when they occur in deaf children's signing as when they occur in hearing children's speech and may be laughed at, responded to, or corrected by others around them. Whatever their reaction, parents and teachers should recognize the importance of such "errors." They indicate that the child is making sophisticated guesses about the grammar of the language and acquiring its component rules.

In deaf three-year-olds, we also see the beginnings of demonstrative pronouns such as THAT, THERE, and THIS, and possessive pronouns such as YOUR, MINE, and OUR. Both types of pronouns appear to occur somewhat later in deaf children than in hearing children, who begin to use them by the middle of their third year (age two-and-a half), but there is very little evidence on this subject. In fact, there is surprisingly little research on the development of sign language in deaf children between the ages three and six years, regardless of whether they have deaf or hearing parents. We know that the order in which new aspects of language are learned by deaf children of hearing parents is consistent with that of hearing children of hearing parents and deaf children of deaf parents, even if it tends to lag some months behind. Beyond that general conclusion, however, there is relatively little information available to parents, teachers, or researchers, as most of the available research has focused on younger or older children.

Deaf Children's Exposure to Social Language

In general, deaf parents show greater awareness of the communication needs of deaf children than do hearing parents. This awareness results in part from their own experiences, but they also are likely to be more sensitive to visual signals from their children, and they clearly will have a better channel of communication with them via sign language. Some hearing parents also are very aware of cues from their young deaf children about the success or failure of communication. Most, however, lack competence and confidence in their signing abilities, and these attributes can make it more difficult for them to adapt to the needs of their children. For their part, hearing fathers tend to have even poorer sign skills than hearing mothers-presumably one reason for mothers taking on a proportionally greater care giving role than they do with hearing children.

Given this greater responsibility of hearing mothers of deaf children, it is important that we consider the language that they use in communicating with their young children. A moment of reflection or observation will reveal that the language that adults use with children frequently is modified to be appropriate for the presumed language capabilities of the young listener.

Sometimes called Motherese, such modification is seen regardless of whether a child is hearing or deaf and regardless of whether signed or spoken language is used. When directed to young children by either deaf or hearing mothers, language tends to be slower, simpler, and more likely to include shortened versions of words or signs than the language directed to older children or adults. Because language development in deaf children of deaf parents occurs in a natural manner, we would expect that deaf mothers' use of Motherese in communicating with their young children would begin just as early as it does in hearing mothers of hearing children, and this turns out to be the case. When their babies are as young as three months of age, deaf mothers use primarily single signs with their babies, frequently with the same kinds of repetition as we see in hearing mothers speaking to their hearing babies. Deaf mothers' signing also tends to be accompanied by smiles and numerous mouth movements, and they use exaggerated facial expressions with their babies even more than hearing mothers. "Baby talk" thus clearly occurs in signing as well as speech.

Speech makes language available to hearing babies regardless of whether they are looking in the right direction. Frequently, however, it appears that a deaf child is not watching his mother, and many hearing mothers are reluctant to sign at those times. Deaf mothers also sometimes report they resist signing to their children unless they have made eye contact, but they commonly move their hands out in front of their babies, rather than moving a child's head or physically changing their position, so that the children will see their signs. Over time, this strategy teaches infants to attend visually to cues in the environment, and deaf babies become remarkably good at picking up on mothers' visual cues across a much wider range of positions than one would expect from a hearing child. In fact, there is now some evidence that deaf children actually are better at detecting visual events in the periphery of their vision than are hearing children. This ability does not result from their being deaf, but from the fact that for them, there are important things happening on the edges of their visual range. Their eyes and brains thus adjust accordingly, with important implications for social and language development. The same phenomenon is seen in hearing children of deaf parents, because such children must also rely on visual cues from their parents.

The ways in which parents accommodate to the language needs of their deaf babies as well as their hearing babies seem to play an important role in determining the effectiveness and interest in communication on both sides of the conversation. It therefore would not be surprising if a lack of sign language flexibility and fluency on the part of hearing parents were to reduce the quality of their social and educational interactions with their deaf children. In fact, when they are signing to their deaf children about a common object of attention, hearing mothers often tend to oversimplify and end up producing language that carries far less information than the language they use with hearing children in similar situations. Similarly, parents often oversimplify language for younger hearing children, using constructions well below their comprehension levels. Such limitations are not unexpected given that most hearing mothers have little more than beginning competence in sign language. When they are extreme, however, lack of parental sign skills can have significant implications for subsequent development.

Summary

This chapter explored the contexts, capabilities, and components of language learning by deaf children. From vocal and manual babbling, to first words and signs, to more complex language, normal language development depends on frequent and regular communication interactions between deaf children and those around them, regardless of whether it is signed or spoken. Deaf children initially babble like hearing children, making sounds that may be responded to by overzealous parents, even if they bear no relation to later language ability. Unlike hearing children, however, their vocal babbling decreases in quantity and variety over the first year of life. Manual babbling also seems to occur in deaf children, although its function and characteristics are not well understood. In any case, babies' vocal and manual babbling appear to have important social roles for hearing and deaf parents, respectively, and lead to conversations that contribute to social and cognitive development as well as language learning.

In young deaf and hearing children, gestures serve practical functions of identifying, requesting, or showing things in social situations. In the case of hearing children, those gesture are obvious and distinct from ongoing spoken language. In the case of deaf children, the fact that gestures and sign language use the same modality makes the two difficult to distinguish. Actually, the gestures used by deaf and hearing children are remarkably similar. Deaf children use more of them than hearing children, but that difference disappears by the time they are adults. As both deaf and hearing children develop, their vocabularies grow and their gestures are replaced with conventional language. This and other evidence suggests that although gestures may have a special role within American Sign Language, they are natural and normal for both deaf and hearing children. There is no evidence that preventing their use by deaf children has any positive impact on their spoken language skills, and it may even work to their disadvantage.

There also is no evidence that early sign language learning impedes or prevents spoken language learning. Sign language may provide a bridge to spoken and written English, and different children will excel in and prefer different modes of communication. Overall, exposure exclusively to spoken language tends not to be as successful for language learning in young deaf children. There are certainly exceptions, and the extent to which speech instruction, or any language instruction, will be successful depends on a variety of factors within the child (e.g., extent of hearing loss), within the parents, and within the language-learning context. My concern is that many deaf children spend years in intensive speech therapy — often to the exclusion of sign language -while missing the critical first years of language learning. This and the previous chapter therefore have raised a variety of issues that need to be taken into consideration before any decision about "the language of choice" is made by parents.

A variety of investigations have suggested that children learning sign language might even have an advantage over children learning spoken language due to differences in the maturation rate of the fingers, hands, and arms relative to tongues, mouths, and vocal tracts. This benefit appears to maintain through the one-word/one-sign stage, but as children start combining words into longer strings, the difference disappears. Increasing complexity and skill in signed and spoken language subsequently follow the same course in deaf and hearing children, even if a lack of early language experience creates a lag in development for some deaf children. If normal language development, whatever its form, requires early and consistent input, hearing parents of young deaf children will most often find it useful and important to learn sign language. If their skill remains limited and their vocabularies concrete, they should not be surprised to see this reflected in their children's language skills, at least temporarily, until the children are exposed to more and better language models. Children with full access to natural languages such as ASL or English will eventually gain fluency. The same cannot be said for artificial languages constructed by committees, such as SEE1 or Esperanto. Most importantly, parents and professionals have to address the needs of each child, as an individual, in the context of the family and educational system.

8

LEARNING TO READ AND WRITE

This chapter is about literacy, specifically the kind of literacy of greatest interest to most parents and teachers of deaf and hearing children: the ability to read and write in English. But there are different kinds and definitions of literacy. The original sense of the term was related to the assumption that anyone who understood the idea of combining letters of the alphabet — the basic building blocks of written language — could use it in a creative, appropriate way to get and use an education. Thus, we refer to people becoming "lettered" or acquiring "knowledge of letters;" and Doctor of Letters is considered a prestigious, if largely ceremonial title for the honorary college degrees conferred on politicians and celebrities.

We now use the term *literacy* in a variety of other ways as well. Educators, for example, refer to students as being computer literate or having mathematical literacy. These terms are related to the original definition of literacy in the sense of having "building blocks" that allow more complex and sophisticated use of the whole, but the content is no longer just language, at least in the literal sense. There is also cultural literacy, which allows an individual access to various aspects of their culture as communicated by others through art, literature, and history. Traditionally, no one was considered truly educated if they were not well versed in literature, that is, in the documentation of knowledge within their language and culture. Of course, we could also talk about literacy within American Sign Language either in the narrow sense, where the components of signs would replace letters, or in the broader sense of providing access to the cultural heritage of the Deaf community.

Although in this chapter, I will be focusing on the more narrow sense of literacy as it relates to English, it will be important to keep in mind yet another distinction: having some basic level of reading and writing competence may be different from having language skills flexible and creative enough to support educational and personal success. Functional literacy is the term most commonly linked to basic reading and writing abilities; the student who is functionally literate has the minimum reading and writing skills necessary to function in society. Traditionally, that minimum referred to a fourth- to fifth-grade level of competence — usually good enough to get a driver's license but sometimes not good enough to understand the warnings on medications or cookbook recipes let alone the manuals that come with home computers. Given the demands of the information age, several educational researchers now argue that an eleventh- to twelfth-grade level of skill for functional literacy might be more appropriate.

The reason why I also referred to literacy "flexible and creative enough to support educational and personal success" is that fourth- to fifth-grade functional literacy may not be sufficient for deaf children to have true access to the free and appropriate education to which they are entitled. To most people, and certainly to parents, true literacy requires fluency in the language used by those who teach us, who write textbooks, and who tell us the news on television — that is, fluency in English. This issue brings us back to the education of deaf children: Do deaf children need to be fluent in English, in ASL, or both to be considered literate? If the question seems a difficult one, consider Hispanic children in the United States who are fluent in Spanish but not English. Unless they learn English, they might not receive adequate education in many parts of the United States, but they would surely be literate: They would have access to world knowledge and Hispanic culture through Spanish. In addition, we presume that Spanish would provide a bridge to learning English, and we would expect that Hispanic students who are encouraged and motivated to learn English should not have much trouble.

Consider now deaf children of deaf parents who learned ASL as their first language. Like Hispanic children who learned Spanish as their first language from Hispanic parents, these children are certainly literate in all senses of the word. They understand the building blocks of the language, they can use them in novel and creative ways, and they have access to much knowledge of the world as well as to knowledge of both Deaf and hearing cultures. In order to gain access to the full body of knowledge available to hearing peers, however, they will also have to be able read and write in English. This situation does not minimize the importance of ASL as a language, any more than it minimizes Spanish. It simply reflects reality: Fluency in sign language, or any minority language, is not enough for full access to the larger culture even if it is sufficient for many of the purposes of family, friends, and day-to-day life.

My reason for laying this groundwork about literacy is not to seek political correctness or claim that a deaf child can be literate even if they cannot read and write English, although that is technically true. Rather, it is to point out the fact that without special attention, most deaf children will not be fully literate in either English or in sign language. The preceding description concerned deaf children of deaf parents. As we will see in the next section, such children generally are better readers than deaf children of hearing parents, suggesting that they are bilingual — literate in both ASL and English. But they represent barely 10 percent of deaf children in this country. What about the other 90 percent.

Compared to hearing children, most deaf children of hearing parents enter school already at a language disadvantage, because they do not have access to their parents' English, and their parents typically are not proficient in sign language. That lag in language skills tends to increase during the school years, as deaf children of hearing parents show slower growth in language development relative to hearing children, even if both show the same general pattern of development. The important question is how we can best use the language skills they have to build literacy in what will most likely be their primary language, sign language, and their second language, English. As the remainder of this chapter will show, I believe that the available evidence indicates that being bilingual, in ASL and English for children in the United States, is the optimal situation, at least as it relates to learning to read and write.

Reading

Current data indicate that on average, eighteen-year-old deaf students leaving high school have reached only a third-grade to fourth-grade reading level, and over 30 percent of them leave school functionally illiterate by the old standard. This compares to a functional illiteracy rate of less than 1 percent among their hearing peers. Accordingly, Gallaudet University recently reported that a large majority of their students do not read well enough to make effective use of first-year college textbooks. That finding did not surprise either Gallaudet students or faculty, and the majority of both groups urged that there be a greater focus on reading English in the curriculum.

Most hearing people take reading for granted only because they learned to read relatively naturally in their first language — much more naturally than they would if they tried to learn another language as adults. This learning seems natural because everyone around us uses the same language, and there is a one-to-one correspondence between words that people utter and what can be written or read in a book. For this reason, parents' reading to their children is one of the most important facilitators of later reading skill, not just because it motivates children by making reading enjoyable, but because it actually teaches them to read at the same time. At a more general level, reading aloud seems like a literate society's equivalent to the tradition of storytelling, a natural behaviour of humans that seems to run through all cultures and times.

Reading is a very complex process that is not fully understood. Consider some of the elements of reading that fluent readers typically do not have to think about. First, reading involves the ability to distinguish arbitrary marks on a background, whether stone, paper, or computer screen. Even before you know what the marks mean, if they mean anything, you have to be able to perceive the marks, for example, through the eye for print or the hand for Braille. Then you have to recognize writing as writing. Only after you discriminate one mark from another do you have to be able to discriminate one kind of mark from another (for example in @&##&@@&) and groups of marks from other groups (for example @&# from #&@ or @@#). Up to this point, you could be looking at Chinese, English, or symbols on your typewriter, and you are doing fine, but you are not reading.

At the next level, there are two possibilities: One is that individual marks can be linked to sounds, which can be built up into larger patterns that you can say to yourself and recognize as words. In this way, you can sound out new words that you may have heard but have never seen or discover new words that you can pronounce but do not know. It is through this process that most readers know what *fowtuhgraf* means, even if it is written strangely. If you do, it probably means that you learned to read by what is called the phonics method: You sound out words according to what are called spelling-to-sound rules. If these phonological rules were not important, I could randomly rearrange the letters in a word, and you would know what it is anyway. Some readers, however, will have no idea what *fowtuhgraf* means. Most likely, those readers learned to read through the whole-word method, either because that was the philosophy of a particular teacher or the school system in which they were educated, or because they had one of many reading disabilities that made letter by-letter reading impossible. For them, *fowtuhgraf* bears no resemblance at all to *photograph*. They also are unlikely to recognize printed words that they have heard but not seen before and thus have to make use of dictionaries more than people who learned via the phonics method.

Assuming that a set of marks is recognized as a word, the next step is to link meaning to it by "looking it up" in some kind of mental dictionary. The hard part, especially for deaf students, is that words have many different meaning as well as different pronunciations, and the correct one cannot be determined solely on the basis of definitions. Depending on how I count them, for example, my *Oxford English Dictionary* has either 10, 40, or 67 different meanings or senses for the word *bow*. These include the bow that shoots arrows, the bow in one's shoelaces, the bow one takes after a performance (which also demonstrates the variability in sound-to-spelling patterns), the bow at the front of a boat, and others. Surely I am not likely to use all of these meanings, and some, like "the stock of cattle on a farm," I have never even heard of. Nevertheless, I was able to read them in the dictionary and I would likely understand most of them in context. To do this, I have to make use of two kinds of rules.

One kind of rule that helps us select the right sense or meaning of words from our mental dictionaries and allows the construction of an infinite number of utterances in a language is a grammatical rule or (syntax). People who are fluent in a particular language have internal sets of rules (grammar) that allow them to combine words into phrases, clauses, and sentences. Those rules allow us to produce completely new utterances, so we can do more than just repeat things that others have said, and to understand new strings of words produced by others. If grammatical rules were not important, I could randomly rearrange the words in this sentence, and it would not affect your interpretation — sentences like "Harry chased Bonnie" and "Bonnie chased Harry" would mean the same thing.

The grammar of English not only allows us to use the language, but it also tells us when someone else does not know how to use it, that is, when they are not using acceptable English. For example, after several years of studying Italian and French, I know enough of their grammars to understood why people from those countries speak English the way they do: They often put English words into Italian or French grammatical structure the same way that Signed English puts ASL signs into English grammar. Even more interesting is the fact that when I am speaking English with Italian or French colleagues, I sometimes find myself doing the same thing! Whether this is an unintentional attempt to make myself clearer or some mixing-up of the languages in my own head, I do not know, but it does seem to improve their comprehension.

So much for understanding sentences. Next is the level of discourse structure. It is at this level that we can identify what pronouns refer to, we can combine ideas into meaningful series, and we actually understand what we read. If discourse rules were not important, I could randomly rearrange the sentences on this page, and it would not interfere at all with your comprehension. Discourse-level rules, like spelling rules and grammatical rules, tell us that order does make a difference to some extent. Just as they acquire grammatical rules, most children acquire discourse rules naturally by watching the correspondence between things and events and the way that people describe them.

With this brief sketch about reading out of the way, we can return to the issue of deaf children's reading skills. It is essential to keep in mind that the above language rules are learned *relatively* easily for *most* readers *most* of the time partly because they acquire them early. That is one of the beautiful, if still mysterious, aspects of both first and second language learning: As long as it happens early, before age four or so for first languages and through adolescence for second languages, it seems to occur with relative ease — even if it takes several years. In contrast, many adults who try to learn other languages find that the rules do not come so easily the second time around. Luckily, we are able to use what we know about our first language to help with the second language, and therefore languages more similar to our first language are usually easier to learn. Imagine, then, what it would be like if you did not really understand the rules of the first language when you tried to learn a second, if the letters and words on the page did not correspond to what people "said," and if you did not see the correspondence of words and events.

History of Deaf Children

Perhaps more than any other area relating to being deaf, the reading and writing abilities of deaf children have been the focus of attention from educators and researchers for decades. Taken together, the results and conclusions of relevant studies provide an enlightening, if disappointing picture of deaf children's skills in this regard.

Many of the behaviours that deaf children exhibit in reading and writing are the same as those made by people learning English as a second language. Over the past twenty years, programmes like the English Language Teaching Outreach Programme (ELTOP) at the National Technical Institute for the Deaf therefore have been developed to instruct teachers of deaf children in methods like those used in teaching English as a second language. Although their reading behaviours and their writing look similar, we need to learn more about *how* deaf children learn to function in English. After all, English is a language in which deaf children will have to function if they are to receive appropriate education and achieve their potentials in the work force and intellectual life of society. First, we have to take into account the variation among deaf children and the influences of early language environments, types of hearing loss, and factors like parent and child motivation. Unfortunately, a large portion of the effort devoted to improving deaf children's literacy has gone into trying to teach them the skills and strategies that work for hearing children, even though it is apparent that deaf and hearing children often have very different background knowledge and learning strategies. As a result, despite decades of concerted effort, most deaf children in this country still progress only about 20 percent as fast as hearing children in learning to read. This means that deaf students leaving school are at a relatively greater disadvantage, lagging farther behind hearing peers than when they entered.

Deaf Children of Deaf Parents

A variety of sources, including a recent report from the National Institutes of Health, suggest that deaf children of deaf parents are, on average, better readers than deaf children of hearing parents. Why? Deaf children's relative lack of early language experience when they have hearing parents clearly plays an important role in their reading difficulties, but earlier chapters have emphasized that there are other differences between the two groups. Deaf and hearing parents may have very different expectations for their deaf children in terms of academic achievement. They also may differ in their ability to help their children in reading-related activities, and we know that children whose parents spend time working with them on academic and extracurricular activities are more motivated and have greater academic success.

In an earlier book, *Psychological Development of Deaf Children*, I did an extensive review of thirty years of studies concerning the reading abilities of deaf children of deaf parents as compared to deaf children of hearing parents. The results were surprising, because I fully expected that deaf children with deaf parents would always come out on top because of their early exposure to language. But it's not really that simple. Deaf children of deaf parents generally are better readers than deaf children of hearing parents. One important factor in this situation is that deaf parents are more sensitive to their children's communication needs. Regardless of whether their parents are deaf or hearing, however, deaf children who are better readers turn out to be the ones who had their hearing losses diagnosed earlier, had early access to language, *and* were exposed to English. At the same time, having a mother who is a good signer appears to be more important than whether she is deaf or hearing or the precise age at which a child learns to sign. So, deaf children of deaf parents will tend to read better than deaf children of hearing parents, but mothers and fathers who learn to sign well can have a powerful impact on their children's reading abilities.

Regrettably, there is no single predictor of reading success that works in all cases, and the combinations of factors that positively and negatively influence reading development are not yet fully understood. It may be, for example, that different environments lead to different strengths and weaknesses (for example, big vocabularies but little grammatical knowledge) depending on when, where, and from whom children learn their first and second languages. For example, deaf children of hearing parents tend to have better speech and speech reading abilities than deaf children of deaf parents, but those abilities do not seem linked to better reading, even though they would seem to support the phonological part of reading. Although it is also tempting to assume that a deaf child's early exposure to language through deaf parents would provide a considerable advantage in learning to read, this advantage may be offset by the fact that ASL vocabulary and syntax do not parallel those of printed English. Consistent with the research findings thus far, this difference supports the suggestion that early exposure to both ASL and Signed English or ASL and Cued Speech might be most beneficial for the reading abilities of deaf children, giving them the advantage of both early exposure to language and English-relevant language experience.

My inclusion of ASL in this language mixture comes from the clear social, cognitive, and linguistic merits of sign language use by deaf children, as described throughout this book. ASL gives young deaf children access to what is happening in the world and provides an effective means of parent child and teacher-child communication. As I mentioned, my inclusion of Cued Speech as a possible English supplement in this mixture draws from some recent research showing that deaf children who are exposed to Cued Speech from an early age show impressive performance in a variety of skills involved in reading. Importantly, those results are most striking when children use Cued Speech consistently both at home and at school. When it was used only at school, gains were much smaller. Although the relative benefits of Cued Speech and Signed English for support of reading skills have not yet been evaluated, it is important to distinguish the potential of these methods from the way in which they might actually be used. That is, Cued Speech has the benefit of providing continuous information to a child, but comprehension may not be complete. Signed English has the benefit of a link to ASL and thus better support for comprehension; but we have already seen that teachers of deaf children who use Simultaneous Communication leave 20 to 50 percent of what they say out of their signing, without recognizing how much information is lost. Such confusion is often cited as one reason to support the use of ASL in educating deaf students, but the problem may be more the fault of Signed English users than Signed English itself. At present therefore, my highest recommendation is for more research and persistence and flexibility on the part of parents and teachers. Use whatever works!

In addition to research on combining ASL and English in teaching deaf children to read, we need to examine the effect of other factors such as motivation, exposure to reading, and the quality of teaching. The effect of early exposure to reading, via parents and early school environments, seems a particularly important area of study given findings indicating that children who read more become better readers, as well as the other way around. Taking a narrower rather than a broader approach to reading, it also is important to consider the various sub skills involved in reading. Deaf and hearing children, or deaf children of deaf versus hearing parents, may differ in these component skills even when their overall reading levels are the same. Alternatively, they may be similar on particular dimensions that create overall differences in reading level. Accordingly, let us spend a little more time with the three primary components of reading — phonology and spelling, vocabulary, and grammar — as they relate to deaf children.

Phonological Knowledge and Spelling

One of the most central and interesting issues in this area concerns how deaf children, especially those who have greater hearing losses, can make use of phonological information in the absence of hearing, because *phonological* normally refers to the way words sound. Even though spelling to-sound skills are enhanced in deaf children with better speech, we know that they are separate from speech skills and cannot be explained on the basis of articulation alone. Rather, the bases for phonological abilities seem to involve some combination of information drawn from articulation, speech reading, finger spelling, residual hearing, and exposure to writing, no one of which is sufficient in itself. Several studies have indicated that the ability of deaf children to decode spelling patterns emerges much later than in hearing children. Skill in the use of such information does not appear directly tied to amount of hearing loss, at least among children with severe to profound losses. Deaf children with this skill are able to make use of phonological information, especially when words follow regular spelling patterns, although they often depend on more global characteristics such as how the word looks on the lips or on the printed page. Interestingly, similar findings are seen in the understanding of finger spelling within sign language: Although letter-by-letter analysis often occurs for new or unfamiliar words, finger spelling is generally seen in terms of overall patterns rather than in terms of component letters for both deaf and hearing signers.

Phonological skill also may contribute to better grammatical skill and better comprehension, because internal speech has been shown to be more efficient than either visual imagery or internal sign language for the memory component of reading. At that level, information about words is held and accumulated until relations among words and relations among events reveal the meaning of a phrase or sentence. We know that deaf children make use of both phonological and whole-word strategies during reading. When words are regular in their spelling, phonological strategies are most likely to be successful. The linkage of such reading strategies to writing is seen in the fact that deaf students sometimes produce phonologically accurate misspellings such as *sizzers*. Similarly, whole-word codes based on how words look may result in a greater likelihood of leaving out letters (writing *orng* for orange) and making letter reversals.

Proficient reading, then, in deaf children as well as hearing children, depends on some underlying knowledge of the characteristics of individual letters. Deaf children in Simultaneous Communication programmes or in exclusively spoken language programmes tend to show more frequent use of phonological information relative to children in more sign-oriented programmes, perhaps explaining some of their early advantage in reading performance. By college age, however, these differences become smaller or disappear. While showing deaf children how words sound may be useful for speech and reading, what is especially important is showing them the link between printed words and their meanings. There is no better way to achieve this than sitting down with a child and reading and signing to them. Books for very young children are also easy enough that they will give hearing parents a lot of good practice in their signing. As one of my colleagues recently pointed out: "Parents of deaf children do not have to act like teachers or trainers; they just have to act like parents!"

Vocabulary Knowledge

Although it has been well documented that vocabulary knowledge is a primary component of reading, consideration of deaf children presents the issue in a somewhat different light. We already have seen that most deaf children come from hearing homes in which they have more limited exposure to language. These children accordingly have been shown to have fewer signed or spoken labels for things around them than hearing children of hearing parents or deaf children of deaf parents. They also are less likely to gain such knowledge from reading. In this context, it is worth mentioning again the fact that more reading makes for better readers, as well as the other way around. The two-way street between how much children read and how good they are at it suggests that we need to make special efforts to expand vocabularies to which deaf children are exposed through print, sign, and speech. The more vocabulary they encounter, the bigger their vocabularies will be, and the bigger their vocabularies, the better they will be able to deal with new vocabulary.

Compared to hearing children, deaf children are more likely to understand and use concrete nouns and familiar action verbs over more abstract or general words with which they may have less experience. This is not just limited to childhood. Several colleagues and I teach a popular course for deaf college students entitled "Strategies for Organizing Word Knowledge." Students enroll in the course because they recognize their weaknesses in understanding such things as the multiple meanings of words, the fact that there can be several words that *almost* mean the same thing, and the hierarchical organisation of word meanings. Apparently, many deaf children get caught up in a cycle of having smaller expressive vocabularies, smaller receptive vocabularies, and fewer opportunities to expand either. Therefore, I frequently urge teachers of deaf schoolchildren to move away from the practice of focusing primarily on practical and familiar concepts. While acknowledging that many deaf students have difficulty with basic vocabulary and related skills, parents and teachers often underestimate the language skills of children – both hearing and deaf. In the case of deaf children, it is especially important to avoid this pitfall, because the bias is even stronger than it is with hearing children.

Deaf children's vocabulary skills typically are better when words have only a single meaning or when they are presented in context rather than in isolation (the latter happens on many achievement tests). Still, their vocabulary abilities tend to lag about a year behind their other reading sub-skills. This mismatch may disrupt reading by interfering with the access to word meaning that is so important for comprehension. In fact, when we observe deaf children's apparent difficulties with grammar during reading, we cannot really be sure that grammar is the problem. It could be that some children have trouble attending to grammatical information because their cognitive resources are overloaded with word finding. In either case, the result would be reduced comprehension and reading speed, as well as a tendency to remember disconnected portions of texts rather than the whole picture, especially when the material is unfamiliar.

Understanding Grammar

During the 1970s, a lot of attention was given to the grammatical skills of young deaf readers. A variety of programmes tried to apply current theories of grammar (or syntax) to deaf children, with little success. Deaf students generally were far more variable than hearing peers in their performance and tended to have particular difficulty with constructions that depended on keeping track of meaning across multiple events and grammatical structures in texts. Pronouns *(he, her, their, that, it, etc.)*, for example, can cause difficulty because the reader has to remember the activities or characteristics of nouns in order to later understand who or what is being referred to. Such findings suggest that more global factors such as concept knowledge, cognitive style, and memory also play important roles in deaf children's reading in ways that cannot always be distinguished from grammatical issues.

At least one research study has directly examined the influence of early language experience on deaf children's grammatical skill. In that investigation, two groups of deaf children who had hearing parents and were exposed only to spoken language were compared to groups of deaf children of deaf parents who communicated with them either via manually coded English or ASL. Overall, the children exposed to sign language consistently outperformed children who were exposed only to spoken English — a finding that is contrary to the expectations of those who support educating deaf children in spoken language only. On the other hand, children exposed to some form of manually coded English by their deaf parents showed better grammatical skills in English than the children who learned ASL. In fact, the ASL group and the intensive spoken language group were roughly comparable — a finding contrary to expectations of anyone who would advocate either approach alone in educating deaf children. As was the case in early vocabulary development, then, it appears that the best approach for optimizing the grammatical component of deaf children's reading is to expose them to both sign language and English, regardless of whether their parents are deaf or hearing. Again, this does not mean that parents need to be training their children. They need to make language available in meaningful and enjoyable ways that will lead children to want to learn to read for its own sake.

Deaf Children's Writing

The intimate relationship of reading and writing is such that it will not come as a surprise to discover that deaf children's performance in the "input" domain of reading is mirrored in the "output" domain of writing. As in reading, deaf students vary considerably in their writing skill, and different criteria for writing may well be deemed important by different teachers at the college level as they are at the elementary and secondary levels. In a recent study involving Gallaudet University students, for example, individual faculty ranged from 5 percent to 75 percent in their estimates of the number of students with "satisfactory" writing skills. Clearly, writing is a very complex skill and one that is difficult to evaluate.

Examinations of writing samples from deaf children show them to produce shorter sentences than hearing peers and to repeatedly use simple subject-verb-object sentences which give the appearance of concrete and literal writing. Sometimes, their sentences are not sentences at all, at least in the sense of being grammatically correct in English. Taken together, such findings have led to the general conclusion, similar to that for reading, that the average deaf eighteen-year-old writes on a level comparable to that of a hearing eight-year-old.

Earlier, I suggested that some characteristics of deaf children's reading and writing might be attributable to the relatively low expectations of parents and teachers. Recent research in classrooms and laboratories, however, suggests that something is missing in all of this. For example, analyses of deaf students' writing has amply demonstrated that it can be rich and creative, even if, as reflected in the excerpt at the beginning of this chapter, it suffers in ways that many English teachers might find unacceptable. Some of my own work similarly has demonstrated that superficial problems notwithstanding, deaf students' writing as early as elementary school is both creative and conceptually well-structured. At the level where events and actions in a story are laid out and interwoven, their writing is fully comparable to that of hearing peers.

Take for example the following story written by a deaf twelve-year-old. As part of a study I conducted with Victoria Everhart, students were asked to write a story about being picked up by a UFO, what would happen, and what the aliens would be like. The following is representative of what we got and fits well with the above description of deaf children's writing.

> *When I get in ufo They look funny. They have long pointed ears and have round face They speak different from our. They brought strange foods and Purple beverage. When I taste it I spill [spit] and begin to cought [cough]. I [It] taste like dog food. But It was very pretty inside with many feather and clothes were very pretty. But one thing people in ufo stare at me because they never see large musclar [muscular] and can pick up Heavy thing like weight,*

people or table. They feel it and said wow and start to teach me how to talk but they speak Russian language. I hate to learn Russian language. So I stay in ufo for 5 hours so they stop to place where they take me and drop their and they sent me a dog with long sharp teeth and was very tame I egan [began] to cry and miss them.

Among the other typical characteristics of deaf children's writing, one of the most noticeable ones in this passage is the frequent omission of words. A variety of studies and surveys have documented the fact that deaf children use fewer adverbs, conjunctions, and auxiliary verbs than hearing age-mates, whereas the frequencies of nouns and verbs are about the same. This characteristic could be taken to indicate that they are patterning written language on ASL, although similar errors are made by many learners of English as a second language.

But now look again. If you ignore the spelling and grammatical errors in this story, something English teachers and many mothers have a hard time doing, you will see that there is a very clear and coherent story underneath it all. The author told us what the UFO and its inhabitants would be like, about their appearance, food, and clothing. She recounted the reaction of others to her, as well as her reactions to them. After an attempt to communicate, the aliens gave up, dropped her off, and sent her a gift for her troubles. After all of these wonders, is it surprising that she missed them when they left? The point here is that when we evaluated these stories on their English characteristics, the deaf students (aged seven to fifteen were found to be writing well "behind" the hearing students. When we examined the conceptual structure of the stories, however, the two groups were functioning at comparable levels. Even if deaf children are not fluent in English spelling and grammar, they still can demonstrate creativity and competence in writing.

Available findings thus indicate the clear parallels between deaf children's reading and writing. Although there are few studies from which to draw conclusions about differences between deaf children of deaf versus hearing parents, it appears likely that the writing abilities of those groups would follow the same patterns as their reading abilities. Deaf college students with deaf parents, for example, show better performance than deaf peers with hearing parents on writing tests intended for people who learn English as a second language. Similarly, deaf college students who learn ASL early from their deaf parents tend to perform better on writing tests than those who learn to sign as adolescents or adults. On the basis of these findings, we would also expect that the writing abilities of deaf children whose parents provide early exposure to both ASL and Signed English or ASL and Cued Speech should surpass those of children who are exposed to only ASL or spoken English. Unfortunately, those studies have not yet been done.

Impact of Social and Emotional Factors on Literacy

Before leaving the topic of reading and writing by deaf children, it is worth re-emphasizing importance of social and emotional factors, such as motivation and desire for achievement, to the development of literacy and to academic success in general. Look again at the excerpt from a student's journal at the beginning of this chapter. Despite its superficial errors, it is clear that Cheryl enjoys writing and finds it interesting to reflect on her attraction to it. In her writing about writing, she shows a motivation to succeed and reveals the importance of having good models. Having a written dialogue with a supportive teacher allows her to improve and learn about writing not by having it corrected, though that happens too, but by analyzing her own writing and the writing of others. To me, this is a true sign of academic achievement: pursuit of knowledge for the sheer joy of learning.

Studies involving hearing children have shown that parents' spending time with their children, facilitating their academic and extracurricular interests, and answering their questions in supportive environments foster academic excellence as well as psychosocial maturity. Regrettably, a language barrier sometimes prevents such interactions between deaf children and their hearing parents, although this varies from family to family. Lower levels of literacy achievement by deaf children also may be related to their relatively narrow orientations toward many academic subjects. This attitude is reflected in the fact that skills learned in one course are not used in other courses, so that, for example, the transfer of algebra to physics or biology to psychology may not occur spontaneously. The reasons for such narrow views are as yet unclear, although I believe they are partly related to the ways in which parents and teachers of deaf children tend to focus on the concrete and familiar rather than on exploration and discovery. Knowledge about language is very abstract, and not everyone finds language as fascinating as language researchers like me. Reading and writing also may be viewed differently from the perspectives of deaf and hearing children. As second language learners, deaf children may be less invested in achieving English literacy due to either their own values or those of their parents — or their parents may not be as good at communicating those values.

Summary

At several points throughout this book, I describe evidence of deaf children's sign language skills being superior to their reading and writing in English. Such findings suggest that writing skills are independent of deaf children's general intellectual abilities and should not be taken as indicators of any general language fluency or language flexibility. Those findings also suggest that literacy should be within their grasp.

The most frequently cited academic difficulty among deaf children is reading. At first blush, one might expect that the hardest part of reading for deaf children would be the ability to decode the spelling patterns of words, a process that normally depends on knowing how letters sound. Many deaf children are surprisingly good in this regard, however, apparently making use of information combined from finger spelling, residual hearing, speech reading, articulation, and exposure to writing. At the same time, deaf children are more likely than hearing children to use visual and whole-word strategies during reading, and the same pattern appears in comparisons of deaf children who are more oriented toward use of sign language than spoken communication.

The most well-documented areas of difficulty for young deaf readers are vocabulary knowledge and grammatical abilities. Limitations in their vocabularies reflect the influence of early nonlinguistic as well as linguistic experience, as deaf children tend to have access to fewer language models than do hearing peers. Slower recognition of words also may affect the ability to make use of grammar in comprehension because the cognitive system may be so busy trying to find word meanings that it will have less "space" to devote to understanding the larger message. Factors like vocabulary and grammatical knowledge run on a two-way street in literacy development: As they improve, children read more and more complex material, which in turns contributes to more skill development. Similarly, deaf children's beliefs about their own abilities and their desires to succeed operate in a two-way manner just as they do for hearing children, so that success breeds success. One essential aspect of academic achievement is that children have to notice that their success in school work is the result of their own efforts. This relation is consistent with the finding that children higher in intellectual achievement tend to feel that they are more in control of their own lives.

Overall, deaf children's reading difficulties do not appear to be the result of any particular orientation in their early language experience. Exactly which variables are the most important ones for predicting their reading success is unclear. At this time, it does not appear that early exposure to sign language is sufficient to account for the observed differences. The best deaf readers appear to be those who receive early exposure to sign language and exposure to the language in which they will eventually learn to read. Finally, the available literature suggests that the sources of difficulty apparent in deaf children's reading performance are also found in their writing. Lags in the development of vocabulary and grammatical skill result in deaf children's writing appearing concrete and repetitive relative both to hearing children's writing and to their own signed productions. At the same time, their writing is clearly well ordered and creative, showing that fluency in English and intellectual ability are at least partially separate. Nevertheless, reading and writing form an essential link to the worlds of social and intellectual interaction, and the consequences of literacy or illiteracy will have increasing impact on all realms of functioning as deaf children grow up.

9

Assessment of Social Competence in Students with Learning Disabilities

For the past two decades, research has addressed critical issues related to the social competence of individuals with learning disabilities (LD). A significant body of literature highlights the social difficulties of youngsters with LD as compared to typically achieving, non disabled peers . Studies have also examined the social development of individuals with LD relative to normal developmental patterns and the extent to which within-individual differences occur over time. According to Killen, the ongoing, active, social processes of interpretation, evaluation, and coordination of social events are central to understanding social development in general. Indeed, most of the social competence research related to individuals with LD could be viewed as examining how individuals with LD interpret, evaluate, or coordinate social events.

Killen also identified three dimensions key to understanding these social processes: context, conflict, and coordination. According to Killen, context influences the type and structure of social interactions. Thus, youngsters behave differently in various social settings, such as their own home, the homes of others, school, and community settings. The issue of context is particularly important when considering the social competence of individuals with LD. We would expect that the context of school would not be particularly "comfortable" for students with LD given their significant academic difficulties in this context and, thus, they may not demonstrate their best social behaviours. In fact, with few exceptions, most of what we know about individuals with LD we know from their behaviour, peer reports, and self-reports at school which are largely about school. Therefore, we believe that comprehensive social assessment of individuals with or without LD must consider relevant contextual factors at school and outside of school.

A second dimension, conflicts, provides an understanding of how an individual negotiates and interprets events and behaviours across settings. Assessment in this area is largely dependent on observation and interpretation, self-reports, or reports from others. Because the collection of observation data is time consuming and expensive, we have relied on the perceptions of others, such as teachers, parents, and peers, to interpret and judge the social negotiations of individuals with LD and on self-reports to understand social interpretations. How an individual interprets events and behaviours is perhaps the most difficult area to assess and interpret, particularly for students with LD who have communication or memory problems. A consistent concern with self-reports is the extent to which individuals are able to tell you what and why a behaviour occurred or their interpretation of what they or other individuals have done. This problem is exacerbated when a student has communication difficulties that inhibit retell or a memory problem that interferes with recall.

Third, the process of social coordination, how one interacts with and responds to others, can be assessed through observation, self-report, or reports from others, often peers and teachers. A limited number of observational studies have examined the interactions of students with LD as compared to students without LD (NLD) and have demonstrated less positive interactions with peers as well as teachers.

Although academic difficulties, by definition, characterize students with LD, there is little question that many students with

LD also demonstrate significant difficulties with social relationships or display inappropriate social behaviours. Researchers and practitioners are quick to point out, however, that not all youngsters with LD have significant social difficulties. In fact, for some students with LD, the social domain is their area of strength, as evidenced by the testimony of an adult with severe reading disabilities: "I could talk my way out of anything. I couldn't read in high school but I always managed to do 'OK' because I could get the teachers to believe anything I told them."

Significant social difficulties are known to characterize students with other types of disorders such as behaviour disorders, attention deficit hyperactive disorder, and social maladjustment. Many of these disorders overlap with LD, making identification of individuals with LD difficult. It is the overlap of these related disorders with LD that has contributed to controversy and debate regarding definitional issues and has made the construct of LD the most difficult disorder to define. This issue is important as we consider the social assessment of students with LD, because social problems are often more pronounced when students have other disabilities as well. When the Interagency Committee on Learning Disabilities was established to determine the state of knowledge regarding LD and to consider the formal definition of LD, they reviewed assessment in the social domain and provided several recommendations. They indicated that optimal social assessment of individuals with LD would be done with an instrument that demonstrates the following characteristics:

1. It is based on empirically validated social skills problems of individuals with LD.
2. It must be psychometrically sound.
3. It could be used in school settings.
4. It must be able to assess individuals across the developmental age range from preschool through adulthood.
5. It must allow for the assessment of all social competence skills.

We agree with Gresham and Elliott that it is highly unlikely that a single measurement tool could adequately demonstrate all of the recommended qualities for social assessment and that multiple assessment tools will need to be used. There are many tools that generate relevant information about the social functioning of individuals. Peer ratings, observational measures, ratings by teachers and parents, and self-reports each provide an important piece of the social competence puzzle.

In both research and practice, social assessment has typically provided a simplistic overview of readily observable social behaviours of a target student from the perspective of a single person (most often a classroom teacher) and in one setting (the classroom). We believe that optimal social assessment should be more comprehensive than that. The process of determining what factors related to social functioning need to be assessed and how these factors are related should be based on a comprehensive model of social competence. This chapter is organized around a theoretical model of social competence developed by Vaughn and Hogan and provides information on assessment tools and practices that best represent this model. Here we discuss the best practices for social assessment for both identification and research purposes.

Discussion emphasizes the importance of comprehensive assessment of social competence from a contextual perspective, that is, considering assessment data within the context in which behaviours and events occur.

Although the assessment tools discussed here may be relevant for a wide range of ages, we focus primarily on their use with elementary-age children because that is the age range in which most students with LD are identified. To the extent that it is possible, we discuss their use with younger and older children but refer the reader to other sources for specific information regarding preschool and adolescent populations.

Social Competence as a Multifaceted Construct

We think of social competence as a multifaceted construct analogous to intelligence in that it is a higher order, elusive construct that cannot be measured or observed directly. This model assumes four dimensions of social competence: effective use of social skills, absence of maladaptive behaviour, positive relations with others, and accurate/age appropriate social cognition. Although we define and measure social competence in terms of its separate components, it is not only the presence of the components but also their interaction that yields social competence. For the purposes of assessment and research, the components must be isolated and measured separately, but it is important in terms of interpretation and understanding of social competence that each component be considered in consort with the others.

For the past few years, we have conducted a number of studies in which we have applied this model of social competence with school-age students with LD to better understand the nature and implications of their social difficulties. Our findings have exemplified the importance of considering multiple factors of social competence, multiple reporters (peers, parents, self), and multiple settings (e.g., home, school, play). Our findings have also highlighted the importance of considering the context in which we measure social competence. For example, although most of our studies have reported lower peer acceptance for students with LD than for NLD students , one study in which subjects were selected from classrooms where teachers were highly accepting of students with LD yielded no significant differences in the peer acceptance of students with LD and typically achieving students across elementary and secondary grade levels . Examinations of social competence across school and non-school setting is valuable to assist in determining the extent to which behaviour that is reported at school corresponds with behaviour in other settings. In another study, we found that, although classroom teachers rated students with LD and other low achievers as less competent in terms of social skills than their typically achieving peers, parents (who view their children in the home setting) did not see their LD or low achieving children as less socially skilled than the parents of typically achieving students .

There are several correlates of social competence that need to be considered as relevant to the measurement of social competence. We are not suggesting that a comprehensive evaluation of social competence should include formal assessment of all related factors. Rather, we feel that such factors are often highly relevant and should be considered when interpreting results of social assessments. Athletic ability, academic ability, physical appearance, and various classroom behaviours are highly related to peer acceptance in school-age children. We know less about the extent to which these factors relate specifically to the social competence of students with LD. It may be relevant to consider these factors and their influence on students' peer acceptance when conducting and interpreting social assessments.

Achievement difficulties are another important factor related to social competence. It is often assumed that when students with LD demonstrate social difficulties it is a function of their learning disabilities. That is, the learning processes that interfere with their ability to effectively read and write also interfere with their ability to effectively interact with others. There is increasing evidence that there is a subgroup of students for whom this is true, however, there is also evidence that social difficulties may be concomitant with low achievement in general rather than causally related to LD. Indeed, our studies have shown that, for four components of social competence (i.e., peer relations, behavioral adjustment, social skills, and self-perceptions), students with LD are very similar to other low achievers who have not been referred or identified as having LD. Thus, we have substantial evidence of the general co-occurrence of achievement difficulties and social difficulties.

The following sections describe each component of the model of social competence as well as what we consider to be the current best practice for assessment within each area. We discuss assessment tools in relation to their purposes and potential uses as well as needs for further research and measure development.

Assessing Social Skills and Maladaptive Behaviours

Although social skills and maladaptive behaviours represent two different areas of social competence, we have converged them in this chapter, because many of the issues regarding measurement of these two areas are similar. Social skills refer to the pro-social and responding skills demonstrated across settings and persons. These include language, nonverbal reactions, and attitudes a person conveys to others. Social skills involves appropriate initiation and responsiveness to others. The *absence* of maladaptive behaviours is another component of social competence. Absence of maladaptive behaviours refers to the ability to refrain from engaging in behaviours considered by societal norms to be inappropriate. Naturally, the frequency and setting in which the behaviours occur influences the extent to which behaviours are viewed as maladaptive.

Maladaptive behaviours are not the opposite of social skills, although they are likely to be highly related. Maladaptive behaviour is not necessarily the ineffective use of or lack of effective social skills, but rather behaviours that would be considered to be inappropriate or maladaptive. For example, hitting another person is not considered to be the ineffective use of a social skill nor is it the absence of an effective social behaviour. It is an inappropriate behaviour. Crying is another example. Although there are situations in which crying would be an appropriate response, a child repeatedly crying in response to normal social situations — such as lining up to go to lunch or another child speaking to him or her — would be considered to exhibit maladaptive behaviour. There are individuals who are capable of demonstrating appropriate social skills and demonstrating maladaptive behaviour. For example, a student with conduct disorders may be able to display highly appropriate social behaviours in selected settings and also display acting out and aggressive behaviours in other settings.

Social skills measures, largely rating scales, assess the extent to which the target youngster demonstrates age-appropriate social behaviours with peers and adults across a range of settings. The existing social skills rating measures report better than adequate reliability and validity. For the most part, measures of social skills are designed for teachers to rate the social behaviours of selected students in their class. However, some of these social skills rating scales do not distinguish between school-related social behaviours (e.g., completing homework, following teacher's directions) and social behaviours related to adequate social functioning (e.g., greeting peers, solving one's own interpersonal problems). Social skills measures have also been designed to assess parents' perceptions of their child's social skills.

Although considerable emphasis has been placed on peer assessments of friendship and like ability, few measures that ask peers to assess the social skills of other peers have been developed. We feel that peers' assessment of the social skills of students is a promising area for several reasons. First, peers witness behaviours of others their own age that are not demonstrated to adults. Thus, they can provide unique insights into social behaviours. Second, social behaviours are not viewed the same by adults and children and, therefore, peers' perceptions of the social skills of their classmates could assist in the interpretation of why some students are not well liked by peers despite their high ratings of social skills by parents and teachers. Third, peers' perceptions of classmates are formed across multiple settings and could provide a more accurate perception of a student's social skills outside of the classroom. In a study conducted by Lancelotta and Vaughn, peer ratings of three subtypes of aggression did not correspond with teacher ratings. However, teachers' and students' perceptions of unprovoked aggression were highly related. One likely explanation is that teachers have little opportunity to observe some types of aggressive behaviour.

School-age youngsters with LD have consistently been found to have higher incidence of behavioral difficulties in comparison to non-LD peers, including higher levels of aggression, distractibility, internalizing or withdrawn behaviour, and externalizing behaviour. Teacher ratings have consistently identified problematic classroom behaviour for children with LD as compared to non-LD peers, such as more off-task behaviour and low rates of responding during instruction . Typically, students with LD have lower rates of behaviour problems than students identified as having behaviour disorders. Some evidence suggests that behaviour problems accompany achievement difficulties in general, rather than being associated with LD per se. In a limited number of studies comparing the behaviour problems of students with LD, low achievers, and average/high achievers, both low-achieving groups (i.e., students with LD and low achievers) have demonstrated similarly high incidence of behaviour problems relative to average and high achievers. Thus, at least when teacher ratings are used as an index of maladaptive behaviour, achievement difficulties and behavioral difficulties often co-occur.

Although teacher ratings of social skills and behaviour problems are usually considered quite reliable, we have three concerns regarding the use of most standardized teacher rating scales for either research or identification purposes. First, we have found that most teacher rating scales of social skills and behaviour problems focus on classroom-oriented behaviour, which is a context-specific view of social skills and ,maladaptive behaviours. For example, the Social Skills Rating Scale for Teachers, which has social skills and behaviour problems sub-scales, includes such items as "Finishes class assignments within time limits," and "Keeps desk clean and neat without being reminded" in the social skills sub-scale. Although these are important behaviours in the social context of the classroom, they are really more related to issues such as compliance or organisation within this particular setting. Students with LD who often display disorganization and difficulty with school work score low on these items, which may not reflect overall social skills difficulties. When using behavioral assessment for research purposes, it is important for researchers to be confident that the measure selected identifies true, generalized social skills or behavioral difficulties rather than school-oriented behaviours such as compliance and work habits. We believe that a comprehensive assessment of behavioral difficulties would include assessment of behaviours considered to be socially unacceptable in the classroom as well as in other contexts.

Our second concern is that the behaviour of students with LD in the school context may not be representative of their behaviour in other contexts. Most teacher rating scales are limited to use in the classroom context and provide the perspective of the classroom teacher. Because these measures are designed to be completed by classroom teachers, setting-specific items that are particularly relevant to teachers make sense. However, this may not provide adequate evidence to identify significant behavioral difficulties. This is particularly problematic when studying students with LD who by definition fail to thrive in school settings. We would expect the classroom to be an environment in which students with LD experience frustration or anxiety feelings that often lead to anger, aggression, or withdrawal. If a student with LD has behavioral difficulties in the general education classroom, but there is no indication of difficulties at home or in a special education classroom, it is highly possible that the difficulties are an indication of frustration relative to the context. Negative teacher ratings may also indicate frustration on the part of the teacher who finds the child difficult to teach. This has very different implications for intervention than when the difficulties occur consistently across settings. It may be possible in some instances to work with the context as well as with the student's context-specific behaviours, whereas implementing an intensive behavioral intervention may be warranted in other cases. For research purposes, it may be helpful to obtain ratings of students' behaviours both in and out of the classroom context, using multiple raters, thus providing cross-validation of results. The Social Skills Rating System, for example, includes parallel forms for parent, teacher, and self-report ratings of social skills and parent and teacher ratings of behaviour problems. In addition, the items are specific to the different contexts in which the raters know the target students. The Child Behaviour Checklist, a parent report measure, also has a corresponding Teacher Report Form as well as a self-report form to assess behaviour problems.

Third, we suggest the use of independent observations in addition to rating scales to minimize the bias inherent in rating scales. Although teachers are knowledgeable of students within the classroom context, they may not always differentiate behavioral difficulties from other concerns, such as social or academic concerns, whereas parents either may not have an awareness of developmental norms for behaviour or may not be willing to rate their child negatively. Few studies have compared teacher or parent ratings with actual observations regarding students with LD. However, in one of our studies, parent and teacher ratings of the behavioral difficulties of youngsters with LD were only moderately correlated. We might not expect teacher and parent ratings to converge because their knowledge of the child involves different settings and experiences. Thus, observation provides a third perspective on children's behavioral difficulties. Best practice for identification purposes might involve observation in and out of the structured classroom context. Although it is probably unrealistic for school personnel to conduct observation in the home setting, it is important to seek information from the family regarding the child's functioning in the home setting. It might also be possible when considering a child for placement in special education to observe the student during a class lesson as well as on the playground or other social context with peers.

For research purposes, observation provides several advantages for assessing behavioral difficulties. First, observation offers an assessment of children's behaviour independent of teacher or parent bias, although observer bias is a potential risk. Reliability is enhanced in observation studies by careful training of observers, interrater reliability checks, and the use of a well-defined data-coding system for either qualitative and quantitative analysis. Probably the greatest advantage is the opportunity to simultaneously observe the child's behaviour and contextual factors such as the reactions or initiations of teachers or peers and contextual events.

Although direct observation has been widely used in developmental research with non-LD subjects, studies using observation techniques with LD subjects are limited in number. Previous studies have examined the frequency and quality of the interactions between LD students and teachers or peers or have investigated the correlates of various social variables such as peer acceptance. Vaughn and Haager provided a review of observational studies of social competence with students with LD.

Methods of observing include naturalistic observation — using either anecdotal recording, time sampling, frequency counts, checklists, or other recording techniques — and analogue or simulated situations designed to elicit specific responses or behaviours, often through role-playing techniques. Naturalistic observation has the advantage of providing an assessment of a child in a naturally occurring environment. However, simulated situations are often selected when the behaviour of interest generally occurs with low frequency or in non-school contexts. Observation is potentially a rich source of information regarding the maladaptive behaviour of individuals with LD. However, both naturalistic and analogue or role-play techniques are costly in terms of personnel and time, which limits the number of observations, length of observations, or both. Comprehensive instruction on implementing observational assessment for both identification and research purposes is beyond the scope of this chapter. Entire university courses, textbooks, and reference materials are devoted to observational methodology. For the purpose of identifying youngsters for special education programmes, we refer the reader to assessment texts and other reviews.

Assessing Positive Relations with Others

The measures that provide perhaps the most relevant insight into the overall social functioning of individuals with LD are those that assess their relationships with others. In particular, the quality and number of friendships and how target students are perceived by peers provides an excellent index of overall social competence.

How youngsters are perceived by their peers has been linked to such outcomes as later adjustment, success in the workplace, and school completion. Peers' perceptions also influence self-perceptions and overall adjustment. These implications are particularly relevant for individuals with LD who are more frequently rejected by their peers and are less well accepted.

Sociometry is the most commonly used method of assessing peer acceptance. Developed by Moreno, sociometry is the study of peer rankings in a group. Most frequently this is done with peer rating scales or nomination techniques. Peer rating scales yield a measure of a target student's likability within a peer group or peer acceptance, whereas peer nominations indicate social status within a peer group, that is, popularity. Examining the nature, patterns, and numbers of friendships among peers is also an important avenue for assessing students' relations with others. This section of the chapter identifies measures and techniques for assessing peer acceptance, social status, and friendship qualities.

Peer Acceptance

Rating scales are the most accepted form of assessing peer acceptance for the purpose of identifying individuals in need of intervention or for research purposes. Because assessing individual students' peer groups would be difficult outside the school setting, peer ratings are most frequently obtained in the classroom. All students within the target student's class are asked to rate on a Likert-type scale each student in the class including the target child. Although different formats such as an easel or card format could be used, we have found the use of a roster of names followed by rating indicators to be most convenient.

In our own work, we use a 3-point scale with youngsters preschool through first grade then convert to a 4-point scale for youngsters second grade and older, through high school (e.g., Vaughn et al., 1992; Vaughn,

How Well Do You Like?

Your Name ______________________________

School ______________________________

Male _____ Female _____ Age _____ Teacher _____

Directions: Please circle the number that indicates how well you like each of the classmates listed. Cross out your own name.

1 = Do not like at at all2 = Do not like very much

3 = Like a little 4 = Like a lot

Student's Name		*How well do you like?*			
1.	Student A	1	2	3	4
2.	Student B	1	2	3	4
3.	Student C	1	2	3	4
4.	Student D	1	2	3	4
5.	Student E	1	2	3	4
6.	Student F	1	2	3	4
7.	Student G	1	2	3	4
8.	Student H	1	2	3	4
9.	Student I	1	2	3	4
10.	Student J	1	2	3	4
11.	Student K	1	2	3	4
12.	Student L	1	2	3	4

We also individually assess children through second grade and conduct small-group or whole-class assessment thereafter. With young children, we use a visual prompt of three faces: a happy face, a neutral face, and an unhappy face. They are instructed that there is no right or wrong answer and that they should indicate how they truly feel. They are also assured their responses will be kept confidential and told that they should not tell others how they have responded. We then provide some examples of the rating procedures and ask the children to point to the face which indicates how they feel about such familiar items as eating pizza, going swimming, cleaning their room, eating cake or spinach. Each face is assigned a point value from 1 for *least positive* to 3 for *most positive*. For older children in a group or class setting, we recommend using similar examples but numbers instead of faces for the ratings, with 1 indicating *Don't like at all,* 2 indicating *Don't like very much,* 3 indicating *Sort of like,* and 4 indicating *Like a lot*. We demonstrate how to circle the numbers on a sample paper. For the younger children, the examiner holds and marks the roster of names, whereas the older children are given the roster and asked to mark it themselves. Once children of both age groups grasp the procedures, they are asked to rate each child in their class, excluding themselves, by indicating how much they like each individual according to the instructions. It should be noted that, even if one is only interested in particular target students such as the students with LD, it is important to obtain whole-class ratings for two reasons. First, the larger the number of raters, the higher the reliability of the ratings. Second, there is potential harm to an individual's self-esteem when including some but not all students in the class in the roster of names. The reliability and validity of peer ratings is moderately high for preschool and elementary students and overall, are higher than for peer nominations.

Typically, the mean score for each target student is calculated and scores can then be used in a comparative analysis or merely examined in relation to those of others. The mean score is indicative of how well a student is liked or accepted by peers. However, mean scores should not be used alone. A list of all the ratings for an individual student will indicate if there are students in the class who like this student a lot (perhaps despite a low mean score) or very little or whether the student is universally liked, viewed neutrally, or disliked.

Despite the ease and usefulness of peer rating information, there are several issues to consider in their use. First, the "stem" that is used to request the ratings should be chosen carefully. The most frequently used stem is "How much do you like." each name on the list. However, other possibilities include "How much would you like to work with." and "How much would you like to play with." or "How much would you like ____ to come to your birthday party?" We would not expect participants to respond similarly using these different stems, due to the fact that they must appraise their classmates on different features for each. For example, a student with LD may be viewed as limited in reading ability and, therefore, might not be rated positively using the "work with" stem whereas they may be athletically skilled and rated more positively using the "play with" stem. In a study conducted by Gresham and Reschly in which non-LD students and students with LD were rated using both "work with" and "play with" stems, the largest statistically significant difference between the groups was obtained with the "work with" stem.

The "play with" stem may be influenced by age, sex, athletic ability, or temperament. Our recommendation is that, if you are most interested in assessing how well a student is accepted by peers, the best stem is "How much do you like." If other stems are used, they should be carefully selected to represent the desired factor to be assessed.

Peer Rating Score Card

	A	B	C	D	E	F	G	H	I	J	K	L
Student A	X	3	4	4	3	3	1	3	4	3	2	3
Student B	3	X	4	3	2	1	1	4	3	3	1	2
Student C	4	3	X	3	3	1	2	4	3	2	1	2
Student D	4	2	4	X	3	2	1	3	4	3	2	3
Student E	3	3	4	4	X	1	2	4	3	4	3	4
Student F	4	2	3	2	3	X	2	3	2	4	2	3
Student G	3	2	4	2	4	2	X	3	2	3	3	4
Student H	2	3	3	3	3	2	3	X	3	3	1	4
Student I	3	4	3	3	4	1	2	4	X	2	1	2
Student J	3	1	4	4	3	2	3	4	4	X	3	3
Student K	3	2	3	3	3	3	2	4	3	3	X	4
Student L	4	2	3	4	2	2	2	3	3	3	1	X
4's rec'd	4	1	6	4	2	0	0	4	3	2	0	4
3's rec'd	6	4	5	5	7	2	2	5	6	7	3	4
2's rec'd	1	5	0	2	2	5	4	0	2	2	3	3
1's rec'd	0	1	0	0	0	4	3	0	0	0	5	0

Figure 9.1 Sample of Students

Sample of a grid used to score peer ratings. Going from left to right, the numbers indicate the scores given by an individual. Going from top to bottom, the numbers indicate the scores received by an individual. Note that subjects do not rate themselves, thus an "X" is placed in the box where the individual's scores given and scores received intersect. The number of 4s, 3s, 2s, and Is received are tallied at the bottom of the form. The mean peer rating for each individual is computed using the scores received as follows: (#4's x 4) + (#3's x 3) + (#2's x 2) +

Social Status

Social status is determined by the number of positive and negative nominations received from classmates. Although there are several methods of obtaining nominations (e.g., name the person you think of as the funniest, smartest), the procedure that yields positive and negative nominations, which then can be used to compute social status categories, is as follows: First, students are asked to write or tell the examiner up to three classmates who they "like most" or would consider to be their "best friends" in the class. These are referred to as positive nominations. Next, students are asked to write or name up to three classmates who they "least like" or would "not want to be friends with." These are considered negative nominations. Using the nominations of the whole class, the number of positive and negative nominations for each target student are computed. These scores can then be used in statistical analyses or for diagnostic purposes. For either purpose, social impact and social preference scores are computed. Social impact is indicative of the extent to which the target student influences the group and is obtained by adding the number of positive and negative nominations. Social preference is the extent to which a target child is highly liked by peers and is obtained by subtracting the number of negative nominations from the number of positive nominations. Note that this could be a negative number if a student receives a high number of negative nominations. For diagnostic purposes, the scores could be compared informally with those of peers. For research purposes, however, the scores are standardized by class by conversion to z-scores and yield social status categories using analysis procedures outlined by Coie, Dodge and Coppotelli. Using these procedures, students are categorized as popular (high positive social impact, high social preference), rejected (high social impact, low social preference), controversial (high positive and negative nominations), and neglected (low social impact). This system of classification provides information about social structure and specific behaviour patterns associated with different status groups and has demonstrated adequate test – retest reliability and criterion-related validity.

Peer rejection is not only associated with interpersonal difficulties, low levels of cooperation and friendliness, and high levels of aggression, but is also thought to be predictive of negative later life outcomes such as poor adult adjustment, criminal involvement, and dropping out of school. Thus, the consistent finding that students with LD are more likely to be rejected than non-LD students is alarming and warrants further investigation. In a recent study, however, we found that low achieving students were over represented in the rejected category, whereas a smaller proportion of students with LD and typically achieving students were classified as rejected, thus indicating that low achievement status may be an important factor.

Friendship Qualities: In addition to considering how the target student is perceived by the group as a whole, it is important to understand the quality of the student's friendships. We know surprisingly little about the nature of friendships of students with LD, but we have hypothesized that, for students with social difficulties, having at least one or two strong friendship bonds may serve as a "buffer" to the ill effects of low peer acceptance and rejection. Bukowski and Hoza presented several key questions to consider that provide a conceptual framework for assessing the quality of children's friendships:

1. Does a child have at least one mutual friend?
2. How many mutual friends does the child have?
3. What is/are the quality of that child's mutual friend?

One way of examining friendship bonds is through identifying *reciprocal* friendships, in which two students name each other as "best friends." This can be done easily through the positive nomination procedure described earlier by examining the nomination forms of those named as "best friends" by the target student to see if they also named the target student. If they did, it is a "hit," if not, a "miss." According to Howes, rejected children had an easier time with peer group entry if they had reciprocal friendships than if they did not. In a recent study examining the reciprocal friendships of students with LD in inclusion settings, overall peer acceptance of students with LD did not increase from fall to spring; however, their number of reciprocal friends increased.

Other measures that assess the quality of friendships are self-reports or interviews. These might be used to answer Bukowski and

Hoza's third question related to the quality of mutual friendships. Bierman and McCauley have developed the Friendship Questionnaire to specifically assess youngsters' peer relations and friendships outside of the school setting. This is a 32-item scale that has three sub-scales: positive interactions, negative interactions, and extensive peer network. Berndt and Perry adapted the Friendship Survey from a structured interview. This 18-item questionnaire was designed to investigate dimensions of children's friendships. Items consist of such questions as, "Do you and your friends get together on weekends or after school?" to which children respond "yes," "sometimes," or "no." The authors identified six dimensions of friendship: play/association, pro-social behaviour, intimacy, loyalty, attachment/self-esteem, and absence of conflicts. However, according to Berndt and Perry, for second, fourth, and sixth graders, the ratings for all six dimensions loaded on a single factor. We, therefore, suggest using the total score on the friendship survey as a measure of the quality of a student's friendships. Whereas peer ratings and reciprocal friendship nominations address only those relationships that occur among classmates, the Friendship Survey gives an index of perceived support from friends irrespective of context and can provide information not tapped by classroom peer measures. We encourage further research regarding the friendships of students with LD.

Assessing Social Cognition

Social cognition refers to the ability to understand and interpret social events and the behaviours of self and others. This requires an understanding of an individual's cognitive processes, an area that is difficult to assess directly. With some academic situations such as math problem solving and writing, researchers have attempted to examine students' cognition by having them "think aloud" while performing the task. However, this technique is not particularly useful in assessing social cognition, because the act of thinking aloud would interfere with the social interaction and alter the situation. Furthermore, even if it were possible to accurately assess an individual's cognition, it would be difficult to know whether the particular cognition assessed are general to all environments or limited to specific environmental situations.

Until social assessment is further refined, we have concluded that it is not possible to assess social cognition directly. Therefore, we suggest the use of self-report assessments that measure some aspect of social cognition, such as self-concept, using measures that require reflective thinking about events or interpretations of events in an individual's experience, to better understand social cognition.

Examining the self-perceptions of students with LD is one way of determining the impact of academic and social difficulties on students' emotional well-being and sense of self. Because students with LD experience repeated academic (and often social) difficulties, we would expect their self-concepts to reflect negative self-perceptions. Although numerous studies have demonstrated that students with LD have less positive self-concepts than NLD students, this is an oversimplified interpretation of years of research. Several other studies have found no differences in self-concepts of students with LD and NLD students. Several factors may help us to understand this apparent contradiction in findings.

First, how self-concept is defined is an important factor. Self-perceptions appear to be domain-specific and results may vary depending on whether the measure used assesses the student's feelings of general self-worth or self-perceptions within specific developmental domains. Harter and her colleagues described six domains of self-perception: scholastic competence, social acceptance, athletic competence, physical competence, behavioral competence, and global self-worth. Several studies have found students with LD to have lower academic-related self-perceptions than NLD students, whereas self-perceptions in other domains did not differ. It is important, then, for the self-concept assessment tool to measure not only general self-worth, but also specific developmental domains.

Age is a second factor that may explain the contradictory findings of previous self-concept research comparing students with LD and NLD. Self-perceptions tend to become more differentiated and refined with age and, generally, self-concept declines through the childhood years. Although we might assume that the self-concept development of youngsters with LD would follow a normal developmental pattern, few studies have provided a developmental perspective. Two longitudinal studies indicated negative self-perceptions for youngsters with LD as compared to NLD peers over time. In contrast, our research following a cohort of children from kindergarten through fifth grade demonstrated that the domain-specific and global self-perceptions of youngsters with LD did not differ significantly at any time from those of typically achieving youngsters. The self-perceptions of the children with LD appeared to follow the same developmental trends of other youngsters. Because we had a small number of LD subjects who remained in the study through the fifth grade, we caution against over interpretation of our findings and encourage further longitudinal research in order to better understand such developmental issues.

A third issue that complicates the interpretation of previous self-concept research is that of setting. As children develop a sense of self and become self-evaluative around the age of 7 or 8 years, they also begin to engage in social comparison, that is, seeing themselves in relation to others. Renick and Harter have proposed that social comparison processes are important to consider when examining the self perceptions of youngsters with LD. Youngsters with LD who are served primarily in a general education classroom have a different social comparison group than those served in pull-out settings. Coleman, Renick and Harter found that when students with LD use the regular classroom as a comparison group they tend to rate themselves lower academically than their NLD peers, but when they are considering themselves in relation to others in pull-out or self-contained special classes they rate themselves more positively.

The three factors discussed earlier also provide some guidelines for best practice for assessment of self-perceptions. It is important to select an assessment tool that differentiates and measures the specific domain(s) of interest. Several published rating scales provide domain-specific assessment. Harter has been a leader in this area with the development of several rating scales that have primarily been used for research purposes. The Self-Perception Profile for Children (ages 8-13) and Self-Perception Profile for Adolescents (ages 14-18) as well as the Self-Perception Profile for Learning Disabled Students (ages 8-18) and the Pictorial Scale of Perceived Competence and Social Acceptance for Young Children (ages 4-7) provide domain-specific self-ratings. Norms have been developed for each of these measures, thus making it possible to compare an individual's score with normative data that might be helpful for assessment related to identification as well.

We also suggest that care be taken to select assessment tools that are developmentally appropriate. Children with LD younger than 7 or 8 years may not have well-defined self-perceptions. The issues that are salient in the formation of self-perceptions vary at different ages. For example, having a large social network may be more critical to the positive self-perceptions of preadolescent and adolescent youngsters than it would be to primary-grade children. Therefore, it is important when selecting or developing self-concept measures to look for a good match between the age of the youngster and the issues included in specific items.

Another important issue in selecting an appropriate measure for use with youngsters with LD is the dependence of self-rating measures on language and cognitive abilities to complete the measures. Instruments that require a great deal of reading or listening may be influenced by the youngster's ability to maintain attention and to process the language involved. A measure with a large number of items may be cumbersome and it may be necessary to take frequent breaks during administration. The examiner should be prepared to explain any item that the individual student does not understand and may have to rephrase or elaborate on specific items. This poses a threat when standardization of administration procedures is desired. It also provides an argument for individual administration even when the instructions indicate the instrument could be given in a group.

Summary

The purpose of this chapter is to provide an overview of issues related to assessment of social competence with students with LD. Additionally, four factors related to social competence (i.e., social skills, absence of maladaptive behaviours, relationships with others, and social cognition) are defined and discussed. Measures that have been developed to assess each of these four factors are described and their use for assessment and research purposes presented. The use (and misuse) of measures designed to assess the social competence of students with LD is explained.

There are several reoccurring themes in this chapter regarding the assessment of social competence of individuals with LD. They are summarized in the following.

Comprehensive Assessment

We have gathered significant evidence to conclude that social assessment from the narrow perspective of one rater (e.g., teachers) or in a single setting (e.g., the classroom) provides an incomplete picture of the social competence of individuals with LD. Furthermore, assessment along a single dimension of social competence (e.g., social skills) provides a limited view of social competence. Whether the assessment is conducted for identification or research purposes, it is critical to obtain a comprehensive measurement of social competence, considering multiple perspectives, settings, dimensions, and other related factors.

Context

The setting in which the student is assessed is critical and must be considered both prior to assessment and in the interpretation of the assessment. This is particularly important for students with LD, because most assessments of social competence occur in the school setting. Thus, it is possible that students social behaviour in the school context is not representative of their social behaviour in other settings. We advocate the use of measures that tap students' behaviour across multiple settings as well as measures that rate school behaviours and other behaviours.

Rater

Who rates the social competence of students with LD largely influences the score. Even when the same measure is used and ratings are completed by the special education teacher and the general education teacher, outcomes will differ. Multiple raters provide multiple perspectives; however, first consideration should be given to selecting a rater that matches the goal of the study or the purpose of the assessment.

Content

The purpose of the measure, content of its factors, and content of relevant items must be carefully considered in the selection and interpretation of social measures. It is important to determine that the measure taps the dimension of interest and that items are worded appropriately.

Characteristics

The characteristics of students with LD may interfere with their completion of or responses on the social measure. For example, students with LD who have attention problems may incorrectly complete measures, thus altering their scores in significant ways that are not related to their social competence. Memory and communication problems, frequently associated with students with LD, often interfere with their performance on social measures and need to be considered when interpreting their responses.

10

Deaf Children to Deaf Adults

Differences in the generality or relevance of social rules for deaf and hearing children can result from the fact that deaf children tend to have fewer playmates during the early years, from their parents having more restrictive rules for behaviour, or from parents not being as able to communicate expectations about social interactions. For example, it is common to see a teacher or parent react to one hearing child hitting another by saying something like "Janie, don't hit Jonathan. How does it feel when someone hits you? It hurts, doesn't it? You wouldn't like it if Jonathan hit you, would you?" This kind of response is more likely to lead to positive changes in behaviour than spanking or yelling "Stop that!" at the child, and it begins the process of internalizing the rules and expectations of the society.

Parents who do not share a common, fluent language with their children cannot engage in such moral teaching as effectively as parents who do. Their children are not as likely to learn the reasons for social rules at home. This is not to say that deaf children will be any less polite or well behaved than hearing children or that parents need to have any special tools for bringing up their deaf children. Quite the contrary: Deaf children will learn about social interactions and will develop personality characteristics in precisely the same way as hearing children. The important issues are who their teachers and role models will be, and how the children see themselves as part of the social world. Growing up is hard enough when it comes to friends, social pressure, falling in love, and "doing the right thing." Growing up deaf adds some extra dimensions.

Emotional Growth during the School Years

Deaf children from deaf families often are more comfortable socially than deaf children from hearing families. Children from deaf families are likely to have had a wider range of social interactions within the Deaf community, and they will have experienced greater understanding and acceptance from others inside and outside the family. Deaf children of deaf parents also are more likely than those with hearing parents to have experienced consistent parenting behaviours and effective communication from an early age. Social interactions with deaf individuals outside of the immediate family thus are more likely to be similar to those within the family. Partly as a result of this consistency, deaf children of deaf families tend to have relatively greater social confidence, self-esteem, and a greater sense of being in control of their own lives. This latter characteristic, known as locus of control, is an important predictor of academic as well as social and career success and has surfaced at various points in other chapters. Deaf children of hearing parents can be just as confident and secure as those of deaf parents, but it may require more conscious planning by hearing parents to ensure that their children have the right kind of personality-building experiences.

As young children become more social, the variety of their relationships with family, peers, and other adults increases far beyond that established with their parents and other family members. Most children will naturally be attracted to other people who will serve both emotional and practical roles in their lives. That is, all children have a need to be liked and emotionally close to others, and so they seek approval and affection from adults and, later, from peers. At the same time, they often depend on others to help them or show them how to achieve their goals. Both of these kinds of attention-seeking are referred to as dependence, and they are normal and healthy parts of children's personalities. Even children who are said to be independent still display appropriate dependence, but they blend dependent behaviour in some situations with self reliance and assertiveness. Children who are overly dependent on others may not feel in control of their own lives and are said to have an external locus of control. Children who blend independent and dependent behaviour and feel "in control" are said to have an internal locus of control.

Children who are physically or psychologically challenged are likely to encounter difficulties in establishing their independence. In part, their need for more assistance from others is a real one, with the kind and extent of such help varying with the nature of the child's handicap. Nonetheless, the frequent overprotection of handicapped children by well-meaning adults creates further barriers to social independence and physical competence, as the children are often able to perform a variety of tasks that others typically do for them. The resulting social immaturity could have been avoided. As Kathryn Meadow-Orlans, a prominent researcher in the field, once noted:

> *Parents generalize from the narrow range of tasks that the handicapped child actually cannot do, and assume that there is a much larger spectrum of tasks of which he is incapable. Eventually, the assumed inability becomes a real inability because the child does not have the opportunity to practice tasks and develop new levels of expertise. In addition, it takes more patience and time for handicapped children to perform the trial-and-error process of skill acquisition — time and patience that parents may not have or be willing to give. For deaf children with deficient communication skills, it takes additional time and patience merely to communicate what is expected, required, and necessary for the performance of even a simple task.*

Meadow-Orlans's suggestion concerning the importance of effective communication between deaf children and their parents and peers is supported by observations of researchers and teachers in a variety of settings. Because they typically receive fewer explanations for the causes of other people's social and emotional behaviours, deaf children may have more difficulty controlling their own behaviour and learning from social experience. Communication barriers also may cause deaf children and adolescents to have less knowledge about social rules, and their lack of social skills may impede the development of independence and self-esteem. Yet another hurdle for social development is the fact that deaf children often lack social role models with whom they can identify and communicate. All of these factors help us to explain the observation that deaf children of deaf parents have greater social maturity than those of hearing parents. Nonetheless, we have to remember that descriptions of whole groups as socially mature or socially immature are broad generalizations, and that many deaf children are just as socially and behaviorally adjusted as hearing children of the same ages.

As in other areas, some children are faster or slower social learners. Some will have families that are more or less instructive with regard to social interactions outside of the home. Deaf children are often seen to be more involved with their families than are hearing children in hearing families. In some sense, family interactions are more important for deaf children than for hearing children, because a greater percentage of their social experience happens with family members than with others outside the home. This makes family members very important as role models. Role modeling plays a central role in development, helping children to learn about different roles, about their cultural heritage, about the values and morals of their family and community, and about more specific things like religion, politics, preferences for particular sports teams, and favorite foods. The ability to identify with others and to model their behaviour first depends on children believing that they are similar to the model. Boys, for example, learn how to act like boys by watching their fathers and other boys, not by watching their mothers and older sisters. As children discover ways they are like others, they try to act like them and think like them, eventually developing similar likes and dislikes. Finding that their parents have the same last name as they do or that they look like one of their parents can contribute to this development in the same way that sharing cultural or ethnic characteristics often makes children act more like others with similar backgrounds.

Perhaps an example will help to make the general point: When I was growing up, my family did not have a strong distinction between "girl" things and "boy" things. We were all involved in cooking, cleaning, painting, fixing, and so on. It was primarily my father who taught me to sew and to cook, and with him as my role model, both activities became very natural for me. A colleague of mine was eager to have his two daughters grow up the same way, and so he made a point of having them help him paint the house and taking them out into the garage to build things with him or work on the family car. It did *not* work. Why? Probably because it was their father who always did the "boy" things with his daughters. If their mother had built the bird houses with them and their father had taught them to cook, perhaps the gender roles would have seemed more flexible. As it is, they are both wonderful teenagers, but they are not very interested in the kinds of activities that we think of as being done by males.

Modeling plays an important role in giving children a sense of identity, both as individuals and as part of a larger community. By sharing characteristics with others in their family or their community, they come to see themselves as part of a group, as *belonging*. Deaf children in hearing families will have a sense of family identity, but their sense of being part of the larger community often will be colored by whether or not they know other deaf people. Deaf children normally will learn about Deaf culture only by being around Deaf children and Deaf adults, and that is why the Deaf community sees residential schools as so important.

Living with Parents and Peers

Early language experience for deaf children has been shown to have a significant impact on their personalities and emotional development, just as it does with hearing children. Most research in this area has focused on the benefits of early exposure to sign language, but the important thing is to have consistent two-way communication, regardless of whether it is spoken or signed. For example, studies have shown that children enrolled in preschool intervention programmes utilizing Total Communication are more likely to respond appropriately to their mothers' requests and use far more communication with them during play. These interactions tend to be longer, more relaxed, and more gratifying on both sides. Deaf children who have established good communicative and social relationships within the family thus will be better equipped to venture out into the social world.

Thinking back to the school years and our social lives during that time, many adults agree that they were the best of times and the worst of times. There are many fond memories of friends and events, but there were also many conflicting pressures. We were supposed to act like individuals, but we also wanted to fit in with the crowd. We were supposed to be successful in academics, but also liked by others. As school and our school friends became major social influences, we started to accept the values of our peers and our role models, sometimes even when those values were in conflict with values of our families. During the school years, we had to face problems of self-esteem, gender identity, and of trying to figure out who we were and what we wanted. Sometimes, it seemed that our parents were not much help.

Deaf children encounter all of the same social problems and find the same social solutions as other children. Depending on their environments, they also might face other challenges. In a public school setting, for example, being deaf makes them different, and parents who think being different in school does not matter are forgetting a lot about their own youth. In residential school or day school programmes, deaf children find others who are like them, but the hearing world is still all around them.

When children share common characteristics and attitudes with others, when they are part of a group, their self-esteem grows. A variety of studies have examined the self-esteem of deaf children and identified factors that promote or hinder its development. Most generally, it is now well documented that deaf and hearing children do not differ, overall, in their self-esteem, a finding that holds from age three all the way through college. Deaf children with multiple handicaps do have lower self-esteem than those who do not, but they are no different from hearing children with multiple handicaps. Deaf children whose parents are better signers have been shown to have higher self-esteem than children whose parents do not sign as well, and for this and other reasons cited above, deaf children of deaf parents have higher self-esteem than deaf children of hearing parents. Deaf children enrolled in Total Communication programmes also tend to have higher self-esteem than children in programmes that focus on spoken language, but the extent to which this is a consequence of communication skill per se rather than improved social relations or other factors is unclear. Similarly, deaf children in residential schools have higher self-esteem than children in mainstream programmes, although the reasons for that relation are undoubtedly complex.

For this and other reasons, most Deaf adults believe that residential schools are a vital source of social growth for deaf children, and available findings linking social development to school placement make it difficult to make a case for any other school setting. Hearing proponents of mainstreaming and inclusion sometimes argue that the "artificial" nature of such schools might result in a narrow view of social responsibility and social interaction, but there is no support for such a position from existing research. Moreover, the fact that many hearing parents do not have fluent communication with their deaf children means that the socialization they receive at home can also be rather narrow, and it is difficult to know which situation would be better or worse for any particular child. The apparent advantages of residential or day school programmes for deaf children's social development do not supersede their need for a secure family life. Nevertheless, special programmes represent a fertile ground for social interactions with peers and deaf adults that go beyond what is available in most homes and preschool programmes. In that setting, deaf children will have more playmates and more communication during play than they will in public schools. They also will be less overprotected and intruded upon by well-meaning adults. Some of the benefits of the larger social circle gained in residential or day school settings may seem trivial: things like going to the mall with a group of friends, telling jokes in the hallway, and flirting on the playground. But I think that the importance of those behaviours for normal social and personality development during the school years cannot be ignored. This kind of experience leads directly to children's acquisition of an accurate assessment of their personal strengths and weaknesses (self-image), leadership skills, and self-esteem. These characteristics, in turn, play an important role in children's desire for achievement and eventual success in academic and social settings.

Clearly, the most important part of raising a deaf child is trying to give them as normal a childhood as possible. Social, language, and educational experiences all enter into the normal mix, but *normal* does not mean *business as usual*. As I cautioned earlier, having a deaf child affects the whole family, and a deaf child in a mainstream setting affects the entire class. This means that some day-to-day activities may have to change if deaf children are to have access to the experiences and opportunities available to hearing children.

Influence of Brothers and Sisters

Most people who have brothers or sisters recognize that siblings have an effect on each other's personalities and development. In general, siblings are less emotionally tied to each other than they are to their parents, and they thus can serve as confidants and behaviour-modifying critics for one another.

Siblings observe and evaluate each other in ways that can contribute to social growth and maturity. They also learn from each other and share resources in a variety of contexts. They can protect each other from emotional or physical harm and serve as a buffer between each other and the parents or outside world. They can make life simpler or more complex, more comfortable or more difficult.

We actually know very little about how sibling relationships might be affected when one child is deaf. Some changes will be subtle, others not so subtle, and all will vary depending on the parents' ability to adjust to having a deaf child. When the parents accept their deaf child, they are more likely to help their other children come to an acceptance of their deaf sibling. Hearing siblings of deaf children, nonetheless, sometimes become angry and resentful toward their deaf siblings. In addition to normal sibling rivalry during childhood, hearing siblings may be frustrated at the lack of communication in the family and at first may not understand what it means to be deaf. Hearing siblings may be jealous of the increased attention that a deaf child receives from their parents and upset at sometimes having to act like caretakers, explaining to people outside of the family that their brother or sister is deaf. At other times, the relationships may be seamless, and deaf and hearing siblings may have especially warm feelings for each other. Positive relationships among deaf and hearing siblings provide deaf children with social and emotional support as well as encouragement in dealing with the implications of their hearing losses outside of the home. Hearing siblings, for example, can serve as helpful resources in social as well as academic contexts. Deaf children with hearing siblings thus often show better social skills than deaf children with no hearing siblings.

With regard to the effects of siblings on deaf children's communication abilities, it is important to note that the quality and quantity of communication in a family with only one deaf child will be considerably different from that of a family with more deaf children. Consider first the situation where there is only one deaf child in an otherwise hearing family, the most common situation. On average, deaf children appear to have more active communication with their hearing siblings than with their hearing parents. Hearing siblings are often more likely to use signed and nonsign gestural communication than their hearing parents, who often try to focus on spoken communication. Hearing siblings thus may serve as intermediaries between deaf children and their parents as well as with people outside of the family. Their possible interpreter role aside, older siblings will provide models of language use, allowing deaf children to "practice" communicating. Deaf children accordingly tend to achieve higher communicative functioning when they have older siblings, either deaf or hearing.

If sharing some mode of communication (either spoken, signed, or a combination) with deaf and hearing siblings has positive consequences for both deaf children and their families, the absence of a common language between siblings can lead either to negative consequences or to the failure to benefit from a potentially positive family setting. For example, it may be too difficult for hearing children to explain to their deaf siblings what is going on in a particular context, how to play a game, or why there is an argument between them. Hearing siblings thus may cut short or avoid more complex social interactions, even if they are on good terms with their deaf siblings. This reduced interaction will not only have a direct effect on social interaction, is will affect the learning of social skills and the ability to resolve conflicts.

Consider now the situation where there are several deaf children in the same family. Such families are likely to have histories of deaf members, indicating hereditary causes of hearing loss. Such families not only will tend to be more accepting of people who are deaf, but they are more likely to accept gestural and signed communication, and may have considerable sign skills. In the promotion of social growth, there is likely to be a considerable difference between a hearing family with only one deaf child, who will tend to be the center of family attention, and a family with several deaf children, which will function more naturally. Growing up with deaf siblings provides a rich environment for modeling and all of the typical characteristics of sibling relationships. Although more research needs to be done, what we know so far indicates that these relationships have only positive effects on deaf children, both socially and cognitively.

Understanding the Feelings

The ability to consider the feelings of other people is intertwined with both social and cognitive development. Over time, children learn to balance social roles, the feelings and goals of others, and the values that their families and culture place on different kinds of behaviour. To behave in a socially appropriate way, children have to consider alternative perspectives in social situations, and role taking therefore is an essential component of mature social functioning.

Traditionally, deaf individuals, and deaf children in particular, have been described as having difficulty taking the perspective of others, thus being emotionally egocentric, lacking in empathy, and insensitive to the needs of those around them. Such reports are common in the literature, but they often overlook the fact that role-taking ability is strongly related to children's language skills. That is, children who have the benefits of early communication are better able to consider the perspectives of others in social situations, probably because they have gotten more explanations of the causes and effects of behaviour. Among such children, any delays observed in their role-taking ability during the preschool years tend to disappear by the middle school years.

Children's understanding the perspectives of others and of their culture is an important part of deciding what is right and what is wrong. Moral development requires that children understand the reasons for avoiding bad behaviours and performing good behaviours. Punishment and rewards can also accomplish this at some superficial level, but unless children internalize the values of the family and society, the effects are often short-lived and limited in generality. When children truly understand how others view their behaviour, they are more likely and more able to try to follow social rules. Moral development thus is related to role taking and, more generally, to children's cognitive development. Research studies over the past twenty years have shown that deaf children lag behind hearing children in their abilities to judge other people's behaviour in terms of their intentions rather than the outcome. For example, they might see a child who accidentally breaks a dish while trying to help in the kitchen as being just as bad as the child who intentionally breaks a dish in a fit of anger. Deaf children are also more likely to behave out of fear of punishment rather than because they understand the principles underlying appropriate behaviour. As a result, they may be more likely than hearing age-mates to be disruptive in school or to get into trouble if they think they can get away with it. Unfortunately, for reasons cited above, deaf children may also be more likely than hearing children to misjudge their chances of getting caught.

Any explanation of the above behaviours needs to take into account the social and cultural context in which they occur. For example, hearing parents may have fewer opportunities to teach their deaf children the family's rules or the culture's morals directly. They also tend to give in to their deaf children's demands when they lack sufficient communication skill to explain the reasons for delays or for denying children something they want. These children will experience inconsistency in responses to their actions when behaviour permitted at home is not allowed in school or neighborhood play settings. Such inconsistency often leads to resistance to parental values by the time children reach the middle school years, thus accelerating the movement to identification with peers. The resulting behaviour will further affect socialization and may be interpreted as indicating underlying psychological problems if it is consistently negative. While there are certainly many more factors that affect the mental health of either deaf or hearing children, the ways they behave in interpersonal interactions are often a primary indicator of psychological well-being or psychological difficulties from the perspectives of concerned parents and teachers. We thus now consider mental health issues in more detail.

Mental Health in Deaf Children and Deaf Adults

In the previous section, we saw that deaf children may lag behind hearing children in recognizing the reasons for other people's behaviour, in part because deaf children are less likely than hearing peers to receive explanations for other people's social behaviours. As a result, deaf children might not always understand why people respond to them the way they do. One investigation involving seven- to eight-year-olds, for example, showed that the deaf children were less successful than hearing peers in matching faces showing different emotions with emotionally related scenes. The deaf children understood and could name the emotions on the faces, but they had trouble connecting the emotions with the right contexts. Findings of this sort suggest that deaf children might sometimes behave inappropriately or misunderstand others' behaviour in ways that can lead to perceptions of emotional difficulty. For example, some people believe that deaf children (and adults) tend to act more immaturely or aggressively than hearing peers. In particular, deaf children are often said to be more disruptive and more impulsive in school, whereas deaf adults are sometimes described generally as oversensitive, depressed, or even paranoid. Is there any truth to these descriptions? As in most areas, the research findings on this issue are mixed and the conclusions we draw may depend on the assumptions we have when we start. Perhaps most importantly, there is a long history of misdiagnosing hearing loss in children as mental retardation, autism, or other psychological disturbances. Mistakes like these are disgraceful and potentially devastating for deaf children and their families, but they do occur. Clearly, they reflect a lack of information about hearing loss on the part of parents, pediatricians, and teachers. Beyond such confusions, however, there is a variety of factors that may put deaf children at risk for psychological stress.

Are Deaf Children Impulsive?

Perhaps the most common psychological problem attributed to deaf children is impulsivity. The term *impulsivity* has two closely related meanings. Normally, we apply the word *impulsive* to people who seem to act without thinking, usually behaving in a way that seems to satisfy their immediate desires without concern for others or for long-term implications. Considering this everyday kind of impulsivity, educators and researchers have claimed that deaf children's behaviour often shows a desire for immediate gratification. This need is reflected either in an inability to wait for what they want or a willingness to settle for less if they get it sooner rather than getting what they really want later. In deaf children, such behaviour is often attributed to the lack of early language interaction with hearing parents and teachers, who may not understand what a deaf child is asking for or may not be able to explain why children cannot have what they want when they want it. Although other possible explanations for impulsive behaviour are considered below, hearing parents of deaf children frequently do yield to demands for attention, assistance, or objects in order to avoid the possibility of temper tantrums. Part of the problem is that once such an episode starts, parents might not have sufficient communication skill to be able to stop it. That is, without enough language proficiency to relate the present to the past and to the future, hearing parents unintentionally might be teaching their children that dependence and demands will be immediately rewarded. This attitude may then be carried over into the classroom, where deaf children are more likely than hearing children to "act up" and get in trouble.

So much for the common use of *impulsive*. When psychologists use that term to describe a child, they normally are not referring to how children behave on the playground, but to the way they solve problems. From the psychological perspective, impulsivity is one end of an impulsivity-reflectivity dimension, one of several dimensions that comprise a child's cognitive style. Although the standard tests of impulsivity-reflectivity examine cognitive or academic problem solving, the underlying dimension also relates to social problem solving. Impulsivity and reflectivity are most easily seen in the trade-off between speed and accuracy in doing a task or in making a decision. Tests for younger children generally involve choosing which of several pictures is the same as or different from a target picture. For preschoolers this might involve a target picture of a bear and a child's having to choose from among pictures of another bear, a horse, a cat, and a mouse. Children in the second grade might be asked to choose from among several clown pictures and pick the one that has exactly the same pattern of striped clothing as the target. Children who make their choices quickly and with frequent errors will fall into an impulsive range, whereas those who take more time to consider the alternatives before making decision will fall into a reflective range Similarly, when older children are asked to trace through mazes printed on paper, those who take longer but stay in the lines are rated as more reflective than those who go more quickly, but bump into lines and have to backtrack out of dead ends. Despite all of the stories about impulsivity in deaf children, relatively few research studies have been conducted to determine whether or not they are really more impulsive than hearing peers in any formal sense. This question is important in part because we know that for both hearing and deaf children, those who are more reflective tend to have better academic achievement scores in school than those children who are more impulsive. The few studies that have been done in this area have suggested that deaf children of deaf parents may be more reflective than deaf children with hearing parents, that deaf children enrolled in early intervention programmes will show better impulse control than those without such intervention, and that deaf children who learn sign language earlier in life may be less likely to be impulsive than those who learned to sign later. There is no evidence that I am aware of, however, linking reflectivity or impulsivity to the presence or absence of hearing. In fact, the only study I know of which actually compared deaf and hearing children is a recent one that I conducted with Victoria Everhart. In that investigation, we compared hearing and deaf children, all of whom had hearing parents, in three different age groups: seven to eight years, ten to eleven years, and thirteen to fourteen years. Our test of impulsivity-reflectivity for all three groups was a standard one, involving tracing paths through mazes. The results were clear: There were no significant differences in impulsivity-reflectivity between the deaf and hearing students in any of the three age groups.

It is difficult to say whether impulsive behaviour on school tasks results in poor performance, or poor performance and frustration in school lead to impulsive behaviour. In any case, given the evidence showing positive relations between (1) early language experience and reflective problem solving, (2) parental involvement with children and academic success, and (3) reflectivity and academic success, it seems safe to conclude that effective communication and involvement of parents in their deaf children's schooling are important for avoiding impulsivity. Impulsivity is not a consequence of hearing loss, but there are avoidable hurdles in growing up deaf that can lead to impulsive behaviour in some children and may have implications for later psychological functioning. The first goal should be to prevent such problems in childhood.

Psychological Functioning in Adolescence and Adulthood

It has sometimes been said that if deaf people did have greater emotional difficulties than hearing people, it would be understandable. After all, some deaf children grow up in homes where there is little acceptance of their hearing losses and less understanding of their special needs. Surely they would be expected to have some anger or to show other effects of such an upbringing. Even in more accepting families, there may be emotional consequences to a lack of effective communication between parents and children. In stressful situations, deaf children may not fully understand what is happening, what is wrong, who was bad, or what their role is in the episode. Similarly, the constant frustrations of not being able to communicate with the hearing-oriented worlds of education and business surely must have some impact on deaf adults, especially when someone is the only deaf person in a company or a small community.

There are also misconceptions by hearing professionals concerning deaf people that may lead to erroneous conclusions about psychological functioning. Difficulties of diagnosis because of communication barriers are well documented. Relatively few qualified therapists are fluent signers, and most deaf people who want counseling or therapy need a sign language interpreter to assist either them or the therapist, depending on your point of view. Some years ago, a deaf acquaintance pointed out to me that it is difficult enough to discuss serious personal problems with a psychotherapist, but sharing them at the same time with an interpreter who may be a neighbor and who works with all of your friends can be very intimidating. Certified interpreters have a very strict code of ethics about such matters, but the situation still can be an awkward one.

Research has shown that the quality of a therapist's sign language skills can directly influence the range of psychological symptoms identified in children and adolescents. In addition to the simple language barrier, most psychotherapists are unfamiliar with deaf people and Deaf culture, and may not understand social and emotional differences between them and hearing clients. This situation can result in the failure of a deaf person to benefit from the therapeutic situation, but it occasionally will lead to misdiagnoses as well. For example, a doctoral student in clinical psychology once came to me concerning a deaf adolescent girl with whom he was working. He was beginning to think that the girl was paranoid, because she reported that her parents were talking about her "behind her back," using spoken language. She also apparently refused to make eye contact with him during their sessions. This was the student's first deaf client, and he was seeking some books or articles on mental health in deaf people, but I sent him back to the girl rather than to the library. He eventually discovered that, as I suggested, the girl's parents actually *were* talking about her when she was present. It seems that neither parent could sign very well, and they had never really discussed their daughter's future with her. Often, however, she would do something that would start the parents talking about their plans and hopes for her future. They would look at her during those conversations, but when she would ask what they were talking about, they would say, "Nothing." Apparently, they were trying to avoid having to explain their parental concerns, and they never realized how much anxiety they were causing their daughter. As for eye contact, moving the interpreter to a seat beside the therapist rather than beside the client solved the problem.

As in other areas, access to mental health services for deaf people is improving in this country, as are the opportunities for deaf people to enter the mental health field. At the University of Rochester School of Medicine, for example, there is a programme that provides doctoral-level training for clinical psychology students who are deaf. Most of those students will later become therapists themselves, with both deaf and hearing clients. Along with other deaf and hearing psychologists, some of them will also conduct research to better understand mental health and mental illness in people who are deaf.

Much of what we currently know about mental health among deaf people comes from relatively old studies, including a famous statewide study in New York in the early 1960s, about which many articles and books have been written. In general, the New York Project suggested that the more severe forms of mental illness, such as psychoses, bipolar disorder, and schizophrenia, are equally frequent among hearing and deaf populations. That finding has been confirmed several times since then in both the U.S. and England.

Other studies have suggested that deaf people may be less likely than hearing people to be mentally retarded or to suffer from severe depression. One study conducted with college students, in contrast, indicated that deaf students were considerably more likely than hearing students to report *mild* depression. What makes this most interesting is that both deaf and hearing students who reported that their mothers were overprotective during their childhood were more likely to report being depressed as young adults. Insofar as we know that hearing mothers of deaf children tend to be relatively overprotective, the greater incidence of mild depression among the deaf students perhaps follows quite naturally. At the same time, this result can serve as another reminder to parents of the need for normal and natural parenting of deaf children.

The finding that deaf college students might experience mild depression more frequently than hearing college students is consistent with findings suggesting that deaf students in mainstream settings may feel isolated and lonely compared to students in special programmes. Similarly, there is some evidence that deaf adults and adolescents may be prone to more posttraumatic stress disorders. For deaf people who are not involved with the larger Deaf community, there may be considerable social isolation that leads to difficulty when parents or other people who are close die or move away. These feelings may be reflected in either depression or posttraumatic stress reactions. Generally speaking, however, even though deaf children might have more frequent behaviour problems than hearing children, there do not appear to be any serious, long-term psychological effects of such behaviour. Some studies have even suggested that growing up deaf might make individuals more resistant to psychological problems. Parents might take some consolation in such findings, but there is still a variety of practical issues to make raising a deaf child a challenge for most people.

Summary

Childhood and adolescence are a time of growth, as personality and social skills emerge from interactions of children with others in their environments. Regardless of whether children are hearing or deaf, they seek the same kinds of emotional and practical support, learn the same kinds of behaviours, and are influenced by the same kinds of factors. Communication plays an important role during these years, as children learn their roles as members of a family, a gender, a community, and a culture. Deaf children who have access to other people's interactions and explanations for behaviours better understand social dynamics. Those who have access to social rules and can consider the perspectives of others develop the moral codes of others who they try to emulate.

In early childhood, parents are the primary source of implicit and explicit teaching about social expectations. As children get older, siblings, playmates, and adults outside of the home take on greater roles in this regard. During the school years, deaf and hearing students seek to be accepted by their peer groups and adopt the values, preferences, and behaviours of children and adults who are their role models. Modeling teaches children about appropriate ways of behaving. They are more likely to model people who are perceived as similar to them, and over time they become more like those models. Having higher self-esteem and a sense of control better enables children to think for themselves and make good decisions about how to act and who to emulate.

Families play a relatively larger role in deaf children's socialization than in hearing children's socialization, if for no other reason than that deaf children are likely to have a relatively greater proportion of their social interactions with family members than are hearing children. Siblings generally have an important role in childhood, providing a safe opportunity to try out new roles and get feedback on behaviour. Deaf children, in particular, benefit from siblings both emotionally and in terms of communication skills.

Other deaf children in residential schools can play similar roles, and that environment provides deaf children with lifelong friends and social-emotional support. Residential schools do not lead deaf children away from their families, but provide them with an important kind of social support that they cannot get at home. There they find children of various ages who are like them and who accept them as brothers and sisters. Meanwhile, deaf adults who work in residential schools can serve as important role models, much like aunts and uncles, promoting accurate self-images and higher self-esteem.

Deaf students often show more behaviour problems in school than hearing students. These can result from inconsistent social experiences, misunderstandings about social rules, and frustration with lack of communication. Behaviour that might be referred to as *impulsive,* however, should not be confused with the psychological sense of *impulsivity,* referring to problem-solving strategies. Contrary to many unsubstantiated claims, there is no evidence to suggest that deaf children or adults are any more likely than hearing peers to have impulsive cognitive styles. At the same time, better communication skills and consistent parenting seem to lead to more reflective, successful problem solving.

Deaf children and adults also do not appear much different from hearing peers in terms of the incidence of mental health problems. More serious illnesses are equally frequent in deaf and hearing populations. Deaf people may be slightly more prone to some mild disorders, but they appear to be less prone to others. Full access to competent mental health services is difficult for deaf people, usually requiring the services of a sign language interpreter in addition to the barriers faced by hearing people. Further, mental health professionals need to become better informed about social and cultural differences between deaf and hearing people if they are to provide effective services and avoid misdiagnoses and lost opportunities.

11

Communication and Interaction with Deaf Infants

In this chapter, we summarize and offer theoretical and clinical interpretations of findings from various analyses of mother and infant behaviours during face-to-face interactions in the first year of life. These results are based on a longitudinal study of deaf and hearing mothers and infants carried out at Gallaudet University beginning in 1988 under the leadership of Dr. Kathryn Meadow-Orlans. Having worked and published in the field of childhood deafness for many years, Dr. Meadow-Orlans recognized the need for greater understanding of the needs and capabilities of deaf infants in order for early interventionists and caregivers to provide the most appropriate environments for these children. In addition, she was aware of the importance of including deaf parents in such investigations in order to gain insights about their natural strategies for interacting with deaf children to optimize visual attention and to maintain communication without relying primarily on vocalizations for this purpose. This resulted in funding for one of the largest studies to date comparing mother-infant dyads in all four hearing status combinations and included gathering observational and interview data over the first 18 months of the child's life.

Several questions were of primary concern to the analyses reported here:

What maternal behaviours support and maintain successful interactive dialogue with a deaf infant?

What characterizes effective responsiveness with a deaf infant for whom access to parental vocalizations is compromised?

In what ways do parents, whether deaf or hearing, intuitively compensate for differences in perceptual abilities in deaf and hearing infants?

From a clinical perspective, are there qualitative differences in the early interactions between deaf and hearing infants and their parents that might be predictive of long-term consequences?

Face-to-face encounters between parents and infants are frequent and expected occurrences in the lives of most families in the Western world. These early interactions provide ample opportunity for researchers to observe the mutuality and reciprocity thought to be so important during parent — infant exchanges. Behaviours that are often used as indices of effective interactions, such as maintaining or breaking eye contact, motherese and infant cooing or babbling, touching and comforting, and expressions of joy or displeasure, have all been documented as part of this study and will be summarized below.

Applications To Deaf Infants

Papous+?ek developed the theory of intuitive patenting in which they describe the skillful yet often overlooked communication strategies used by parents when interacting with their babies — nonconscious behaviours that in fact are ideally suited to support the human infant's natural inclination to adapt to its social world. In addition to furthering our understanding of typical parent — child exchanges, this perspective also has the potential to illuminate our perceptions of parenting in exceptional populations. As a guiding model behind the current research, intuitive parenting has thus been applied to variations in parenting behaviours that may be related to deafness on either side of the dyad, parent or child, but can have important consequences regardless of the origin. Of course, interactive difficulties can result when disruptions occur in those subtle parenting behaviours that normally require very little thought and yet are necessary to sustain and enhance the parent-infant relationship. On the other hand, this theory also helps researchers become more observant and aware of the many nonconscious ways in which parents may be compensating quite appropriately for a child's hearing loss and may therefore lead to useful insights for early intervention personnel and educators of deaf children.

One example can be seen in the ways deaf parents modify their sign language when communicating with an infant. The patterns noticed by Erting, Prezioso and Hynes, for example, are strikingly parallel to those documented in vocal motherese: Signs are simplified and highly repetitious but also more influenced by the partner's gaze than sign communication among deaf adults. In other words, when the infant is looking at the mother, her signing is likely to occur near her face rather than within the larger space used among adult signing partners; when the infant looks away or at another object, the deaf adult is more likely to sign near the object or to reach into the infant's visual field for effective communication. This finding has been supported by similar observations in other cultures, such as reported by Masataka in regard to Japanese Sign Language directed to deaf infants. Spencer and Lederberg also provided evidence of syntactic simplification, visual displacement of signs, and use of shorter signed utterances to younger deaf children.

Compensations when an Infant is Deaf

The developmental and educational delays experienced by some deaf children may be the result of difficulties hearing parents and teachers have in making the necessary adaptations or providing the scaffolding needed to help transmit knowledge and skills to the deaf child. This Vygotskian emphasis on the dialectical nature and social imbeddedness of the child's early interactive experiences also informs the research of Jamieson. Observing hearing parents with deaf preschoolers, she found that even after effectively establishing eye contact prior to giving instructions, these parents often proceeded as if the child's auditory capacity was completely intact. As a result of using a simultaneous auditory-visual style of teaching, these parents essentially made very little adaptation to the deaf child's perceptual and learning needs. As Jamieson noted, "It appears that hearing adults, both parents and teachers, face a tremendous challenge in trying to unlearn habitual communication patterns and to replace them with patterns more appropriate to the visual mode".

These conclusions may also be relevant to interactions with the younger deaf subjects who have been the focus of our own investigations. However, an earlier study by Wedell-Monnig and Lumley stressed the early visual compensation observed between deaf infants and their hearing parents, noting that this may in fact contribute to delayed diagnosis if hearing parents misinterpret the infant's heightened visual sensitivity as response to environmental sounds or voices. That is, these parents may achieve a level of communication with their deaf baby through eye contact, facial expressions, and touch, especially in the early months. According to Wedell-Monnig and Lumley, however, a "common symbolic language" may still be missing in these dyads, with potentially deleterious long-term consequence.

A number of researchers reported that hearing mothers tend to be highly directive with deaf children and as a result may not be sufficiently sensitive to the child's need to explore the surroundings visually. As Spencer observed, overly directive efforts to elicit and sustain a deaf infant's attention preclude the parent's sensitive responsiveness to the baby's cues. The same authors showed that deaf mothers with deaf infants are more likely to wait for the infant to look at them before signing or responding to the child's focus of attention. Such coordination of gaze patterns is of particular importance for the deaf child who must rely on vision for both receptive language input and for exploration of the external world.

Deaf parents with deaf children may provide important insights for hearing parents and early interventionists regarding optimal strategies for communicating with a deaf infant. Having grown up themselves without hearing, these deaf parents may in fact model intuitive parenting in ways that have to date been largely unexplored. Even deaf parents who do not use a formal system of sign communication appear to incorporate gestures extensively during spoken interactions with their deaf children; de Villiers, Bibeau, Helliwell, and Clare interpret this as an unconscious facilitation of the child's access to parental language input. Similarly, Spencer et al. report that dyads in which both mother and child are deaf often utilize strategies rarely observed among hearing partners, but that result in highly responsive and contingent interaction patterns.

Some of the more varied and multi modal forms of stimulation observed particularly by deaf parents in our own analyses include highly animated facial expressions, visual-gestural games (and of course sign communication), and frequent, vigorous tactile contact. Furthermore, many hearing mothers with deaf infants also become quickly adept at enhancing their usual visual and tactile stimulation. This represents an important adjustment by hearing mothers to the heightened visual needs of a deaf child, even though it may not occur immediately or automatically. (We note for example, that these adjustments appeared more frequently among the mothers of 9-month-old deaf infants in our study than when the infants were younger.) Many infants had only recently been diagnosed as deaf at the time of our 6-month observation, so their hearing mothers may have required some time to accept this news, understand its implications, and begin to modify their behaviours in ways that better met the deaf infant's perceptual and attention needs. A variety of parental modifications in other modalities add to the list of intuitive behaviours observed in parents with deaf children or parents who themselves are deaf, as elaborated on next.

Maternal Vocalizations

It is difficult indeed for caregivers not to respond to the coos, babbles, and pleasant vocalizations of a human infant. These social signals typically elicit imitative and nurturing responses from caregivers and often lead to some of the infant's first lessons in turn taking with a social partner. Vocal exchanges thus play an important role in furthering and refining interactions between parents and their offspring, even before infants are themselves able to imitate the language to which they are exposed. A deaf child with hearing parents may, at least until the parents are able to make informed decisions about their preferred method of communication, be affected by the lack of experience with an accessible language system; the effect may extend to the socio-emotional realm, with negative consequences in areas such as affect regulation, self-awareness, and self-esteem.

Parental vocalizations clearly influence and shape the emerging language skills of infants, but their significance is even more far reaching. Early vocal exchanges also provide important affective information and cues to help the infant identify significant figures in the social world. As Fernald asserted, the characteristics of motherese, evident in so many languages and cultures, make speech particularly salient for human infants and contribute in important ways to the infant's development of meaning, particularly the understanding of affective messages. According to Kirkman and Cross, "Deaf children, even more than hearing children, need to have their attempts at vocalization reinforced by incorporating them into the development of an affectional bond; such imitative babbling has both linguistic and emotional ramifications".

In an analysis of the acoustical patterns of both deaf and hearing mothers in the Gallaudet study , we were surprised by the extent to which Deaf mothers modified their own vocalizations depending on the hearing status of their infant. In other words, and lending further support to the application of intuitive parenting concepts to this population, it is apparent that deaf mothers use their voices more and incorporate more features of motherese when interacting with a hearing baby. On the other hand, it is the hearing mothers with deaf infants who appear to exaggerate their pitch excursions the most, as if to compensate for the infant's limited auditory perception. It is important to add, however, that concomitant facial expressions, head movements, and use of other sensory channels while vocalizing may also function to make these maternal utterances more salient even to a deaf child.

Another finding from this study, indicating that hearing mothers increase their use of vocal games when interacting with a deaf baby, is consistent with this view. Again, this demonstrates parental efforts to make vocal communication more salient and accessible to an infant with a hearing loss. *Vocal games,* as we define them, typically involve animated visual and often tactile cues and thus represent an important compensatory adaptation when interacting with a deaf baby. In these interactions, parental vocalizations are augmented by exaggerated play with sounds, perhaps accompanied by visual stimulation such as in peek-a-boo games, as well as animated facial expressions particularly when eye contact is achieved. Vocal games are by definition multi modal events and therefore more easily perceived by the deaf infant. It is encouraging to see that hearing mothers are already using such strategies with their 9-month-old deaf infants.

Tactile Contact

Numerous researchers have demonstrated the importance of touch during interactive dialogues between caregiver and child. In addition to soothing or comforting a fussy baby, tactile contact contributes to the child's emerging awareness of boundaries between self and other, and to the development of reciprocity and communication skills in a variety of modalities. However, relatively little is known about the patterns of this early tactile contact that may contribute to its effectiveness, characteristics across different cultures, or the extent to which caregivers rely on touch in various contexts.

Gusella, Muir, and Tronick instructed mothers to use vocal and facial expressions but no touching while interacting with their 3-month-old infants. Results indicated a gradual decrease in the time infants spent smiling and gazing at their mothers. That is, when touch was removed from the interaction altogether, mothers were less able to maintain their infant's pleasure and participation. Stack and Muir also observed infant smiling and gaze behaviours while eliminating the mother's facial affect and vocalizations rather than touch; in this case, the role of tactile contact took on an even greater significance. That is, mothers resorted to more active patterns of touch in their efforts to maintain the infant's positive affect and eye contact.

As mentioned earlier, studies of spoken language directed to infants have increased researchers' awareness of the variety and complexity of parental behaviours — in the case of speech, the patterns of melodic contours, pitch ranges, rhythms, and repetitions all contribute to the infant's heightened responsiveness to motherese. We examined parallels in the ways in which deaf and hearing parents touch their babies, focusing on duration of tactile contact during interactions and characteristics such as intensity and active or passive types of touch.

Dyads in which one or both partners are deaf offer a unique opportunity to observe the possible functions of touch in terms of optimizing or enhancing communication when the auditory modality is limited. In these dyads, touch may play an even more important function than usual as it is often necessary for eliciting visual attention, alerting the child that signed communication is forthcoming, or maintaining contact and providing reassurance even when the deaf child has looked away. Deaf mothers, having grown up with the need to rely on multiple sensory modalities for communication, provide interesting insights into the use of tactile contact during early interactions with either a deaf or hearing infant; in either case, the child needs to be attentive to various kinds of nonauditory communication occurring within the deaf family. Such naturally occurring adaptations provide impressive examples of parents' nonconscious compensatory behaviours that support the attentional needs and the emerging interactive skills of the young infant.

Mothers with deaf infants appear to use somewhat more active patterns of tactile contact with their infants, an adjustment that represents an important means of intuitively compensating for an infant's hearing loss. This use of a highly salient sensory channel for eliciting and maintaining visual attention is particularly necessary for a child learning to communicate in a visual-gestural modality. That is, touch may be even more important when a visual-gestural mode of communication is being used as it frequently serves to regain the infant's visual attention to a signing partner. Analyses reveal that deaf mothers with deaf infants in our sample emphasized short duration touches with infants at both 6 and 9 months of age. Brief episodes of tactile contact such as this appear to be examples of a tap-sign strategy used to alert the infant to forthcoming sign communication.

Clearly there are numerous subtle adjustments that parents make without any conscious awareness or planning but that in many cases may serve to support the perceptual, linguistic, and cognitive capabilities of a child without hearing. Of course the parent-child relationship is not a one-way street, and there may be equally subtle cues on the part of the infant that in turn help to instruct the relatively naive parent about strategies that are effective, pleasurable, and which the child would like to have repeated. In the process of learning how to communicate with each other, parents must also be sensitive to this feedback from the infant. We now turn our attention to some of the behavioral contrasts we observed between deaf and hearing infants, highlighting those that were somewhat unexpected or particularly important for parents who have not had previous experiences with deafness.

What Infants Contribute to these Interactions

Repetitive Movements

We observed that infants who are deaf, as well as those whose parents are deaf, spend more time engaging in repetitive physical activity such as kicking, rhythmically extending and flexing the arms or hands, and so forth. One possible interpretation is consistent with the idea of attunement as described by Stern in which the similar activity levels reflect a sharing by deaf mothers and their infants of each others' level of physical engagement during these early interactions. Of course, the deaf mothers we observed were frequently signing to their infants, so their infants may have been responding by mirroring this repetitive activity — that is, by frequently moving their own hands and arms. This activity by the infant may then be interpreted as a precursor to sign communication and responded to with praise and encouragement. In fact, this may occur regardless of the infants' hearing status: Those who are born into deaf families will most likely grow up using sign language at home, even if they themselves are able to hear.

Eye Gaze

Maintaining eye contact or visual attention to the social partner is of particular importance for a child who is deaf or for one who is interacting with a deaf caregiver. As Robson pointed out, visual flxation and following are among the earliest volitional acts of the infant. The visual modality allows the infant to control sensory input by closing the eyes or looking away so as to eliminate external sensory input even within the first months of life.

In our studies, we found that 6-month-old infants with deaf, signing mothers alternate their gaze back and forth between mother and the surroundings more frequently but sustain their gaze to their social partner longer than do those with hearing mothers. By contrast, infants at this age whose mothers are hearing spend more time looking around the room. By age 9 months, it is apparent that hearing infants with hearing mothers look away from the mother most frequently during interactions. It should be remembered, however, that for this group eye contact is least important to the success of an interaction as hearing infants can access spoken language input regardless of their focus of visual attention.

Self-Regulation

Infant self-regulatory behaviours offer important insights into the child's ability to modulate responses to distress, over-stimulation, or displeasure and may also reveal the degree to which an infant perceives a particular experience as distressful. Using the maternal still-face paradigm, we compared these regulatory mechanisms in both deaf and hearing infants, revealing some interesting differences. We noted, for example, that 6-month-old deaf infants display more self-regulatory behaviour during actual face-to-face interactions with a hearing mother than do infants in the other groups; however, these same infants decrease this behaviour during the still-face episode, which is when infants usually increase their self-regulation strategies. By 9 months of age, both groups of deaf babies (that is, with either hearing or deaf mothers) spend more time in self-regulatory activities in general than do their hearing peers. As would normally be expected, 9-month-old infants in all hearing status groups increase their use of these strategies during the still-face episode as compared to the interactive episodes.

Another interesting finding is that infants with deaf mothers appear to be the most distressed during the still-face episode, as seen in greater displays of negative affect. Deaf mothers themselves are often highly active and animated with their infants and may thus be more entertaining and engaging as partners; if so, then the still-face episode that disrupts this responsiveness may be a greater deviation for the infant, therefore eliciting a more negative reaction. Infants with hearing mothers, on the other hand, appeared to increase their protestations more gradually over the three episodes we observed.

Infant Vocalizations

Deaf as well as hearing infants produce vocal sounds such as cooing. In the Gallaudet study, for example, we found essentially no differences in the amount of effectively positive or negative vocalizations emitted by deaf or hearing 9-month-old infants. In the presence of caregivers, these sounds often initiate a dialogue, with parents responding as if the baby is already a conversational partner. With hearing parents, early dialogues require listening to the infant, imitating or prompting the infant to vocalize again, and pausing or waiting for the infant to take a turn. The hearing infant therefore experiences what Papous+?ek refer to as a modeling/imitative frame, receiving feedback and reinforcement for vocalizing and encouragement for the further development of conversational skills. There are innumerable opportunities for hearing infants to expand their vocal repertoire in response to spoken linguistic feedback. This process includes not just the imitation of language units but learning how to control relevant aspects of sound production such as tone of voice, melodic contours, volume, temporal patterns, and consonant-like sounds. Both infant and caregiver must be viewed as part of a variable and dynamic system, as proposed by von Bertalanffy in which every utterance as well as every pause has potential meaning.

For hearing parents, the diagnosis of deafness in a child can have a profound and unsettling effect on their confidence as parents, particularly in their ability to communicate effectively: "The diagnosis of deafness forces hearing parents abruptly to confront basic differences between themselves and their child, with the knowledge that there is a fundamental way in which they cannot share that child's experience". In a more recent study, Gregory observed that hearing parents sometimes refrained from speaking to their deaf child, assuming there was simply no point and finding that spoken communication was difficult. As we described previously however, many important and salient features of early communication with an infant co-occur with language input and may be of particular significance during interactions with a deaf child.

Clinical Implications

This section focuses on the clinical impact that the specific maternal and infant behaviours under investigation in our research can have on the quality of parent-infant interactions, particularly when deafness is a factor. Ultimately, the parent-infant relationship as a whole is affected when there is a perturbation or situation on either side that interrupts the normal sequence of development or the positive flow of social and emotional exchange between the two partners. Maternal behaviours that appear to compensate for sensory modality differences between themselves and their infants are particularly relevant for early intervention with clinically at risk parent-infant dyads.

The clinical observation of parent-infant interactions requires a skilled eye that is attuned to the dialectical give and take inherent in a family systems approach, as described earlier. It is difficult to conceive of other instances in behavioral science research in which the saying "the whole is greater than the sum of its parts" could be more true, regardless of an individual's perspective as observer, child participant, or parent participant. Even the brief observations used in our research reveal many examples of well adapted interactions and the multiple ways, both subtle and overt, in which each partner responds to and shapes the other's behaviour. Gradually, behaviours coded as discrete acts of parents and infants merge to form impressions of signals and reactions that appear to be either smooth and well organized, or disconnected and frustrating on both sides. Researchers and clinicians alike may notice the distinct subjective experience of no longer observing individual actions and reactions but rather the fluid psychological motion of the dyadic unit as a whole.

Many clinicians hold the belief that disturbances in the early parent-child relationship significantly influence future development of the young child. The strength of this belief is reflected in the fact that relationship disorders is one of the five axes listed in the *Diagnostic Classification of Mental Health and Developmental Disorders of Infancy and Early Childhood*. The *Diagnostic Classification: 0-3* manual indicates that formal clinical assessment of the parent-infant relationship should involve an evaluation of the behavioral quality of the interactions, the affective tone of the interactions, and the degree of psychological involvement. We stress that these features of parent-infant interactions are important regardless of whether deafness is a factor. However, our research findings primarily address each of these areas of parent-infant interactions within the context of a deaf partner in the dyad.

Behavioral Quality of the Relationship

The behavioral quality of the parent-infant relationship includes aspects of mutual responsiveness, sensitivity, and emotional regulation similar to some of the dynamics observed in our own research. The concept of intuitive patenting offers important insights regarding the optimal patterns that clinicians seek to observe, quantify, and describe in their attempts to rate the behavioral quality of any parent-infant relationship.

As previously discussed, this perspective addresses communication strategies that parents use intuitively to meet the adaptive needs of their infants. The particular features of a parent's communication style that may be expressed for this purpose are far ranging and complex. Nonetheless, it can be said that the nonconscious aim of the deployment of intuitive patenting strategies is to support and enhance the behavioral quality and the adaptive needs of the parent-infant relationship. The question then becomes in what ways do parents intuitively adjust their own behaviours so as to support their infant's early adaptive needs, particularly when either the parent or the infant is deaf.

It is difficult to measure and operationalize the rather abstract qualities such as sensitivity, reciprocity, and responsiveness that reportedly contribute to the behavioral quality of the parent-infant relationship. However, our research findings suggest that there may be a constellation of behaviours that have particular relevance for operationalizing these concepts for deaf infants. The results imply that these particular maternal and infant behaviours may contribute significantly to the fluid functioning and reciprocal exchanges with the dyad in these cases. When this occurs, state regulation, emotional predictability, and a generally positive affective tone should follow.

Nevertheless, it is to be expected that there will also be cases in which these compensatory behaviours do not appear, perhaps due to stress or depression or lack of support experienced by the parent. Our results lead us to conclude that the behavioral quality of the early relationship between a deaf infant and hearing parent may be enhanced by education awareness, information dissemination, and of course modeling techniques. For example, playback of carefully selected videotaped observations, drawing the mother's attention to specific moments when she did achieve mutual attention and shared positive interactions with her baby, may improve her sense of self-efficacy and effectiveness as a parent with a deaf child. On the other hand, showing hearing parents videotaped examples of deaf parents' intuitive modifications of their behaviours, such as signed motherese or tapping the baby before a signed communication, may also be an effective intervention strategy. It is particularly important in this case, however, to do so with a great deal of care and awareness of differences between deaf and hearing cultures in regard to such matters as personal space and tactile contact during interactions.

Affective Tone: Affect is a clinical term that refers to the communication of meaning beyond the physical display of a feeling state. The affective tone of the parent-infant relationship is of critical importance because it determines the overall mood of the dyadic exchanges. The clinical concern regarding the affective tone of the parent-infant relationship is one of intensity and the degree to which intense affect serves to dysregulate the quality of the interactions.

For example, a dyadic exchange between parent and infant may involve behaviours such as verbal teasing and tickling, initially leading to positive affect such as laughing or squealing. However, if these exchanges remain intense over time, the effect can be *dysregulation:* Very similar actions now take on a negative quality, better characterized as verbal and physical intrusiveness and resulting in negative affective exchanges — grimacing, scowling, or crying on the part of the baby. The result is the establishment of a negative or hostile mood. This is pertinent to some findings regarding hearing mothers with deaf children indicating a tendency to be more directive and even intrusive when compared to mothers with hearing children. Although this may be a natural result of the parents' efforts to maintain attention and elicit responses from the deaf child, clearly the possible outcome of negative affect during these early interactions is neither desirable nor rewarding for either social partner.

The most relevant findings from our research regarding the area of affective tone involve maternal facial and affective expressiveness, infant affective responses, and maternal and infant vocalizations. Our findings suggest, for example, that parents modify their facial and affective expressiveness and their vocalizations in response to the hearing status of their children — in particular, appearing more animated and incorporating a greater variety of modalities during communication with deaf infants. Again, the intuitive parenting model and the clinical framework for examination of parent-infant relationships suggest that parental adjustments are made to meet the adaptive needs of the infant and thereby support and enhance the behavioral qualities of the relationship overall. In this case, animated behaviours that serve to make the mother's communication and play more salient to a deaf child appear to be highly appropriate modifications of the usual parental repertoire.

Psychological Involvement: Psychological involvement as a concept applied to the assessment of parent-infant relationships focuses on the impact that "parental attitudes and perceptions of the child" can have on the relationship . The literature in infancy studies is replete with findings addressing the effects of parental attitudes and expectations on child development in various domains of functioning, including cognitive and motor abilities.

Although it is difficult to operationalize the construct of psychological involvement for the purpose of assessing the parent-infant relationship, we believe our research has in fact succeeded in providing a unique example of how this might be done.

Our findings involving repetitive movements by deaf babies, and the distinctly different meaning attributed to these movements by deaf mothers as compared to their hearing counterparts, have strong implications for the concept of psychological involvement. As previously discussed, we observed that deaf mothers tend to interpret their infants' repetitive hand and arm movements as a precursor to sign communication, regardless of the infant's hearing status. As a result, deaf mothers respond to this type of rhythmic activity with praise and encouragement, whereas hearing mothers do not (hearing mothers, in fact, reported a somewhat negative interpretation in which they perceived this physical activity as a sign of their infant's hyperactivity). This is a case in which the consequences of even a subtle behaviour on the part of the infant can play a significant role in the subsequent emergence of these cues into more recognizable forms of communication.

The most direct explanation for these differential responses to repetitive movements is rooted in the varying life experiences of deaf and hearing mothers and in the way these experiences affect their perceptions and expectations of their infants' behaviours. Deaf mothers with deaf children do not typically experience the same struggles and conflicts reported by hearing mothers with deaf children in regard to methods of communication, schooling, or cultural identity. Even in the case of deaf mothers with hearing infants, there is likely to be encouragement of the use of gestures and manual forms of communication, assuming that in both families the primary language will be visual-gestural. The many opposing philosophies and opinions about education of children who are deaf present a confusing and often stressful picture to hearing parents. It is almost inevitable that this bewilderment will in some way be communicated to the young child, even if it is only in the parent's hesitancy to respond to the infant's early use of gestures to communicate needs, desires, and feelings. As Spencer and Lederberg noted, many of the hearing parents in this same study changed their minds about a preferred mode of communication with their deaf infant during the course of our observations. It seems reasonable to assume that this ambivalence alone must have some impact in terms of potential disruption of the compensatory parental behaviours that seem so important to establishing effective communicative exchanges with a deaf infant.

Summary

From the 1960s to the 1990s, there has been a vast amount of research on parent-child interactions, with most investigation focusing on presumably normal mother and child dyads. Some questions and insights resulting from these efforts, such as the degree to which an infant is securely attached to the caregiver, have received much attention not only in the academic literature but also in the popular press. Society generally acknowledges the impact of the caregiver-child relationship on the developing child. Increasingly, the influence of fathers, siblings, and out of home caregivers is also being examined, so that gradually a more complete picture of the socio-emotional world of the infant is emerging.

As part of this expanding knowledge, research must necessarily include those dyads and families in which one or more individuals experience some kind of disability or challenge to their normal functioning. Although many Western societies have made impressive strides in accommodating and including persons with disabilities in all areas of life – schools, the work place, athletic competition, and so forth – there is still relatively little comprehensive data regarding the early development of children who are deaf or who grow up in families with deaf parents. In this chapter, we take some initial steps to rectify this situation by providing an overview of some of the most interesting results of our observations comparing deaf and hearing infants in their first year of life as they interact with their hearing or deaf mothers.

12

Impact of Child Deafness on Mother Interaction

The presence of a deaf child has considerable impact on a hearing family. As early as infancy, there are reports of disruption in the development of reciprocal interactions between hearing mothers and their deaf infants. A few investigators have found these differences minimal, but their findings are atypical.

> *Most research investigating the impact of deafness on early mother-child interaction has compared hearing mothers and their deaf infants or toddlers to hearing children and hearing mothers. Those studies, almost without exception, found hearing/deaf interactions problematic compared to those of hearing/hearing dyads.*

These quotes are representative of the prevailing view of the impact of child deafness on early hearing mother-deaf child interaction, but the picture they convey may be unduly ominous. Because of our training, behavioral scientists tend to focus on results that show significant differences between groups, perhaps because behavioral scientists know the null hypothesis cannot be proven. However, this may result in a more negative picture than exists in reality. The goal of this chapter is to review research on interactions between hearing mothers and deaf toddlers to identify positive, as well as negative, aspects of adaptations by hearing parents with deaf toddlers during the second year of life. Strengths, adaptive behaviour, and signs of resiliency observed in hearing mother-deaf child interaction are noted, as well as aspects of early interaction that are problematic or detrimental to development.

This goal, to identify strengths and weaknesses in the relationship between deaf children and their hearing mothers, is a particularly appropriate topic for this volume because it follows in the tradition of the trail-blazing book *Sound and Sign* by Schlesinger and Meadow. We are most concerned with deaf children born to hearing parents because they represent the vast majority of deaf children. From the late 1970s to the late 1990s, earlier identification of deaf children, particularly those of hearing parents, and stronger legal requirements for early intervention have resulted in their enrollment in early intervention programmes at younger ages than ever before. Before the age of 3 years, many early intervention services focus on supporting and facilitating the child's interactions with his or her parents. Professionals in these early intervention programmes clearly are limited in the time they have with parents; they need to identify those aspects of the mother-child interaction requiring intervention and those developing along a typical pathway in order to provide the most useful parent education in a timely and cost-effective manner.

It is our contention that understanding the positive aspects of interactions between hearing mothers and their deaf children is as important as identifying areas in which deaf children and their hearing mothers experience problems. By depicting hearing mothers in the literature as deficient in their interactions with their deaf children, researchers bias professionals working with these mothers to focus on negative aspects of hearing mother-deaf child interaction. A balance of fostering hearing mothers' natural competencies to communicate with and meet the needs of their deaf children, along with identifying aspects of mother-child interaction that need modification, is most likely to prepare mothers to benefit from intervention programmes.

Three methods have been used to identify strengths and weaknesses in mother – child interaction. First, the majority of research compares hearing mother – deaf child dyads with hearing mother-hearing child dyads. This comparison allows an individual to draw conclusions about the ways in which hearing mother-deaf child interaction is impacted by the child's hearing loss. Differences in dyadic functioning are seen as strengths or weaknesses depending on whether they are facilitative of development. Some of the differences may be positive adaptations to the child's needs, whereas others may be seen as areas of concern.

Second, deaf child-deaf mother dyads are included in some studies, providing an opportunity to tease apart the impact of hearing loss and the lack of a common communication system on the interaction between parent and child. Studies including Dd dyads are important to developmental theory because they also allow researchers to determine if communication modality has a significant impact on development. More importantly, from an interventionist's point of view, the observation of interaction patterns in Dd dyads provides a model of the kinds of positive adaptations possible when parents interact with their deaf children. As a result, these studies can be useful in interpreting the strengths and weaknesses in Hd dyadic interaction.

Third, characteristics of the Hd dyadic interaction can be related to outcome measures to determine which aspects are related to a positive developmental outcome. Cause and effect cannot be determined in correlational research, but these studies serve as a starting point from which important variables can be identified for later empirical research.

The review of research presented in this chapter relies heavily on two longitudinal studies that complement each other. The Infancy Research Group at Gallaudet observed four groups of infants: Hd, Hh, Dd, and Dh dyads at 9, 12, and 18 months. Lederberg, Everhart, Mobley and Prezbindowki observed Hd and Hh dyads at 22 months and 3 and 4 years of age. Thus, the studies have the potential for allowing us to capture the impact of child deafness on hearing mother-deaf child interaction from infancy through preschool. In this chapter, we primarily focus on the findings during the second year of life to gain a more complete description of the impact of child deafness at this young age. For years, Meadow-Orlans and Lederberg have been puzzled about why their results conflict in a number of ways, with Meadow-Orlans' research showing more differences between Hd and Hh dyads than Lederberg's research. In this chapter, we present supplemental analyses conducted on these data to elucidate the factors that resulted in the different pattern of results.

Both studies described mother-child interaction in multiple ways, used similar coding schemes, and included samples of a reasonable size. In order to achieve a large enough sample, they included children who varied in degree of hearing loss and communication method. They included only infants or toddlers already identified and enrolled in early intervention programmes and excluded children with other disabilities. Therefore, children in these two samples are advantaged in comparison to the general deaf population, but they are representative of a large proportion of deaf children who are in early intervention programmes.

There are some notable differences in the studies' samples. Families participating in the Infancy Research Group's study were more highly educated than the families in Lederberg's study: 70% of mothers in the Infancy Research Group's sample had a college degree and 35% had additional postgraduate education, in contrast, only 41% of mothers in Lederberg's sample had completed college and only 7% had postgraduate education. There was greater racial diversity in the Lederberg sample; 20% of the children were minorities, but there were no minorities in the Hd dyads in the Infancy Research Group. The dyads in the Infancy Research Group represented greater geographic diversity. They came from five different metropolitan areas across the country, and the Lederberg sample came from only one.

We include other studies to complement the findings of these two studies where appropriate. However, we purposely excluded studies that have small samples. Although these studies are invaluable in identifying *potential* strengths and weaknesses, we believe it is misleading to use the characteristics of a few dyads to describe a whole group because of the wide variability of functioning.

These studies examined the impact of child deafness on mother-child relationships by comparing Hd and Hh dyads on attachment and three components of mother-child interaction: the quality of interaction, maternal communicative control, and dyadic joint attention. In addition, individual differences within Hd dyads are examined to document relations between the quality of maternal behaviour and outcome variables.

Attachment

Since the 1970s, assessment of the quality of the attachment bond has become a widely accepted way to describe the quality of the early mother – child relationship. The quality of attachment, as described by Bowlby and Ainsworth, is usually assessed by the "strange situation" procedure, which consists of seven 3-minute episodes during which the infant is separated from his or her caregiver twice. Classification of the quality of mother – infant attachment is made based on the infant's behaviour during these separation and reunion episodes and is conceptualized according to the infant's feeling of security in the presence of a caregiver.

Securely attached infants will use their caregivers as a secure base of exploration and venture out to examine an unfamiliar environment when their caregivers are present. When under stress, securely attached infants will, on reunion, seek proximity to their caregivers and be comforted by their presence. Infants who do not seem to derive the same sense of security from their caregivers will show one of two patterns of behaviour. Avoid insecurely attached infants do not seek to be in contact with their caregivers when stressed. In fact, they frequently actively avoid contact with their caregivers on reunion by turning their backs or even crawling away. Ambivalent or resistant insecurely attached infants will usually seek proximity on reunion, but they will show their ambivalence about their caregivers by turning away from the caregivers or by angrily batting away offered toys. These infants also frequently will not get the comfort they seek by the presence of the mothers and continue to be upset throughout the reunion episode.

Research suggests that security of attachment is derived from the infant's experiences with his or her caregiver. Secure attachments are developed when care giving is characterized by prompt responsiveness to crying, sensitivity to infants' signals during feeding and play, contingent and consistent interactions, and warmth and affectionate behaviour. All of these maternal characteristics have been related to infants' security of attachment.

In addition to the importance of attachment as a way of describing infant's relationships with his or her caregiver, quality of attachment seems to have broad impact on infants' socio-emotional adjustment. Theorists posit that attachment contributes to the infant's development of a sense of self and to the development of a working model of the infant's effectiveness in relationships that persists throughout childhood and adulthood. An infant's security of attachment, as assessed at 12 or 18 months, is associated with increased motivation and independence in problem-solving situations at age 2 and more positive peer and adult relations during early and middle childhood.

There are several reasons why deaf children have been hypothesized to be at increased risk for developing insecure attachments: Increased stress and depression associated with the diagnosis of deafness may cause a hearing mother to neglect her deaf infant; Deaf infants may perceive their hearing mothers as insensitive because their mothers' natural way of comforting them is through the voice; Poor communication between infant and mother may lead to a sense of insecurity; Controlling, dominant types of interaction by hearing mothers of deaf children appear insensitive.

Contrary to our hypotheses, there is now evidence that child deafness does not interfere with the development of a secure attachment. Lederberg and Mobley found almost identical numbers of securely attached deaf and hearing toddlers. Koester and MacTurk from the Infancy Research Group also found no differences in security of attachment in their Hd and Hh dyads.

Table 12.1 Proportion of Securely Attached Toddlers in Lederberg and Mobley and Koester and MacTurk

	Group	
Sample	*Deaf Toddlers*	*Hearing Toddlers*
Lederberg and Mobley		
Complete sample	56% (23/41)	61% (25/41)
Noncollege graduates	42% (11/26)	50% (12/24)
College graduates	80% (12/15)	76% (13/17)
Koester and MacTurk	75% (15/20)	90% (18/20)

Deaf and hearing toddlers seem equally likely to perceive their mothers as providing sensitive, responsive emotional support.

Therefore, although parents may be depressed due to their children's recent diagnosis of hearing loss and communication may be less than optimal between hearing parents and their deaf children, these data suggest that parents are able to change their interaction patterns to meet the emotional needs of their deaf infants. Koester, Papougek, and Smith-Gray suggest that much of early interaction is based on intuitive parenting, which is a system mutually regulated by infant and parent. This includes both parents attending to cues signifying that their infant is alert and ready to interact as well as parents using appropriate visual and vocal strategies to gain and maintain their infant's attention. Hearing parents do appear to adapt to their deaf infants' needs as evidenced by an observed increase in the amount of visual communication and behaviour hearing mothers use with their deaf children.

It is possible that the similar rates of securely attached deaf and hearing toddlers in these studies may be a result of the Hd dyads being enrolled in intervention programmes. However, Lederberg and Mobley found that the length of time the deaf toddlers were in the intervention programme did not relate to security of attachment. In addition, the high rate of insecurity among the dyads in the Lederberg and Mobley study suggests that some intervention programmes were not particularly successful.

Although deaf and hearing toddlers showed similar rates of secure attachments in each of these studies, the studies varied considerably in the percentage of children who were securely attached. Whereas Koester and MacTurk found less than 20% of their toddlers insecurely attached, almost 50% of the deaf and hearing toddlers were insecurely attached in Lederberg and Mobley's study. The high proportion of securely attached infants in the Gallaudet study is most likely due to their advantaged sample. Research with hearing infants shows that, in large samples, typical levels of secure attachment average 66%. Among children at high risk due to socioeconomic circumstances, secure attachment drops to closer to 50%, but advantaged samples can have more than 75% secure attachments. In the Lederberg and Mobley sample, the proportion of infants who were securely attached to their college educated mothers was similar to the Gallaudet sample and significantly higher than the proportion of infants securely attached to their non college educated mothers, $X^2 (1, N = 82) = 8.30, p \ll .01$.

Thus it seems, it is the mother's characteristics rather than her child's deafness that is the cause of the insecurity. Sensitive parents seem to be able to adapt to a variety of special needs of their infants and toddlers in such a way as to make them feel secure in their care, with maternal characteristics impacting on whether they provide sensitive parenting. This finding is consistent with the conclusions reached by van Ijzendoorn based on a meta-analysis of attachment studies: "In clinical samples, the mother appears to play a more important role than the child in shaping the quality of the infant-mother attachment relationship".

In sum, although child deafness does not put a child at risk for developing an insecure attachment, this research suggests that among infants and toddlers in any intervention programme, just as with a group of typically developing hearing children, there will be infants who have an insecure attachment to parents who are not able to meet their needs.

Mother-child Interaction

The impact of child deafness on mother-child relationships has traditionally been examined by noting defining features of maternal and child behaviour during free play. Researchers have used a variety of different methods to capture the impact of child deafness on these interactions. We include three lenses in this chapter: global ratings of the quality of mother-child interaction, use of communication to control the child, and development of joint attention. Each will be described in turn.

- Quality of Interaction
- Comparisons of interaction between Hd and Hh Dyads

Schlesinger and Meadow pioneered the use of rating scales to capture the impact of child deafness in the way hearing mothers socialize and play with their deaf children. Observers rate the characteristics of mother — child interaction using 5-point Likert-like scales after watching a videotape. These rating scales are designed to describe individual differences in the quality of mother — child relationships.

In the Gallaudet research study, Meadow-Orlans and Steinberg rated mother-infant interaction for five maternal characteristics, four infant characteristics, and three dyadic characteristics. Child deafness influenced the quality of hearing mothers' behaviour. Hearing mothers of deaf infants were less sensitive, less flexible, less warm, and showed less consistency in their interaction than mothers of hearing infants. Infant and dyadic ratings were not significantly different. In a follow-up study, Meadow-Orlans found that the quality of the behaviour by deaf mothers of deaf infants did not differ from that of hearing mothers of hearing infants. Thus, it is not child deafness per se that impacted on maternal behaviour but rather the mismatch between maternal and child hearing status.

Lederberg and Mobley rated mother-toddler interaction for 10 maternal characteristics, 9 child characteristics, and 3 dyadic characteristics. Ratings of Hd and Hh dyads differed significantly only on ratings of communicative competence. Contrary to Meadow-Orlans and Steinberg, the quality of maternal behaviour was not significantly different in the Hd and Hh dyads. The differences in the outcomes for these two studies may be attributed to differences in samples and statistical designs and differences in the definition of maternal sensitivity and responsiveness. An examination of each of these follows.

First, we approximated a replication of Meadow-Orlans and Steinberg's study by reanalyzing the data from Lederberg and Mobley using a statistical design closer to theirs. We conducted a multivariate analysis of variance on the three maternal rating scales from our study (sensitivity, positive affect, stimulation) that most closely resemble three used by Meadow-Orlans and Steinberg using only child hearing status as the between-subject variable. Because Meadow-Orlans and Steinberg's sample was primarily college educated, we also split the Lederberg and Mobley sample into college graduates (n = 32) and non-college graduates (n = 50). Table 12.2 displays the means and standard deviations of these scales for Meadow-Orlans and Steinberg's sample and Lederberg and Mobley's two sub-samples.

Analyses of the subgroups in the Lederberg and Mobley study revealed a significant difference in maternal sensitivity between the Hd and Hh dyads for the college graduates but not for the noncollege graduates. College graduates with hearing toddlers were rated significantly more sensitive than college graduates with deaf toddlers. The one-point differential was very similar to that found by Meadow-Orlans and Steinberg. This effect seems to be due to the extremely high ratings that the college graduate mothers of hearing toddlers received.

Table 12.2 Mean Ratings of Maternal Behaviour in Meadow-Orlans and Steinberg and Lederberg and Mobley

Meadow-Orlans and Steinberg			*Lederberg and Mobley*				
	All Dyads			*College Educated Dyads*		*Noncollege Educated Dyads*	
Ratings	Hd	Hh	Ratings	Hd	Hh	Hd	Hh
Sensitivity	3.3	4.2	Sensitivity	3.9	4.8a	3.9	4.1
	(1.4)	(1.0)		(1.1)	(0.4)	(1.2)	(1.3)
Affect	3.2	4.0	Positive	3.5	3.4	2.9	3.5
	(1.4)	(1.2)	Affect	(0.8)	(1.0)	(1.4)	(1.1)
Involvement	3.6	4.0	Stimulation	3.4	3.9	3.2	3.5
	(1.3)	(1.3)		(0.8)	(0.8)	(1.1)	(1.0)

[a]Difference between college educated Hd and Hh dyads, t (30) = 3.13, p « .01.

The ratings of college graduates with deaf toddlers were much more variable (2-5) as were noncollege graduates of either deaf or hearing toddlers. These results suggest that highly educated mothers are almost universally able to be sensitive to their hearing toddlers' cues in this free play situation, although some highly educated mothers were much more likely to be out of tune with their deaf toddlers, as were some non- highly educated mothers with either deaf or hearing toddlers.

The second major source of the discrepant results from these two studies was the definition of maternal sensitivity. Meadow-Orlans and Steinberg defined *highly sensitive mothers* as those who are responsive, do not interrupt their infants' activities, pace appropriately, and play instead of teaching their infants. In Lederberg and Mobley, overall sensitivity was defined more narrowly as the mother's ability to be in tune with her child by accurately perceiving her infant's signals or cues and responding appropriately to his or her interests, activities, or affective states.

Lederberg and Mobley then rated mother-child interaction on three additional scales thought to contribute to maternal sensitivity:

(a) *intrusiveness,* the frequency with which a mother's behaviour interrupts or abruptly interferes with the child's ongoing activities; (b) *pacing,* the ability to appropriately time changes in activities; and (c) *developmental appropriateness,* mother's engagement in activities that are too hard or too easy for the child. Meadow-Orlans and Steinberg's study incorporated these three aspects of mother-child interaction into their definition of maternal sensitivity rather than analyzing them separately.

Although, like Meadow-Orlans and Steinberg, Lederberg and Mobley conceptualized maternal nonintrusiveness, pacing, and developmental appropriateness as components of overall sensitivity, the pattern of results suggests that this was only true to a limited degree. Correlations between sensitivity and the other scales ranged from moderate (intrusiveness, r (80) = .53, pacing, r = .59) to low (developmental appropriateness, r = .18, because mothers were almost always appropriate). Furthermore, some mothers were perceived as insensitive but nonintrusive by the raters.

Although there was an impact of child deafness on the overall sensitivity of college educated mothers, there was none for intrusiveness, pacing, or developmental appropriateness. Thus, in the Lederberg and Mobley study, what seemed to distinguish the college educated mothers of deaf toddlers from those of hearing toddlers was not intrusiveness but rather how sensitive they were to their children's signals. This is consistent with Koester's suggestion that one of the major tasks of intervention programmes is to help hearing mothers learn what their deaf toddlers' cues or signals mean.

Pressman, Pipp-Siegel and Yoshinaga-Itano studied the quality of mother-toddler free play using another sample (n = 42) of deaf or hard of hearing (HOH) and hearing toddlers. These authors used two rating scales, sensitivity and structuring/intrusiveness, developed by Biringen and Robinson to measure "maternal emotional availability in mother — child interactions". *Maternal sensitivity* included responsiveness to child cues, positive affect, and affect regulation. *Maternal structuring/intrusiveness* was defined as the degree to which the mother provides optimal support of learning by following the child's lead and structuring the interaction appropriately and by not interrupting ongoing activity. These scales seem similar to the sensitivity and intrusiveness scales used in Lederberg and Mobley . Pressman found that mothers of deaf and hearing toddlers did not differ in their sensitivity or intrusiveness during free play. These results suggest again that child hearing loss does not have a consistently negative impact on hearing mothers' sensitivity or intrusiveness. The impact of child deafness on maternal sensitivity may depend on the sample studied and the definition of sensitivity used.

Relations between Maternal Responsiveness and Outcome Variables

Although child deafness may not consistently influence maternal sensitivity, a different and perhaps more important question is what impact differences in the quality of maternal interaction have on the deaf or HOH child's development. To address this question, relations between the quality of maternal behaviour and outcome variables are examined. Even in studies where there were no differences between mothers of deaf and hearing toddlers, mothers within each group differed in how responsive, warm, and so forth they were with their toddlers. Research has studied relations between the quality of mother — child interaction and attachment, child's play, and language growth.

Attachment: Laderberg and Mobley hypothesized that the quality of maternal behaviour would be related to the toddlers' security of attachment. However, security of attachment was only minimally related to maternal behaviour. Although mothers of securely attached toddlers reinforced their children more than did mothers of insecurely attached toddlers, they did not differ on measures of sensitivity or affect. In fact, surprisingly, mothers of insecurely attached and securely attached toddlers were rated the same on sensitivity (insecure, $M = 4.06$, $SD = 1.15$; secure, $M = 4.13$, SD 1.04), intrusiveness (insecure, $M = 3.94$, $SD = 0.89$; secure, $M = 3.98$, SD 1.12), pacing (insecure, $M = 3.91$, $SD = 0.89$; secure, $M = 4.08$, $SD = 0.96$), and developmental appropriateness (insecure, $M = 4.79$, $SD = 0.59$; secure, $M = 4.81$, $SD = 0.39$). Koester and MacTurk also found no relation between attachment security and Meadow-Orlans' maternal ratings. Thus, the sensitivity or responsiveness measured in both studies seems different from sensitivity that contributes to the development of a secure attachment. This may be because mothers were observed in a free play situation, and infants' feelings of security may be more related to maternal sensitivity during stressful situations.

Play: Although the quality of maternal behaviour in the free play situation did not relate to attachment, it does seem to be important for other aspects of development. Research with hearing children supports the hypothesis that mother's behaviour influences the sophistication of her child's play. Spencer and Meadow-Orlans analyzed the relation between maternal responsiveness and the deaf and hearing infants' level of play at 12 and 18 months. Maternal responsiveness did not relate to infants' play at 12 months. However, maternal responsiveness was a significant contributor to differences in the amount of time spent in the highest subcategory of pretend play — preplanned pretend play -- at 18 months. This type of play, which is based on symbolic representation, was the most cognitively advanced play observed at 18 months. This suggests that maternal responsiveness may encourage deaf and hearing toddlers to engage in a higher level of play, which could in turn facilitate their general cognitive development.

Language: The quality of maternal behaviour may be related to deaf and HOH children's language development. Spencer found that maternal sensitivity at 12 months correlated with deaf or HOH 18-month-olds' language. Pressman found that maternal emotional availability at 2 years significantly contributed to the amount of language growth deaf or HOH children experienced over the next year. Interestingly, in this study, maternal sensitivity seemed to contribute to language growth for deaf but not hearing children. Lederberg did not find maternal sensitivity at 2 years to be related to deaf children's language level at 3 years. This may be because Lederberg's sample was much more language delayed than either Spencer's or Pressman.

In summary, maternal sensitivity in free play does not seem to relate to the development of a secure attachment, but it does seem to have a significant impact on deaf toddlers' symbolic play and language development.

Maternal Communicative Control

Another dimension of maternal behaviour that has been studied more than any other is maternal directiveness. Unlike the previous dimensions, directiveness has traditionally been studied by examining the characteristics of maternal communication and language rather than overall interaction style. These studies almost uniformly find that mothers of deaf children are more directive than mothers of hearing children. This increased directiveness has been cited as a contributing factor to deaf and HOH children's language delay and to child passivity. However, during the 1990s researchers have realized that maternal directiveness or control is not a unitary dimension and that some types of control may have a positive impact on development whereas others may have a negative impact.

Tannock proposed that there are three distinct ways mothers may control interactions with their children:

> Response control *refers to a mother's tendency to use commands, questions, and other behaviour to elicit a response from the child.* Topic control *refers to the mother's tendency to redirect the child's attention to mother-selected topics by using utterances or turns that are unrelated to the child's ongoing activity or topic.* Turn-taking control *addresses the extent to which mothers dominate the interaction by contributing long and frequent turns.*

Each of these different types of control seems to be caused by different factors and have different effects on child development.

Response Control: Research consistently suggests that mothers of oral deaf or HOH children (2 1/2-5 years) use more response controls than mothers of age-matched hearing children. Lederberg and Everhart also found mothers of deaf toddlers used more action and attention-getting directives than mothers of hearing toddlers. Although some have suggested that the use of response controls is a reaction to a sense of powerlessness, research suggests that it is an intuitive adaptation to deaf children's linguistic delay; mothers of deaf children use the same amount of response controls as mothers of language-matched hearing children.

Research on the impact of response controls on language development is complex and contradictory; research with deaf children has shown both positive and negative relations between the amount of response controls mothers use and their deaf children's language. The effect of response controls on language may depend on the child's level of language and mode of communication. However, results are so inconsistent that Musselman and Churchill concluded:

> *The obtained patterns of relationships, however, are complex, suggesting that parent training programmes should be selective when attempting to decrease parents' overall levels of control. Taking into account the overall pattern of findings, directiveness should vary with children's language level and other characteristics. The findings for TC children are congruent with those from other studies that suggest that high control strategies are beneficial for children at the one-word stage.*

In sum, hearing mothers of deaf children seem to make an intuitive adaptation to their children's level of linguistic competence by being more directive. However, it is not at all clear that this behaviour should be interpreted as positive or negative.

Topic Control: Research with hearing children suggests that maternal language that is following or contingent on the young child's attention facilitates early language learning. Spencer found that communication and social behaviour by mothers of deaf and hearing toddlers was highly contingent on their child's attention. At 12 and 18 months, approximately 80% of mothers' visually based social responses to deaf and hearing infants were contingent on the infants' attention. Although the spoken communication of mothers of hearing infants was significantly more contingent than that of mothers of deaf infants, they were both highly contingent (88% vs. 82%, respectively). In their sample, Lederberg and Everhart found no effect of child deafness on mothers' topic control. Communication by mothers of deaf and hearing children was highly responsive to their children's attention (88% and 90% of utterances, respectively, were contingent). In addition, the majority of new topics started by mothers were in response to their children's attention or actions (deaf = 59%; hearing = 60%). This research is encouraging. It suggests that many hearing mothers are sensitive to their deaf infants or toddlers' interests and attention, and, therefore, maternal topic control, at least as defined in these studies, is not the source of most deaf toddlers' language delay.

Turn-Taking Control: Turn-taking control or dominance is usually measured by the proportion of communicative utterances contributed by mothers. Although research suggests that mothers of deaf preschoolers are more dominant than mothers of hearing preschoolers, this does not seem to be the case with younger deaf children. Neither Spencer nor Lederberg and Everhart found differences between the Hd and Hh dyads in how much mothers contributed to the interaction. For both deaf and hearing infants and toddlers, mothers contribute the vast majority of communications at this young age.

In sum, child deafness did not seem to impact on maternal topic or turn-taking control during infancy and toddlerhood. In addition, although mothers of deaf toddlers seem to use more response controls than mothers of hearing toddlers, this may not have a negative impact on deaf children's development.

Joint Attention: Research with typically developing toddlers suggests that another important way to characterize mother-child interaction is to examine the child's engagement/attention states. In the first year of life, infants primarily attend to only one aspect of their environment. However, during the second year they spend increasing amounts of time in joint attention, attending to both objects and people in the environment. Joint attention is considered an especially important engagement state because the infant integrates his or her attention to two or more aspects of the environment, enabling parental input to influence his or her perceptions of the environment.

There are three different ways that infants achieve joint attention. Initially, joint attention is scaffolded by caregivers' facilitation of infants' interactions with objects in the environment without the infants' acknowledgment of the mothers' participation, called *supported joint attention*. As infants mature, they become capable of engaging in more complex forms of joint attention. Specifically, infants begin to actively alternate their attention between interactive partners and objects in their environment, called *coordinated joint attention* (e.g., infant stacks rings while alternating gaze between rings and involved mother). Then, as language develops, children integrate language into episodes of joint attention. In other words, receptive and expressive language begin to mediate interaction between mothers and children, with language influencing the children's behaviours and thoughts, called *symbol-infused joint attention*.

Spencer and Waxman examined joint attention in Hd, Hh, and Dd dyads at 12 and 18 months. All three types of dyads spent similar amounts of time in joint attention at each age, with an increase from

12 (38%, 35%, and 37%, respectively) to 18 (54%, 58%, and 61%, respectively) months. However, analyses of the different kinds of joint attention revealed some group differences. Dd dyads spent significantly more time than Hd dyads in coordinated joint attention, the engagement state in which children actively attend visually to both people and the environment. Coordinated joint attention is especially important for deaf children who access communication through the visual modality. Other researchers in this volume have shown that deaf Mothers of deaf children are very good at scaffolding deaf infants' visual attention to themselves. Although this heightened visual vigilance was not present in Hd dyads, Hd dyads did not differ significantly from Hh dyads in the time spent in these prelinguistic joint attention engagement states.

Prezbindowski, Adamson, and Lederberg examined engagement states of Hd and Hh dyads at 22 months. Table 5.3, a composite of the results of Spencer and Waxman and Prezbindowski et al., displays the means and standard deviations of the proportion of time dyads spent in the different types of joint attention states at 12, 18, and 22 months. A comparison across these studies suggests that both Hh and Hd dyads increase the time they spend in joint attention from 18 to 22 months. However, by the age of 22 months, Hd dyads do not increase the time spent in joint attention as much as Hh dyads and, consequently, fall significantly behind Hh dyads in time spent in joint attention. This difference is due to the fact that by 22 months, Hh dyads spend about one third of their time in symbol-infused joint attention and the Hd dyads spent almost none. Thus, by the end of the second year of life, the use of language qualitatively changes the nature of mother-child interaction in Hh dyads but not in Hd dyads.

Table 12.3 Mean Percent Time Spent in Engagement States at 12, 18, and 22 Months

	Group							
	Hd			Hh			Dd	
Age in Months	12	18	22	12	18	22	12	18
Total joint attention	38	54	66	35	58	77	37	61

(Contd.)

	Group							
	Hd			Hh			Dd	
Supported joint attention	30 (20)	23 (18)	19 (14)	20 (12)	19 (14)	14 (11)	19 (9)	19 (13)
Coordinated joint attention	8 (9)	31 (23)	45 (20)	15 (14)	39 (23)	33 (19)	18 (17)	42 (19)
Symbol-infused joint			2 (3)			30 (29)		

Hd dyads compensate somewhat for their lack of symbol-infused joint attention by spending significantly more time in coordinated joint attention. In fact, at 22 months, Hd dyads spend almost 50% more time in coordinated joint attention than they do at 18 months. Thus, the extent to which deaf children actively include their mothers in their exploration of the world increases as they approach the end of their second year, but that increase is not as much as that which occurs with hearing toddlers.

These results suggest that language provide a unique means to attract and hold children in episodes of joint attention, which cannot be replaced by nonverbal communication. Because most of the language that these hearing mothers used was inaccessible to their deaf children, language did not serve as a means to attract and maintain the children's attention in joint attention states. This limitation prevented Hd dyads from engaging in a similar quantity and quality of joint attention compared to Hh dyads. As a result, mothers of hearing children enculturate their children more (via parents' demonstration of problem-solving strategies and transmission of cultural information within this context) than hearing mothers of deaf children.

Summary

The comparison of Hd and Hh dyads informs us whether child deafness places an Hd dyad at increased risk for nonoptimal outcomes. Gallaway and Woll summed up the prevailing view in the field:

> *Findings from these studies gave rise to the notion that deaf children might be suffering the secondary handicap of controlling, discouraging, and negative interactions with their mothers, which*

would provide a less facilitative environment for language acquisition and for social and cognitive development.

Similar to Gallaway and Wolf, we caution people from accepting this conclusion. The research reviewed here suggests that child deafness does not have general negative impact on mother-child *social* relationships in a number of areas, including attachment, quality of maternal affective behaviour, and maternal control. Thus, as Koester argue, many mothers may be able to intuitively adapt to a variety of different affective needs during early development. Our review suggests that negative interactions may be specific to certain samples and limited to subsets of Hd dyads. At this stage, however, any conclusions must be tentative. Although the three studies reviewed here had relatively large sample sizes, there is still not enough research to make firm conclusions.

Although Hd dyads may not be generally characterized by negative affect or nonreciprocal interactions, we do not mean that interaction in Hd dyads is the same as interaction in Hh dyads. Research suggests that interactions in Hd dyads are more likely to be interrupted than those of Hh dyads because of communication breakdowns. Thus, although these communication breakdowns were not associated with increases in negative affect, they did result in a decrease in the amount of interaction between mother and toddler. Hearing mothers of deaf children seem to make some adaptations to their child's communication needs by using more visual communicative devices and increasing the amount they touch their children. However, these accommodations are insufficient to result in optimal communication. In addition, once language starts to mediate interaction between hearing toddlers and their mothers, the nature of these interactions differs for the Hh and Hd dyads. We are proposing that it is specifically the difficulty with communication, rather than the social relationship between hearing mothers and their deaf toddlers, that disrupts development.

Optimal communication with deaf children is more intuitive for deaf parents. Observations of deaf mothers communicating with their deaf children provide the foundation for intervention programmes such as the one developed by Mohay. These programmes provide intensive training for parents on nonintuitive strategies that help hearing caregivers communicate more effectively with their deaf children. For example, parents are instructed on ways to gain their deaf children's attention and taught strategies to make language visually accessible and salient.

The conclusion that child deafness does not have a major impact on several areas of the early social relationship does not mean that these areas are not important for the development of deaf children. On the contrary, individual differences *within Hd dyads* in the quality of the mother-toddler relationship affect developmental outcomes in multiple ways. For example, although child deafness per se did not put the child at risk for developing insecure attachments, some deaf children do develop insecure attachments, and an insecure attachment has an impact on the child's social development. In Lederberg and Mobley, security of attachment had a stronger influence than hearing status on the toddler's social behaviour. Although ratings of deaf and hearing toddlers did not differ, securely attached toddlers initiated more, responded more, showed more affective sharing, had a longer attention span, and were more likely to show pride after completing a task than insecurely attached toddlers. Thus, interventions that attempt to improve the quality of attachment may be appropriate for some Hd dyads. Research reviewed here suggests that maternal responsiveness during free play cannot be used to identify insecurely attached dyads. Instead, observations of maternal responsiveness to toddlers during times of stress may be more useful for identification of problem dyads.

Although differences in maternal responsiveness during free play did not relate to attachment, differences in maternal responding did relate to deaf toddlers' language, play, and joint attention. Although we feel that intervention programmes for deaf toddlers need to make language learning their top priority, language learning needs to occur in a warm and responsive context for optimal development to occur. For individual dyads, increasing maternal responsiveness may be an important goal of intervention. Overall, however, dissemination of information to parents suggesting that intuitive parenting is sufficient to support typical growth in many areas of development may provide parents with a sense of competence in their ability to meet their children's needs in the months following the diagnosis of a hearing loss. This initial sense of mastery may help parents meet the challenges of learning nonintuitive ways of creating a language-rich environment for their deaf toddlers.

13

Role of Mother in Development of their Young Deaf Children

Many in the profession have looked eagerly to the gradually accumulating body of research with deaf mothers for models and information that can be used to help hearing parents of deaf children who need guidance in interacting in the visual mode. Now that a number of aspects of deaf mothers' behaviour have been identified that show great promise as a basis for assisting hearing parents, it may be worth asking whether there is any variation in what deaf mothers do. In other words, how much leeway do professionals have in advising hearing mothers? Do the requirements of communicating in the visual mode strongly shape deaf mothers' ways of handling interaction with their infants, leading to a great degree of similarity between them? Do all deaf mothers — or even all deaf mothers who are clearly skilled in interacting with their children — proceed in the same way to foster turn taking? Or, is there a range of behaviour that can nurture this development? These questions led to this study of mother-child interaction in deaf mothers whose interactions with their infants were rated positively and whose infants had learned to share attention between their mothers and objects. This investigation was made possible by the major contribution of Dr. Meadow-Orlans and her colleagues, namely the longitudinal study of mother-infant interaction conducted at Gallaudet University and the wealth of information contained in its videotaped data.

Requirements of Visual Communication

For deaf people, the visual channel must be used both to take in language and to inspect objects and events in the environment. Given this constraint, helping a deaf child develop conversational turn-taking skills is something of a hurdle, even for a deaf parent. The problem is heightened because at 5 or 6 months of age all children start to focus on objects and may go through a period when they actually avoid looking at their mothers. The new interest in objects changes and complicates interaction for any mother, but the stakes are particularly high when the mother and child are deaf because mature communication relies to a great extent on attention to the face. For deaf people, having eye contact with those they are talking to is also very important emotionally. Thus, as Kyle and Ackerman put it, when the child becomes focused on objects, "The deaf mother . . . has to contend with a child who is not 'attending' and who is psychologically limiting the nature and extent of her utterances".

Another basic problem for the mother to contend with is that young children do not have long visual attention spans. The duration of visual fixations normally decreases sharply with development, with older infants' fixations being three to four times shorter than those of younger infants. Deaf children must learn to sustain visual attention if they are to receive linguistic input and be able to participate in signed conversations of any length.

Despite these complications, Spencer found that deaf infants from deaf families, observed at 9, 12, and 18 months, spent at least as much time in coordinated joint attention as hearing children and significantly more than deaf children from hearing families. Moreover, anecdotal evidence suggests that by the time the child is 2 or 3 years old, interaction between deaf children and deaf mothers is often characterized by a remarkable synchrony and fluidity of turn taking, even in the presence of objects or books. The fact that this synchrony is not typically seen in hearing mother-deaf child dyads tells us that it does not just arise naturally, as a by-product of a deaf child's development. What is it that deaf mothers do to foster such fluency of turn taking in their children?

Characteristics of Mothers

A number of characteristic behaviours of deaf mothers interacting with their young children have been identified, all of which, in concert, may contribute to the successful acquisition of turn taking. In addition to their ability to provide accessible linguistic input from birth, noted earlier, deaf mothers instinctively accommodate their children's perceptual abilities by communicating in a Motherese register, namely signing larger and more slowly than in conversation with adults and employing more repetition. They also use a great deal of positive facial expression , as well as touch, and modify the placement of their signs; for example, by signing on the child's body, directly in the child's line of sight, or in the peripheral field until the child acquires the habit of shifting visual attention back to the mother's face.

Maternal Responsiveness

Another dimension that may be important in supporting turn-taking development is maternal responsiveness. For example, differences have been found in deaf and hearing mothers' responses to spontaneous looks from their children. Koester, Brooks, and Traci examined face-to-face interaction when infants were 9 months old and found that "deaf mothers were significantly more likely than hearing mothers to respond in the visual modality when the infant directed eye gaze toward the mother." The mothers' responses were "exaggerated facial expression, head-nodding or looming, finger play, gestures, etc.", as well as sign language. Prendergast and McCollum, studying mothers' interactions with 18- to 28-month-old deaf infants, also found that deaf mothers responded to significantly more of the child's looks than hearing mothers. Kyle, Woll and Ackerman observed that deaf mothers treat their child's eye contact almost as a request and suggested that for hearing mothers "the idea that requests from the child come through eye contact is rather alien", which may cause them to miss many of the child's early bids for communication.

Deaf mothers have also been found to be responsive to their children's attention focus in communicative interaction. A study of the language of randomly selected deaf mothers in the Gallaudet sample showed that the majority of the mothers' comments were related to what the child was looking at or holding, and that responsiveness was in turn positively related to the number of signs the child produced.

Another sort of responsiveness is seen in deaf mothers' ability to wait for their children's attention without intervening when the child is looking at something else. Examinations of mothers' behaviour when their infants looked away from them revealed that at both 9 months and 12 months deaf mothers often simply waited for the child to look back at them. At the 12-month observation, comments were made related to the child's previous focus of attention after his or her gaze returned to the mother.

Overt Attention Getting

Responsiveness notwithstanding, deaf mothers are often very active in seeking their children's attention. Kyle and Ackerman noted that deaf mothers of deaf infants will "break the child's gaze overtly by moving into the line of sight" in order to try to get their visual attention. They observed that "the 'game' seems to become 'how to get the child to look at me' rather than how to get the child engaged in long interaction". They also observed that whereas hearing mothers of hearing 9-month-olds tend to play far-near games of moving toys closer and closer to a child with simultaneous "gonna get you" commentary, these games are "almost completely missing in the deaf mothers at the same age" and commented that the "same games for the deaf mother seem to exploit the visual space allowing the child's eyes to track the object with less opportunity for linguistic intervention by the mother". Deaf mothers, however, do manage to get their children beyond a focus on the objects alone and to bridge the gap between nonlinguistic and linguistic interaction around objects.

One of the most salient features of deaf mothers' behaviour is the use of overt attention getting, for example, tapping the child or waving, which is part of the communication repertoire for deaf adults. Spencer found that for dyads with deaf infants, mothers' attention getting at 18 months was moderately correlated with both coordinated joint attention and language level.

It is worth remembering that the ability to respond to a tap as a signal for attention to another person is not present from birth and is in fact a cognitive skill. Even learning to achieve joint attention by following another person's gaze or pointing gesture is not always straightforward. For example, a study by Grover of children's visual responses to adult pointing found that at 6 and 9 months the children were as likely to look at the adult's hand as to follow the point. But at least other people's gaze or pointing gestures are potentially focusing attention in the actual direction of a present object or location. By contrast, a tap on the body is not meant to direct the child's attention to his or her own body, but to the person doing the tapping and usually to their communication. There is thus a kind of disjunction between the place where physical contact occurs and what the contact represents, and in that sense a tap is arbitrary and symbolic.

The available information confirms that tapping in the early months of a deaf infant's life is not very effective for attention getting. Harris reported that in the earliest observations of the deaf children of deaf parents they studied, namely 7, 10, and 16 months, the mothers' attempts to direct the children's attention by tapping — or even by physically moving them — were "usually unsuccessful". In short, the child must learn that such a signal means "look at me" or "pay attention to what is going to come next."

Waxman and Spencer looked at maternal attention-getting strategies in mother-child dyads of the four possible combinations of hearing and deafness, in groups of approximately 20 dyads. The behaviours coded were presenting or moving objects, tapping objects, tapping the child, and waving or hitting the floor. Using the movement of objects to attract attention was far and away the most frequently used strategy for all groups at all ages, though it declined significantly between the 9- and 12-month and the 12- and 18-month sessions. The strategy of tapping the child directly was used significantly more by deaf mothers of deaf children than by mothers in the other three groups during the 9- and 12-month sessions; by the 18-month session, the deaf mothers of hearing children had increased their use of tapping so that both groups exceeded the two groups with hearing mothers. Tapping in deaf mothers of deaf children did not change significantly over time. For the forty 15-second time segments sampled, the deaf mothers tapped their deaf infants in an average of 8.4 segments in the 9-month session, 10.7 segments in the 12-month session, and 8.7 segments in the 18-month session.

Both Waxman, Spencer, Prendergast and McCollum found considerable variability in the amount of attention getting that deaf mothers did, which suggests that examination of individual dyads' behaviour over time might reveal information that is lost in group data. Waxman and Spencer also noted their impression that the "nature" or "degree of insistence" of deaf mothers' attention getting changed over time and urged further, qualitative investigation of the phenomenon. The purpose of the investigation described here was to look at skilled deaf mothers' attention-getting behaviour in individual dyads over time in order to examine individual patterns of attention getting.

Descriptive Study of Deaf Mothers

This study looked at the communication of nine deaf mother-deaf child dyads selected from a sample that was part of the Gallaudet longitudinal study. The dyads were chosen on the basis of the children's communication development as indicated by their ability to share attention between their mother and objects, a state referred to as coordinated joint attention. In this state, the child actively divides attention between an object and a communication partner as evidenced by shifting gaze between the two. The nine children studied were in the upper half of the sample on this measure at 18 months. Out of a possible 600 seconds of interaction, the amount of time spent in coordinated joint attention at 18 months ranged from 248 to 488 seconds, with a mean of 333 seconds. Five of the nine children were already spending some time in coordinated joint attention with their mothers at 9 months.

The mothers in the sample also had high global ratings on a composite measure of maternal behaviour that included sensitivity and flexibility, when the child was 18 months of age. The mean rating for the mothers was 4.3 (SD = 0.5).

Demographic characteristics of the subjects are presented in Table 13.1 . All children had been identified before 9 months of age, were in parent-infant programmes by 12 months of age or earlier, and were functioning within the normal range. Four of the children had profound hearing losses, three had severe-profound losses, and one had a moderate-severe loss. Information about hearing loss was not available for one of the children.

Eight of the nine mothers used ASL with their children, primarily without voice. One mother whose child had a moderate-severe loss signed and spoke with her child. This child was observed in one instance orienting to voice plus tap at 9 months.

Table 13.1 Demographic Characteristics of Dyads

Dyad	*Sex*	*Child Hearing Loss*	*Etiology*	*Maternal Hearing Status*	*Maternal Education*
1	F	Moderate-severe	Heredity	Deaf	16 yrs.
2	M	Profound	Heredity	Deaf	18 yrs.
3	F	Severe-profound	Heredity	Deaf	20 yrs.
4	M	Unavailable	Heredity	Deaf	18 yrs.
5	F	Profound	Heredity	Deaf	18 yrs.
6	M	Profound	Heredity	Deaf	18 yrs.
7	F	Profound	Heredity	Deaf	18 yrs.
8	M	Severe-profound	Heredity	Deaf	14 yrs.
9	M	Severe-profound	Heredity	Deaf	15 yrs.

The mothers' education ranged from 14 to 20 years, with six of the nine mothers having at least 18 years of education. Clearly, then, this was a privileged group of mothers and children.

The Context of Data Collection

The source of the data was videotaped interactions of mother-infant play with toys, recorded at 9, 12, and 18 months in a laboratory setting with one-way mirrors on two sides of the room. Interaction between mothers and children was taped for approximately 15 minutes at 9 and 12 months and for 20 minutes at 18 months. Parent and child sat on a mat on the floor with toys. Mothers were asked to interact with their children as they normally would at home.

Coding and Analysis of the Data

For the purposes of this investigation, 15 minutes of interaction were transcribed for each of the sessions. For the sake of comparability with data from other studies, 10 minutes of interaction were coded for maternal use of attention getting (e.g., tapping the child, waving, wiggling fingers in peripheral vision, patting a surface near the child, such as a mat or table).

For the count of maternal attention getting, instances were recorded and totaled. In the case of tapping, an instance was a tap or multiple taps bounded by a pause. The most common pattern of signaling was a two-beat tap, which was counted as one instance. On rare occasions, a mother tapped as many as 9 or 10 times in quick succession until a child finally turned; like the two-beat taps, this was counted as one instance. However, if a mother tapped, stopped, and then tapped again, it was counted as two. Jiggling or shaking the child to get attention was not counted, nor was tickling, with or without a toy in hand. In a few instances a mother used an object to tap a child to get attention, and this was included in the count.

The entire 15 minutes of interaction was used in order to obtain more data on which to base percentages of the children's responses to attention getting, as well as for qualitative description. Instances of attention getting were coded as *child responds after tap,* (meaning the child oriented visually either to the mother's face or signing hand, or to an object she was holding), *no response,* and *other* (including cases where the mother tapped the child when he or she was already oriented in the mother's direction, and no clear response could be seen; taps occurring when the child's back was to the camera, and a response could not be observed; etc.). In order to compute percentages reflecting the children's tendency to respond to a signal, instances of attention getting in the *other* category in which the child's response could not be observed were eliminated. The percentages of child responses to attention getting thus reflect the number of instances of clear responses divided by the total instances of attention getting for which a judgment about the response was possible.

It should be noted that the mothers typically tapped the child and then signed or pointed, or tapped the child and then presented an object. It was not practicable to determine what the child was responding to, that is whether to the tap, the following sign or presentation of the object, or some combination of the two.

For three of the taped segments , intrarater reliability for the coding of occurrences of the mother's signals and of the child's response to those signals was 90%, 100%, and 89%.

Mothers' Use of Attention Getting

Frequencies of mothers' attention-getting behaviours in a 10 minute period appear in Table 13.2 . The mean frequency of instances of maternal attention getting was approximately 15 in the 9-month session.

Table 13.2 Number of Instances of Attention-Getting by Deaf Mothers In 10 Minutes

Session *Mother*	*9 Months*	*12 Months*	*18 Months*
1	3	11	44
2	9	15	11
3	30	27	8
4	7	11	14
5	4	15	11
6	5	9	39
7	35	9	15
8	20	30	21
9	24	27	16
M	15.2	17.1	19.9
SD	12.2	8.5	12.8

The high variability of this behaviour is reflected in the fact that standard deviations approached the mean for the 9-month and 18-month sessions. Only at 12 months was maternal behaviour somewhat more consistent across the group.

Looking at the nine dyads individually across the sessions reveals three distinctly different patterns of maternal behaviour. Two mothers in the sample used attention getting infrequently during the 12-month session and increased it dramatically in the 18-month session. By contrast, three mothers engaged in frequent attention getting in the first session when the child was 9 months of age, with less signaling in the 18-month session. Three of the mothers used attention getting more evenly across the three sessions without a high rate of signaling at either 9 or 18 months. Subject 8 was also fairly consistent across the three sessions but with a higher rate of signaling.

Children's Responses to Attention Getting

Percentages of responses to attention-getting signals are shown in Table 13.3 . The mean percentage for the number of attention-getting signals the child responded to was approximately 23% at 9 months, 50% at 12 months, and 78% at 18 months.

Table 13.3 Percentages of Attention-Getting Signals to Which Child Responded

		Age	
Child	*9 Months*	*12 Months*	*18 Months*
1	14	45	64
2	17	33	69
3	33	69	64
4	43[a]	31	87
5	0	60	77
6	17	36	93
7	31[a]	67	88
8	32[b]	64	81
9	19	43	82
M	22.9	49.8	78.3
SD	13	15.3	10.6

[a]12-13 mins., [b]10 mins.

The children's responses to attention getting were much less variable than the mothers' use of signals, particularly at 12 and 18 months. In most cases, the percentage of the individual children's responses to attention getting increased from 9 to 12 months and from 12 to 18 months. One exception was Subject 4, who had his own agenda in the 12-month session and consequently resisted responding to his mother. There was also a slight drop in responding for Subject 3 in the 18-month session; however, this was based on responses to only eight taps by her mother and, given her overall attentiveness to her mother's communication, may well be a result of sampling error.

Qualitative Observations

It should be noted that the nature and intensity of the mothers' attention-getting signaling changed somewhat over time as the children became more responsive and tuned in to communication. In the 9-month session, the children were not yet visually tuned in to their mothers for the most part. The children's spontaneous looks to their mothers consisted primarily of brief glances, though three of the children were already exhibiting some clear shifting of visual attention to their mothers. A fourth child was still producing only very brief looks, but she often tossed toys in an uncontrolled way and then immediately looked at her mother as if startled. If the mothers wanted to use the children's glances as an opportunity to communicate, they had to rush to sign, and often the infants looked away immediately.

During this first session , the mothers were obviously working, to a greater or lesser extent, to get their children's visual attention. In addition to the adult forms of attention getting, two of the mothers produced noncanonical attention-getting waves, or gently wiggled the fingers in peripheral vision to try to get attention. In the 9-month session in particular, there were also more instances of a tap accompanied by other kinds of touch, for example, taking the child by the shoulder or arm and trying to get him or her to turn, jiggling, and so forth. Occasionally there were prolonged attempts to get attention where the mother tapped repeatedly on various parts of the body jiggled an arm or leg in between and sometimes finished with a hug or tickling as she gave up the struggle.

While communicating, mothers often leaned close to the child and angled their heads around to try to get eye contact. Between these features and the signs themselves, there were multiple cues for the children to respond to. There was also a great deal of use of toys. Mothers exploited their child's ability to notice and track moving objects in order to get his or her attention to their faces or to the toy beside their faces. In sum, the mothers adapted in various ways to the fact that their children were not yet responsive to taps as signals in themselves.

By the 12-month session, all nine children were producing at least some clear shifts of visual attention to their mothers, some of them very frequently. These spontaneous looks had become longer and more obviously communicative. For example, children often accompanied looks to the mother with smiles, or picked up something and then looked at her, or signed and then looked at her. All but one of the children produced some signs in the 12-month session, though for two the only sign noted was clapping. Subject 4 was the child for whom visual attention to his mother was comparatively rare at 12 months. For part of the session, he was determined to look at something on a table in the corner of the observation room, and she was trying to reengage him and get him back to the play interaction. In a brilliant stroke, after a long period of tapping him, tugging at him, patting the table, and signing NO in his line of sight, she put a block on the table in front of him and a line of blocks on the floor leading back to the mat, then removed the blocks one by one so that his attention was led back to her and the toys.

By the 18-month session, mothers could typically use the conventional two-beat gesture and get the child's visual attention without additional efforts. In that session, we begin to see some of the smoothness of turn taking that characterizes slightly older children. Turn taking appeared to be more rapid, with children more often responding quickly and crisply to taps as well as shifting gaze frequently to their mothers. However, even at this age there were instances of mothers making repeated efforts to get the child's visual attention and finally giving up.

Discussion

The data confirm that there are strong individual differences in the attention-getting behaviours that skilled deaf mothers use with their children and that there is indeed a range of attention-getting behaviour that can be used to support the deaf child's development of joint attention and turn taking, even in this highly select sample of a select population. The mothers of the children varied both in how much signaling, they did and at what child age they chose to do the most signaling. Despite these differences, all three patterns of maternal attention getting were associated with children's success in coordinating attention between persons and objects, as measured at 18 months, and, by extension, in the development of turn taking.

A question of interest is what caused the differences in the mothers' approaches. One possibility is that they may have had different philosophies or beliefs about infants' cognitive capacities and about the best way to get them to adult-like turn-taking behaviour. Another possibility is that they were responding to individual differences in their children's development.

Unfortunately, no information is available about the mothers' beliefs and philosophies specifically related to the development of turn taking. The efforts that some mothers made to get their children's visual attention in the 9-month session suggest that they were attempting to teach their children to attend visually, though a lean interpretation might be that they were just trying to get their children to look at them. On the other hand, the variation in the mothers' performance tells us that they did not all treat attention getting, particularly tapping, as a way to train the children visually.

One possible explanation for individual differences in attention getting is differences in maternal directiveness. However, Wilson and Spencer's study, conducted with many of the same subjects, found that deaf mothers' language was related to the child's attention focus a majority of the time. The study also found that this topic responsiveness and the number of attention-getting attempts by the mother were not related to one another, either positively or negatively. Inspection of the interactions of the present sample reveals that the mothers often used attention getting before making comments related to the child's attention focus as well as before initiating a new topic or activity. Thus, though attention getting involves directing attention, it does not necessarily mean that the mother is being directive, or unresponsive to the child's focus.

When the relationship between the actual amount of time the children spent in joint attention at 18 months and the mothers' signaling patterns at different ages is examined, the results again suggest that attention getting is not the only important factor. The two children highest in coordinated joint attention at 18 months were Subjects 6 and 1. Both of their mothers signaled infrequently at 9 months and increased their signaling dramatically at 18 months. However, before jumping to the conclusion that it is best to refrain from much signaling early on, consider that Subject 3 was almost identical to Subject 1 in time spent in joint attention at 18 months , yet her mother's pattern was the opposite: frequent signaling at 9 and 12 months, which decreased markedly by 18 months.

When we attempt to assess the virtues of frequent early signaling, we find that there were 3 other children besides Subject 3 whose mothers signaled frequently at 9 months, and all of them spent approximately 100 seconds less in coordinated joint attention than she did. Such variability suggests that there is no direct, simple relationship between amount and type of attention getting and joint attention for this subgroup of the larger sample. The lack of such a relationship also suggests that attention getting is only one component in a larger constellation of maternal behaviours — and hence of the children's communicative experience — that foster the children's coordinated joint attention and turn-taking abilities.

One way to consider the relation between attention getting and developmental factors in the children is to look at the individual differences in performance in the 9- and 18-month sessions. In the 9-month session, none of the children was signing, and though some of them exhibited occasional shifting of visual attention toward the mother, it was not with any degree of fluency or automaticity. By 18 months, all the children were carrying on signed conversations with varying degrees of sophistication, and all were attention switching. Despite this comparative consistency with regard to the children's behaviour, there was a high degree of variability in the mothers in both sessions. Mothers attention getting ranged from 3 to 35 instances in the 9-month session, and from 8 to 44 instances in the 18-month session.

The children in dyads 1 and 6 may be taken as counter evidence for a relationship between attention getting and spontaneous attention-switching ability. In both cases, their mothers signaled infrequently during the 9- and 12-month sessions, yet the children were very clear attention switchers by 12 months, suggesting that the latter ability does not depend on mothers' use of signaling. Then, in the 18-month session, with attention switching already well established, we see the dramatic jump in the amount of signaling by the mothers. In the case of these children, it may be that the mothers were using the tapping to speed up the conversational exchange, or to further train the children in adult turn-taking behaviour. At that stage, using tapping frequently was evidently a choice for those two mothers, not a necessity. Their tapping had the character of a conventional signal, as opposed to an attempt to teach the children to look.

Unanswered Questions

Some interesting questions are what determines a mother's decision to use an attention signal, and why she does or does not persist until the child looks. There were some indications that the mothers were careful about the signaling they did. At times mothers prepared to tap their child, but stopped when they saw that the child was about to do something else, or held their hands poised in position for a tap for several seconds before tapping the child, or tapped the child once or twice but then gave up when they saw that the child was absorbed in something else. As noted earlier, the cases where a mother persisted and produced many rapid taps in succession until the child finally turned were comparatively rare. The mothers were also not heavy handed, in a literal sense; for the most part, the tapping appeared to be light and delicate (though there were exceptions in the early sessions at moments when the mother apparently really wanted the child to look and used a series of taps on various parts of the body interspersed with more emphatic jiggling.)

It is evident that the use of signaling also depends partly on context. For the mother of Subject 3, once turn taking had been well established, by the 18-month session, there was infrequent tapping while mother and child were in face-to-face mode (partly because the child was walking around); however, in a later segment where they were looking at a book together, and the child was on the mother's lap (facing away, with the possibility of the mother signing in front of the child and not requiring visual attention), she tapped the child frequently to get her to turn and look at her. Another example is the sixth dyad in which 35 of the 39 signals in the 18-

month session occurred in approximately 7.25 minutes of the interaction, while the mother and child were sitting together interacting around toys. After that, the child got up to pull a toy cart around the room, and the mother waved only infrequently during the rest of the 15 minutes coded.

Another question is what response mothers are actually seeking when they tap the child. In most cases, it appears that it is visual attention: Mothers tap and then present an object for the child to orient to, or tap and then sign, or both. However, the notions of attention and visual attention can be separated, in principle, and it is possible that some taps are meant just as a general alerting signal as opposed to a signal to turn and look — particularly in the early sessions when the mother was still signing in the child's peripheral field. (Certainly the mothers often accepted the child's not looking in response to a tap.) At times mothers also tapped the children when the children were already oriented in their direction or were oriented toward an object that the mothers then commented on. Occasionally a mother tapped a child lightly, without looking at him or her, while reaching for an object to present. In such cases, the subjective impression is that the purpose of the tap was to alert the child to an upcoming change of activity or topic similar to the function of "hey!" in speech. At any rate, taps of the more conventional sort were often used to signal an upcoming activity.

How Deaf Mothers Support Turn Taking

As the study shows, mothers' signaling behaviour does not appear to determine whether children acquire either spontaneous attention-switching behaviour or turn taking (given that children whose mothers did not signal much when they were 9 months old had acquired attention switching by 12 months and that some mothers did not tap frequently until 18 months, when both attention switching and turn taking were very well established). If this is true, how do children learn these things? Possible contributors include physical rhythms of interaction, experienced very frequently over time, which may create unconscious expectations about the occurrences of turns and responses, and sources of information in peripheral vision, such as the mother looming in, or changing her position in small but marked ways as she focuses her own visual attention on the child. Presumably the redundancy of these cues helps the child learn what to expect and to anticipate the handing back and forth of turns.

As noted earlier, the interactions include a great deal of tactile activity in addition to the use of taps, particularly in the first two sessions. In addition to hugging or patting the child, this included things like tickling or jiggling or running a wooden car over the child's body, as well as signing on the child. Also, in contrast to Kyle and Ackerman's findings for their British sample, far-near games were used by seven out of nine of the Gallaudet mothers in the 9-month session. In these routines, which combined visual and tactile aspects, mothers sometimes held toys high in the air and brought them wiggling down to the child's face or hopped a toy toward the child at varying rates of speed ending with tickling the child. Both the physical contact and the games might be thought of as an attention-maintaining device or one of many means of maintaining a certain level of stimulation and activity that the mother may feel is necessary for communication.

In addition, it is obvious that both the mothers and children were sensitive to visual events of various kinds, and these things became incorporated into quasi-conversations, that is turn taking. For example, when the children happened to notice themselves or some movement in the mirrors in the room, the mothers often bounced or moved their heads jauntily in response, looking at the mirror, sometimes engaging in a kind of movement dialogue with the child. Some mothers used their child's name sign while they looked in the mirror together, labeling the child and themselves. Occasionally, though by no means always, mothers imitated an involuntary flapping arm movement by the child or made a movement corresponding to "boom!" after an object fell. Likewise, if the child did something, such as take the lid off a bucket, and then turned to the mother, she generally responded in the visual mode even if she did not sign: often with a wide open mouth and wide eyes, sometimes a large two-handed gesture, or a sudden movement forward, and so forth. Finally, peekaboo games were accompanied by very positive, engaging facial animation.

Attracting and maintaining the child's visual and cognitive attention with toys is clearly also an important part of the story. As noted earlier, Waxman and Spencer , examining the various modes of attention getting in infancy, found that the movement of objects was by far the most common for deaf as well as hearing parents, even when the child was 18 months of age. Whereas attention to an object without accompanying communication can be a dead end, as Harris and Mohay observed, deaf mothers use objects to attract the child's attention for purposes that seem both interactive and linguistic. Researchers need to pin down how deaf parents use objects to draw children into communication.

Finally, it should not be forgotten that the child's attention to the mother is supported by the language the mother produces around their joint experiences, as well as by her nonverbal communicative responses. As communication develops, both mother and child are rewarded by increasing amounts of verbal communication.

In summary, skilled deaf mothers support the development of communication in their children through a multifaceted complex of behaviours, which include active attention getting to varying extents, depending on the mother and the age of the child. Though the visual mode creates certain constraints in terms of interacting around objects, there is in fact more than one way to help the child learn the process of visual turn taking.

In addition to the substantial variability found even among deaf parents who are skilled communicators, close investigation of the phenomena of interaction can help professionals retain a degree of latitude and flexibility in what they recommend to hearing parents. It seems clear, viewing the interactions, that the mothers respond to the states of their children on a moment to moment basis as they make decisions about when to signal and that these decisions may relate to their knowledge of the child's temperament and capabilities, as well as their own preferred styles of interacting.

14

Deaf Education in India

Introduction

Deaf education in india is provided b various organisations, NGOs. In this chapter we are discussing about one organisation which is providing education to deaf students and also engaged in the benefit of deaf students.

DEAF REACH was founded in 1991 by J.S.K.Rao, with guidance from Mrs. Christine Lazarus, chairperson and M.L.A.'89-94, and initiated with five deaf youth, Hari Kumar, Anil Kumar, Ritesh Kumar, Nagesh and Moosa Kutty. Deaf Reach began by identifying potential leaders in the Deaf community in Hyderabad and focused on empowering them with skills and training to better serve their community. For several years now, part of this time in cooperation with UNICEF, Deaf Reach has been implementing unique leadership training and mentoring programmes in the Indian State of Andhra Pradesh. Present day Programmes include Leadership training, Adult Education, Computer training programme, AIDS awareness, Job Placement, Interpreters training, Sign Language training, Deaf Awareness and counseling.

Some years back, Deaf Reach pioneered India's first ever AIDS Awareness Programme for the deaf, entitled "Relationships and

Health". The first such programme was coordinated with Project Sign Post of Mumbai, the organisation that first developed this unique non-verbal health education curriculum for the deaf. Project Sign Post has since turned this project over to Deaf Reach

An estimated 193,600 deaf Indians are HIV positive. This is the largest HIV positive deaf population in the world, and the one least likely to receive life support resources, information, education and communication. The "Relationships and Health" workshop is the only method currently available for helping the deaf understand health and safety within relationships. This workshop is attended by deaf youth from which some are chosen to be Deaf Peer Educators (DPE's), to train deaf people in the towns and cities of south India.

Key benefits: Empowering deaf women and girls to protect themselves, and help the deaf make informed choices about relationships, as well as health awareness.

Deaf Reach's Teacher Training programme for Deaf adults is the first of its kind in India. Currently they have students from four cities. The one-year course trains deaf adults to be teachers in deaf schools. It is also the only programme in India to offer a Bilingual approach to Deaf education, that is, using Indian Sign Language as the first language to learn other languages.

The consultant to their programme is Dr. Madan Vashihsta, a prominent Deaf Educator from Gallaudet University, Washington DC (Gallaudet University is the world's only University for the Deaf.) Their programme is being watched very keenly by the Rehabilitation Council of India and other government bodies, and is expected to be replicated in other parts of the country.

The year 2002 started with the inclusion of DEAF REACH in the GITEX EXHIBITION held in Hyderabad from January 1st to the 9th with a special stall donated by the Secretary, IT Shri Satyanarayana IAS to project the work of and for the Deaf and hailed by the Governor and Lady Governor as one of the best stalls. The week long exhibition highlighted social responsibility and recognition of the deaf as potential workers in the IT Sector. As of Jan 2002 Ms. Candice B.Sc Computers MBA Finance/PG/HRD has consented to serve part time as the CEO.

The CMD requested the Parents Teacher Association to be more responsible in the affairs of DEAF REACH and to take initiative in the activities, including helping the Deaf with housing facilities, ration cards, bus/railway passes etc.,

In March Their records were inspected in connection with the grant of first installment received from GOI. The sudden death of the CEO and Founder of Deaf Reach Shri JSK Rao had serious repercussions. Immediately on confirmation of the renewal of the grant efforts plans are being made for community based rehabilitation for the Deaf. This programme will assure maximum empowerment for deaf young people with the courses on English, Bilingualism (sign & written) relationships & health and life skills training and jobs for those who have been trained as teachers.

The new financial year brought changes: 4 members trained and experienced took up the responsibility of teaching and training.

In April the Commissioner Disabilities informed the Chairperson of Deaf Reach of the government backlog vacancies to be filled by the disabled. The members were directed to meet the deaf and the CMD will meet the CM to request certain exemptions and considerations:

1. That the filling up of 1% of the 3% for disabilities be mandated only for the profound deaf
2. That the technical training to be acknowledged as equivalent to intermediate; in view of the fact that there is only one junior college for boys in Baptla for the entire State and with a request for a college at district headquarters.
3. That the deaf be interviewed with an interpreter in view of the use of sign language
4. Consideration of special schools proposal submitted for pre and primary schools for deaf children before integration with hearing children.
5. Grant of lease of land requisitioned in 1997/1999 through the Collector RR District.
6. Request for release of funds to assist some of the deaf leadership to attend the DEAF WAY II in USA.
7. State Assistance to NGOs for special services.

In May orientation classes were held for teachers of the deaf in English.

In June 02 Their CMD approached the Governor of AP & First Lady who immediately consented to host the Helen Keller Birthday Celebrations and present the Anne Sullivan Awards to teachers of the deaf and blind, the activists also of the deaf and blind and their supporters. DEAF REACH organized the entire programme with support from the PTA.

Excellence Awards for Teachers for the Deaf

Every year on 27th June, They celebrate Helen Keller's birthday by hosting the Anne Sullivan Excellence Awards for Teachers for the Deaf. This event is an annual feature eagerly anticipated by the teaching community there in Hyderabad.

One of their long-standing dreams was also realized this past June 27th with the opening of the DEAF REACH Pre School for the deaf, the opening also officiated by the Commissioner. The Preschool is housed on property donated by Mrs. Christine Lazarus, former State Legislator and our Chairperson. The property required renovation and construction and many individuals and companies came forward and donated construction materials. The preschool is unique in that all the teachers are Deaf adults teaching deaf children. They have an initial class of five deaf children.

Other Centres

Centre for Research, Education and Empowerment for the Deaf (C.R.E.E.D.)

DEAF REACH launched the Centre for Research, Education and Empowerment for the Deaf (C.R.E.E.D.) in April 2001. The new centre was inaugurated by the First Lady of the State, Mrs. Haripriya Rangarajan. The centre, is housed on the 7th Floor of an office building comprising of two rooms. The office space was given by Mr. Bashiruddin Babu Khan a prominent builder and former Minister. The centre will house a computer centre, a Sign language lab and library.

Entrepreneur Development programmes will also be conducted at this centre. Intergraph Corporation donated 15 used computers for the centre. Sign Language Classes, the first of its kind in the country will also be offered at this centre. Currently the centre is offering free computer training to deaf school children from poor families.

More Deaf Reach Activities

First National Seminar on Billingualism in Deaf Education: Deaf Reach hosted the first ever National Seminar on Bilingualism in Deaf Education in March of 2001. This seminar is an historic one in that for the first time a seminar was conducted on Indian Sign Language (ISL) and its role in deaf education. This seminar was sponsored by the Rehabilitation Council Of India (R.C.I.). For a long time Sign Language was suppressed in India thus denying the Deaf in India access to education in their native tongue. This seminar paved the way for official recognition of ISL. The seminar was conducted by eminent Deaf Educator Dr. Madan Vashishta, former Superintendent of the New Mexico School for the Deaf and currently teaching at Gallaudet University, Washington D.C. and Dr. Ulrike Zeshan, a linguist from Germany who has done pioneer research on ISL. Several academics presented papers. Around 120 people participated including principals of Teacher Training Centre, teacher, professionals, parents and deaf people.

The Governor of Andhra Pradesh, Dr. C. Rangarajan and the First Lady Mrs. Rangarajan hosted a tea at the Governor's Residence for all the participants as well as 100 deaf children form various schools. They took this opportunity to give awards to all those individuals who worked hard to research, promote and disseminate Indian Sign Language, the first time such awards were given in recognition of those working on Sign Language. These awards, named the DEAF REACH awards, were given to 10 individuals from India and abroad. They also gave scrolls of honor to their friends who have supported them in their work these many years. Several National TV channels broadcast the event in their news bulletins and all the newspapers national and regional covered this event.

India's first National Orientation Course for Sign Language Interpreters: FCF Project Manager, J.S.K.Rao, was asked by the Rehabilitation Council of India to conduct India's first National Orientation Course for Sign Language Interpreters. The 12-day workshop was held in Chennai (Madras). The goal of the workshop was to train teachers, social workers and others working with the Deaf in India in Sign Language Interpreting. This is the first in a series of three workshops to train potential interpreters. This workshop is a historic event in that Sign Language is being finally recognized by the Indian Government and a long standing demand for making communication accessible to the Deaf in India will finally become a reality.

International Week of the Deaf Celebrations: Deaf Reach organized the 44th International Week of the Deaf Celebrations, which is the International Day of the Deaf. The week-long celebrations was inaugurated on September 30th by the Governor of the State of Andhra Pradesh and the First Lady of the State, Dr. Mrs. Haripriya Rangarajan. The Governor commended their efforts which he termed truly innovative and pioneer efforts in the field of Deaf education in India. Later The First Lady inaugurated the website of the Indian Sign Language Online Dictionary. This website was designed and created by deaf staff and students of Deaf Reach. Their dance troupe of 25 deaf boys and girls performed to the song" Diye Jalte Hain" from the CD "Flame". Later this troupe traveled to four cities and performed everywhere to rave reviews. The Governor later gave away the Deaf Indian 2001 awards to 7 Deaf Achievers.

Bibliography

American Association for the Advancement of Science. (1989). *Science for all Americans*. Washington, DC: Author.

American Association for the Advancement of Science. (1993). *Benchmarks for science literacy*. New York: Oxford University Press.

Berenfeld B. (1993). A moment of glory in San Antonio. *Hands On!*, 16(2), 1, 19-21.

Biehler R. (1993). Cognitive technologies for statistics education: Relating the perspective of tools for learning and of tools for doing statistics. In L. Brunelli & G. Cicchitelli (Eds.), *Proceedings of the first scientific meeting of the International Association for Statistical Education* (pp. 173-190). Perugia, Italy: Università di Perugia.

Carpenter T. P., & Franke M. L. (1998). Teachers as learners. Principled practice in mathematics and science education, *NCISLA/Mathematics & Science Semiannual Newsletter*, 2(2), 1-3.

Cleveland W. S. (1993). *Visualizing data*. Summit, N.J.: Hobart Press.

Cobb P. (1998). Individual and collective mathematical development: The case of statistical data analysis. Paper presented at the annual meeting of the International Group for the Psychology of Mathematics Education, Steelenbosch, South Africa.

Cobb P., Wood T., & Yackel E. (1989). Young children's emotional acts while engaged in mathematical problem solving. In D. B. McLeod & V. M. Adams (Eds.), *Affect and mathematical problem solving: A new perspective* (pp. 117-148). New York: Springer-Verlag.

Coulter B. (1997b). Tracking migratory animals: Going online for environmental education. *Green Teacher* 53 (Fall), 20-21.

Data explorer [Computer software]. (1998). Pleasantville, NY: Sunburst.

Dewey J. (1929). *The quest for certainty*. New York: Minton, Balch & Co.

Driver R., Guesne E., & Tiberghien A. (1985). *Children's ideas in science*. England: Open University Press.

Fathom Dynamic Statistics [Computer software]. (1999). Emeryville, CA: Key Curriculum Press.

Feldman A. (1994). Connecting classrooms. *Hands On!*, 17(1), 20-21.

Feldman A. (1997). Digital kids: There's no turning back. *Hands On!*, 20(2), 1, 16-17.

Finzer B. (1997). *E-mail correspondence to C. Konold*.

Fitzpatrick C. (1997, Fall). Can young students use GIS? *ESRI ARC News*, p. 33.

Gal I., Rothschild K., & Wagner D. A. (1989). *Which group is better? The development of statistical reasoning in elementary school children*. Paper presented at the meeting of the Society for Research in Child Development, Kansas City, MO.

Hancock C., Kaput J. J., & Goldsmith L. T. (1992). Authentic inquiry with data: Critical barriers to classroom implementation. *Educational Psychologist*, 27(3), 337-364.

Harasim L., Hiltz S. R., Teles L., & Turoff M. (1995). *Learning networks: A field guide to teaching and learning online*. Cambridge, MA: MIT Press.

Healy J. (1998). *Failure to connect. How computers affect our children's minds – for better or for worse*. New York: Simon & Schuster.

Howard E. (1998, August 18). Personal communication with Bob Coulter.

Hunter B. (1993). Collaborative inquiry in networked communities. *Hands On!*, 16(2), 16-18.

Johnson R., Brooker C., Stutzman J., Hultman D., & Johnson D. W. (1985). The effects of controversy, concurrence seeking, and individualistic learning on achievement and attitude change. *Journal of Research in Science Teaching*, 22(3), 197-205.

Julyan C. (1988). The creation of a curriculum. *Hands On!*, 11(1), 6, 20.

Julyan C. (1990). Lunchroom garbage: Findings from student-scientists. *Hands On!*, 13(1), 11-14.

Julyan C. (1993). Mapping a journey to understanding. *Hands On!*, 16(2), 4-7.

Karlan J. W. (1995, April 4). *E-mail message to National Geographic and TERC.*

Karlan J. W., Huberman M., & Middlebrooks S. H. (1997). The challenges of bringing the Kids Network to the classroom. In S. A. Raizen & E. D. Britton (Eds.), *Bold ventures: Case studies of U.S. innovations in science education* (pp. 247-394). Dordecht: Kluwer Academic Publishers.

Kilpatrick W. H. (1918). The project method. *Teachers College Record,* 19, 319-351.

Lajoie S. P. (Ed.). (1998). *Reflections on statistics. Learning, teaching, and assessment in grades K-12.* Mahwah, NJ: Lawrence Erlbaum Associates.

Lave J., & Wenger E. (1991). *Situated learning: Legitimate peripheral participation.* Cambridge, England: Cambridge University Press.

Logical journey of the zoombinis [Computer software]. (1996). Novato, CA: Broderbund.

McMahon T. (1996.) *From isolation to interaction? Computer-mediated communications and teacher professional development* (unpublished doctoral dissertation, Indiana University). Indiana: Author.

Mehan H. (1979). *Learning lessons: Social organization in the classroom.* Cambridge, MA: Harvard University Press.

National Commission on Excellence in Education. (1983). *A nation at risk: The imperative for educational reform.* Washington, DC: Government Printing Office.

National Council of Teachers of Mathematics. (1989). *Curriculum and evaluation standards for school mathematics.* Reston, VA: Author.

National Gardening Association. (1991). *Indoor gardening: Advice from GrowLab classrooms.* Burlington, VT: Author.

Oppenheimer T. (1997, July). The computer delusion. *Atlantic Monthly*, 280(1), 45-62.

Panel on Educational Technology. (1997). *Report to the President on the use of technology to strengthen K-12 education in the United States*. Washington, DC: President's Committee of Advisors on Science and Technology.

Papert S. (1980). *Mindstorms: Children, computers, and powerful ideas*. New York: Basic Books.

Rosebery A. S., & Warren B. (Eds.). (1998). *Boats, balloons, and classroom video*. Portsmouth, NH: Heinemann.

Roth W.-M., & Bowen G. M. (1994). Mathematization of experience in a grade 8 open-inquiry environment: An introduction to the representational practices of science. *Journal of Research in Science Teaching*, 31, 293-318.

Rowe M. B. (1983). Science education: A framework for decision-makers. *Daedelus*, 112(2), 123-142.

Scardamalia M., & Bereiter C. (1996). Computer support for knowledge-building communities. In T. Koschmann (Ed.), *CSCL: Theory and practice* (pp. 249-268). Hillsdale, NJ: Lawrence Erlbaum Associates.

SimCity [Computer software]. (1994). Walnut Creek, CA: Maxis.

Simon M. A. (1995). Reconstructing mathematics pedagogy from a constructivist perspective. *Journal of Research in Mathematics Education*, 26(2), 114-145.

Soloway E., & Wallace R. (1997). Does the Internet support student inquiry? Don't ask. *Communications of the ACM*, 40(5), 11-16.

Tabletop [Computer software]. (1995). Novato, CA: Broderbund.

TERC. (1986). *KIDNET*. A proposal submitted to the National Science Foundation. Cambridge, MA: Author.

Varelas M. (1996). Between theory and data in a seventh-grade science class. *Journal of Research in Science Teaching*, 33(3), 229-263.

Vesel J. (1998, January 13). Interview with Nancy London and Alan Feldman.

Von E. Glasersfeld (1984). An introduction to radical constructivism. In P. Watzlawick. (Ed.). *The invented reality* (pp. 17-40). New York: Norton.

Walters J. M. (1996). *Final report on the EnergyNet project* (unpublished report). Cambridge, MA: TERC.

Wasser J. D., & Bresler L. (1996). Working in the interpretive zone: Conceptualizing collaboration in qualitative research teams. *Educational Researcher*, 25(5), 5-15.

Watson J. M., & Moritz J. B. (1998). *The beginning of statistical inference: Comparing two data sets* (unpublished manuscript). Hobart, Tasmania: Author.

Wenglinsky H. (1998). *Does it compute? The relationship between educational technology and student achievement in mathematics.* Princeton, NJ: Educational Testing Services.

Whitehead A. N. (1929). *The aims of education.* New York: The Free Press.

Williams J. (1995). *USA Today weather almanac.* New York: Vintage Books.

Yager R. E. (1984). Toward new meaning for school science. *Educational Leadership*, 41(4), 12-18.

Young V., Haertel G., Ringstaff C., & Means B. (1998, October). *Evaluating global lab curriculum: Impacts and issues of implementing a project-based science curriculum* (review draft). Menlo Park, CA: SRI International.

INDEX